NO WAY OUT

MAJOR ADAM JOWETT

with Geraint Jones

NO WAY OUT

The Searing True Story of Men Under Siege

SIDGWICK & JACKSON

First published 2018 by Sidgwick & Jackson
an imprint of Pan Macmillan
20 New Wharf Road, London N1 9RR
Associated companies throughout the world
www.panmacmillan.com

ISBN 978-1-5098-6470-6 HB
ISBN 978-1-5098-6472-0 TPB

3 5 7 9 8 6 4 2

A CIP catalogue record for this book is available from the British Library.

Typeset by Palimpsest Book Production Ltd, Falkirk, Stirlingshire
Printed and bound by CPI Group (UK) Ltd, Croydon, CR0 4YY

Visit www.panmacmillan.com to read more about all our books
and to buy them. You will also find features, author interviews and
news of any author events, and you can sign up for e-newsletters
so that you're always first to hear about our new releases.

This book is dedicated to
the men of Easy Company,
the Artillery, and the aircrew
who answered the call.

THE PEGASUS ETHOS

As British Airborne soldiers we place the mission, and our comrades, before ourselves. Our bravery is founded upon determination, endurance, and selflessness. We are supremely disciplined and that discipline is primarily self-imposed. We take pride in being part of an elite, and we understand our responsibility to strive for the highest standards of achievement, turnout, and attitude. We wear Pegasus with humility, recognizing our obligation never to demean or diminish the value of others. We are a compassionate friend, but a ferocious enemy. In battle, in barracks, and at home, we always do the right thing.

THE REGIMENTAL CHARTER

The Parachute Regiment provides the capability to deploy an infantry force at short notice, in the vanguard of operations and in the most demanding circumstances. As such, it is trained and ready to form the spearhead for the army's rapid intervention capability.

Its watchwords are professionalism, resilience, discipline, versatility, courage, and self-reliance.

It is light by design, because this confers speed of reaction, and is expert at air–land deployments, by helicopter, aeroplane or parachute. It is trained to conduct a range of missions, from prevention and pre-emption tasks, to complex, high intensity war fighting. It is also trained to provide direct support to United Kingdom Special Forces, with whom it maintains close links and to whom it contributes a very significant proportion of manpower.

In sum, the Parachute Regiment's approach to the training and selection of its soldiers continues to foster those qualities of resilience and versatility recognized by its founding fathers as the rock on which its particular value is built. It remains a force for good and for all seasons in the army.

UTRINQUE PARATUS – Ready for Anything

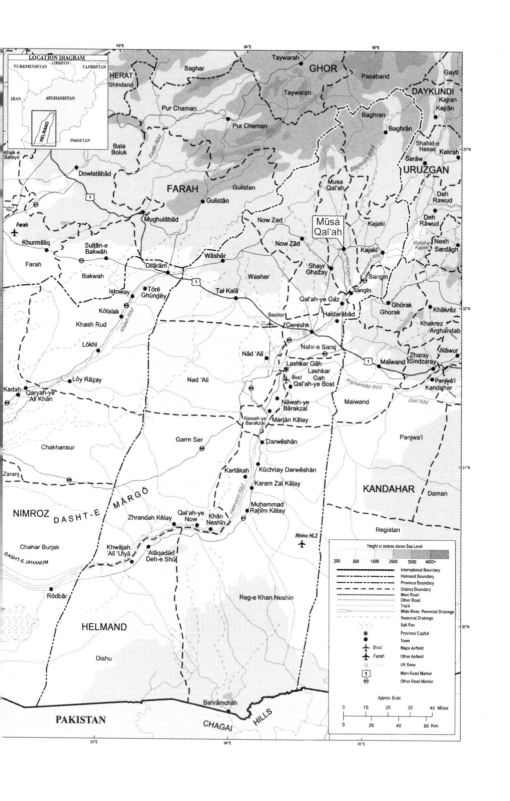

Glossary

2IC – Second In Command
ACM – Anti-Coalition Militia
ally – (al-ee) irregular, unissued kit or appearance celebrated amongst the Paras
ANA – Afghan National Army
ANP – Afghan National Police
ANSP – Afghan National Standby Police
belt-buckle – expression for being as low as possible to the ground
casevac – casualty evacuation
CIMIC – Civil Military Cooperation
CSM – Company Sergeant Major
danger close – the closest point at which friendly fires can be brought without striking your own position
DC – District Centre
double tap – to fire two rifle rounds in quick succession at a target
EOD – Explosive Ordnance Disposal
FOB – Forward Operating Base
FOO – Forward Observation Officer
FSG – Fire Support Group
FST – Fire Support Team
gen – to brief
gimpy – general purpose machine gun
gimpy link – the belt of ammunition for the general purpose machine gun
GPMG – General Purpose Machine Gun
green zone – irrigated and vegetated area bounding rivers and tributaries

HCR – Household Cavalry Regiment

headshed – headquarters element informal

hesco bastion – mesh fortification

HLS – Helicopter Landing Site

HMG – Heavy Machine Gun .50 Calibre

ICOM – radio intercept

IDF – Indirect Fire

IED – Improvised Explosive Device

IO – Intelligence Officer

IRT – Immediate Response Team (CH-47 borne)

ISAF – International Security Assistance Force

I-STAR – Intelligence Surveillance Target Acquisition

JDAM – Joint Direct Attack Munition

JOC – Joint Operations Centre

JTAC – Joint Terminal Attack Controller

KIA – Killed In Action

LAV – Light Armoured Vehicle

LEWT – Light Electronic Warfare Troop

LMG – Light Machine Gun

LZ – Landing Zone

MOG – Manoeuvre Outreach Group

MSQ – Musa Qala

NCO – Non-Commissioned Officer

nine liner – the format for reporting casualties

NVGs – Night-Vision Goggles

OC – Officer Commanding

OP – Observation Post

ops room – operations room

pax – personnel

PF – Pathfinders, 16 Air Assault Brigade's reconnaissance
platoon

PKM – Pulemyot Kalashnikova (machine gun), Soviet
equivalent to our general purpose machine gun

PRR – Personal Role Radio

replen – replenish or resupply

RHA – Royal Horse Artillery

RIP – Relief In Place. Process of rotating troops in a FOB or AO

RPG – Rocket-Propelled Grenade

sangar – fighting position with varying degrees of protection

shemagh – Arab headdress

Soldatenglück – soldier's luck

SOP – Standard Operating Procedures

tab – tactical advance to battle. Moving fast with kit

Terry – Taliban

Toms – young paratroopers

WIA – Wounded In Action

Prologue

To move was to die.

The air above our heads was being torn apart by the supersonic zipping and cracking of bullets, splinters from the wooden structure of the sangar thrown up into the air. Hot sand from the leaking bags poured onto my neck and into the back of my body armour. My senses felt assaulted, the smell of cordite and dust thick in my nostrils, my ears ringing from the boom and blast of RPGs; the rattle of machine guns, friendly and enemy; the frantic shouts of command; the crump of mortars. Even after weeks of furious fighting, it was the heaviest weight of fire I had ever experienced. The most intense battle.

And, from the sounds and sights around me, I knew that we were losing.

It had all started so casually. The front gate sangar had requested a battery replen, and I had told my signallers that I would run them out in their place. Using the cover of buildings, and sprinting between open spaces, not a single round had come at me from the enemy-occupied buildings just fifty yards away. Compared to what we had faced so far, such an easy crossing of the compound felt like bliss. A true walk in the park.

'Morning, boss', the smiling Ranger Russell had greeted me, his eyes red from days of gun smoke and nights of little sleep.

'Morning, Russ', I replied, taking in our defences at the compound's front gate, a collection of metal sheets and wire that was more *Mad Max* than British Army. 'All quiet?' I asked.

The words were hardly out of my mouth when the trio of RPGs fired, the sound of their launch and detonation overlapping as they slammed the short distance into our defences. The heavy weapons were the signal for the enemy to start their attack, and within moments the ghost town had been turned into an inferno of gunfire.

'Down!' I shouted at Russell, pulling him into the corner of the sandbagged position. 'Stay down!' I told him as he bravely tried to fire back at the enemy.

Fuck! I screamed to myself. *Fuck!*

This was the enemy's heaviest weight of fire to date, and as the company commander I should be in a position to co-ordinate my men, and to smash the Taliban's attack with air and artillery power. Instead, I was pinned down completely in an exposed fighting position, and there was no doubt in my mind that to raise my head would mean immediate death. To run to the closest building would be impossible. The air was choked with bullets, rounds churning up dirt and smacking into mud walls like acid rain.

I turned to look at the young soldier beside me, expecting that he would need some encouragement. 'Why are you laughing?' I found myself asking instead.

'You started it, boss,' Russell replied, grinning, and I realized that he was right, the chaos of the situation and adrenaline forcing the reaction from me in long barks. The laughter cleared my head, and I crawled my way to the edge of the fighting position so that I could look back across the compound; I saw my men fighting from the roof of the ops room, but it was clear that the weight of the enemy's fire was suppressing them, and pinning us all into cover. Easy Company were losing this firefight, and if the Taliban could keep our heads down for long enough, then they would be at our walls. We had already had to fight them off with grenades. Would today be bayonets?

Every battle has a tipping point, and for the first time I felt with dread that the decisive advantage was about to be given to the enemy. I needed to be with my artillery and air controllers. I needed to be calling in the firepower that would break this contact. I had already lost soldiers in the battle for the town, and I had no intention of losing more.

I looked south, where the men of Somme Platoon were valiantly fighting their way from cover to cover, attempting to ease the pressure on the western perimeter. My stomach was in my throat as I watched them run, expecting that at any moment I would see one of my soldiers fall. The trail of RPGs left dirty streaks across the sky above them, one exploding in mid-air, and I felt my heart pound in relief as I saw that the air burst had caused no casualties.

We could not be so lucky forever, I knew.

I looked back across to the north-west corner of the compound, where the fire was thick, heavy and deadly. To move was to die, but to stay in cover was to fail my men.

'Keep your head down,' I told Russell, feeling as if I had a gun held against mine.

And then I ran.

1

For me, the siege of Musa Qala did not begin in the dust and heat of Helmand Province. It began in the snow and chill of the South Atlantic. It began with crowded ships leaving Portsmouth to cheering crowds. It began when I heard names like Mount Longdon, Wireless Ridge, and Goose Green. It began when I saw grimy, hard-looking men on the BBC news. Men in maroon berets.

Paras.

I was an eleven-year-old schoolboy in Surrey when the Falklands campaign was fought, but, looking back, I can see without doubt that it was the stories and images of those men that led to me commanding my own soldiers in war more than twenty years later. In Afghanistan, it would be I whose grimy face was on the news. It would be I who wore the maroon beret of the Parachute Regiment. It would be I who had the honour of commanding British soldiers who would not give an inch in the face of a furious enemy, and it would be I who had to make decisions that would see some of those men paying the ultimate price for their heroism and duty to their comrades.

My family is no more of a military one than any other in Britain. My favourite uncle had been a Royal Marine in the Second World War and, like most of my generation, so had my grandfather. As an infantry soldier, he had fought the Germans in Europe. Badly injured, he had been taken prisoner during the Battle of the Bulge, and I always yearned to hear my grandfather's war stories.

He never spoke of them.

Whilst my grandad held his silence, there were other veterans who did share their experiences. My parents were the owners of the local bookshop, and I devoured any war memoir or action novel that arrived on our shelves. I pictured myself in the kind of African adventures that Wilbur Smith was writing, and by the time I was a teenager I knew that my future lay beyond the British borders. I wanted new frontiers and experiences that would test me mentally and physically. I was an accomplished cross-country runner, and I threw myself at anything that hinted of the outdoors. Like thousands of other schoolchildren with itchy feet, I gravitated to the Duke of Edinburgh's award scheme. Reading Ordnance Survey maps and pitching tents in muddied fields scratched that itch, and it was without hesitation that I took the chance to join a British Schools Expedition Society journey to Alaska at the end of my A Levels. The year was 1989, and that winter was spent pulling sleds across glaciers and climbing rock faces. To protect against bears the expedition was equipped with shotguns and pistols. Working out of an old copper mining 'town' in the mountains, I had found the adventure that I was looking for. I knew that a normal career path back home would feel like a noose about my neck, and so, as did almost every other member of the expedition, I elected to join the military.

More specifically, I elected to join the army and the Grenadier Guards. I hadn't forgotten the Paras, but I was influenced by a family friend and mentor who had served with the Grenadier Guards up to the rank of colonel. I chose his regiment and I chose the infantry because I wanted to be in the thick of whatever was happening should I deploy. Even as a civilian I was aware that the infantry were the ones on the sharp end, with all the other combat and support arms there to support them in one capacity or another. If I was joining the army for a challenge and adventure, then I wanted the biggest one that it could throw at me.

The adventure started at the Royal Military Academy Sandhurst, where civilians are turned into army officers. I soon took to the structure and challenge that it provided both physically and mentally; at Sandhurst, quick wits and fitness counted for as much as academia, and I felt as though the sands of education had shifted in my favour. At school I had been an able pupil, but never one who shone. In Sandhurst, I led the way on endurance events and loved the chaos of command appointments, where students would be pushed and pulled by the college's veteran instructors. I felt I was going somewhere, that I had something to do.

It was exactly what I had been looking for.

I was in my senior term at Sandhurst when I first heard the name Saddam Hussein. As I had been during the Falklands War almost a decade earlier, I was once again glued to the TV screen and newspapers as reports of impending hostilities filtered back from the desert. Of course, this time I was in uniform, and, like my fellow students at the military academy, I prayed that peace would hold until I could join my regiment in the field. War seemed to be something that fell every decade or so, and I felt sick knowing that if I missed the invasion of Iraq in 1991, then I was likely to be doomed to a military career of parade squares and training areas. Through no fault of my own, I felt as though I would miss the real test of combat. Without war, could I ever truly consider myself a soldier? Would I ever know if I had what it took to face enemy fire? Could I make myself break from cover, and run towards the enemy?

The world didn't wait to satisfy my sense of adventure. In 1991, after weeks of seeing bombs flash on the television screen, I watched, green with envy, as an entire British armoured division punched through the Iraqi army. The war was over quickly, but redeploying such a large force was not achieved so speedily. When I joined the Grenadier Guards at their German base, the faces of the returned soldiers were still dark from the sun, their stride and swagger full of the confidence of men who have faced war, and have returned alive and triumphant.

As a young officer, I took over a platoon of thirty such soldiers. Many were older than myself, and almost all were more experienced. I hoped that my training at Sandhurst and my own character would help me to prove myself, but as the battalion was relocating to England, there was little for me to do but oversee the paperwork of vehicle maintenance and logistics. It was hardly the adventure I was looking for. At least newly reunified Germany had something to offer for someone raised in Surrey, but it was a brief look at a new world before my hobnailed boots were tramping against the gravel of Horse Guards Parade, as the regiment took up its ceremonial duties, desert pattern helmets replaced with thick shaggy bearskins.

OP Banner offered a break from the monotony of the parade square. Banner was the name given to the army's mission in Northern Ireland, and though the violence of the Troubles had mercifully dropped, it was still a time of patrols, checkpoints, and threat. There was an enemy in the province, and my overwhelming feeling during the deployment was one of bewilderment. I had been raised as a Christian, and still held my faith. I prayed, I attended church, and I could not fathom how it would be possible for me to hate my friends of other denominations because we held slightly differing views on theology. The province was a puzzle to me, and I was thankful that my time there was quiet. I was desperate for combat, but not at the price of peace for my countrymen. Unfortunately for civilians in the Balkans, their own soldiers held no such qualms.

The UN Protection Force (UNPROFOR) mission in Bosnia was two years old when I arrived in 1994. I deployed alone, having spotted and been released for a junior staff officer vacancy at the multinational headquarters in Gornji Vakuf. I arranged the transfer myself, and hitched rides on convoys from the airbase in Split, Croatia. There was a Wild West feel to the enterprise, the air sometimes creased by the crash of distant explosions or the crackle of gunfire, but always thick with rumour and tales. My job was to run the operations room and report back to our Permanent Joint Headquarters (PJHQ) in London. I had some control over how and where I went out from headquarters, and I used this freedom to join convoys and requisition helicopters. In Sarajevo, sprinting between ruined buildings to avoid sniper fire, I knew that I had found adventure at last. With reflection, it sounds really selfish and crass to say such things. I was enjoying myself in the midst of a war that had ruined the lives of thousands, and I was not blind to this dichotomy at the time. But I didn't feel guilty – it was not my actions that had caused the suffering, and I did believe my being in Bosnia was doing something to help overcome the violence that neighbours had visited on themselves. There was no shortage of the signs and reports of atrocity, and I was proud that my country was amongst those who had stood against such darkness.

When I returned from Bosnia, I felt as though my career in the army had run its short course. I had attended Staff College, but had no real desire to serve in a headquarters room, knowing that the freedom I had so recently experienced was the exception, not the rule. But an intervention of one of my superiors kept me from signing my discharge papers. It had always grated on me that I had not earned the coveted maroon beret worn by those hard-looking men at Goose Green and on Mount Longdon, and so when I was offered the chance of a secondment to 3 Para – as the Third Battalion of the Parachute Regiment is known – I grabbed at the opportunity with greedy hands.

The road to 3 Para was paved with assault courses, loaded marches, and the infamous P-Company – culminating in a week of demanding challenges designed to test the physical and mental aptitude of the wannabe Para. Only on passing P-Company is a soldier awarded the distinctive beret, and I wore it proudly as I attended the subsequent parachute course, and learned how to fall out of aircraft without dying, all whilst having a load as heavy as a small horse strapped onto me.

Now a fully fledged paratrooper, though still belonging to the Guards, I took up the position of 3 Para's intelligence officer. I'd barely had time to unpack when 1 Para were warned off for a possible UN/NATO intervention in Kosovo. I volunteered to take part, and along with C Company of 3 Para, I moved across to join the men who were preparing to deploy, taking up the role of A Company's second in command. Finally, I was with the Red Devils made famous at the battles of Normandy, Arnhem, and Goose Green. Finally, I was a paratrooper on the verge of deployment and combat.

It was everything that I hoped it would be.

We flew into Skopje, where 4 Mechanized Brigade were preparing to punch through Serbian forces if needed, and to push through to Pristina. To facilitate their movement 1 Para would leap forward in a series of helicopter moves whereby we would secure vital high ground, crossing points, and junctions. In time-honoured Para tradition, we began the deployment by stealing as much ammunition as possible from the heavy units that were already in place. We were only in Macedonia for a couple of days before our orders came to board the Chinook helicopters and to enter Serbian airspace.

It was thrilling. The whump of the rotors was almost drowned out by the happy chatter of the soldiers. Every man aboard had dreamed of such moments from childhood, and there was no fear when we ran from the ramp and onto soil that could prove hostile – there was only excitement.

From the high ground of the vital Kaçanik Defile I got my first look at the huge armoured formations of the Serbian army. The guns of their tanks and fighting vehicles were silent, their massed divisions cowed by the power of NATO. They knew that, should they stand and fight, their vehicles would be reduced to smoking hulks from the jets above us. And so, angry and bitter, their heavy columns rumbled back towards Serbia, but danger did not leave with them. Serb paramilitary forces sought to settle scores and loot before they crossed the border, raping and murdering until NATO forces swept across the country. As we landed in Pristina, 1 Para was quickly put to the task of restoring order and ensuring peace. We rushed to the sounds of trouble, directed there by the pleading cries of the locals or the crack of gunfire. The days went by in a blur of sprints and shouted orders as we disarmed fighters and reassured citizens. Then, as the Kosovo Liberation Army fighters slipped from the mountainsides and into the cities, we were tasked with keeping our allies in check as they sought to take vengeance on their Serbian neighbours.

Though that time was a rush of adrenaline and welcome chaos, there was one incident that etched its way through the blur of the deployment and into my mind. It concerned a group of Serbian paramilitaries who had abducted a Kosovar family. They planned to rape the daughters in front of the parents before killing the entire family – a horrifically common occurrence in those dark days. I was made aware of the crime by aggrieved locals who sought our help, having quickly learned that the hard-looking men in the maroon berets could be trusted. Anxious to live up to this standard, I took three Paras from A Company's HQ and made best speed to the house that the militants had occupied. They fired on us, but seeing our resolve to storm the building and to kill them if forced to, they soon threw up their arms. The young girls and their parents were saved from rape and murder, and my chest almost burst with pride to be in the company of men who had selflessly put themselves in danger to rescue others. It was the experience I needed to keep me in uniform, and I made my transfer from the Guards permanent.

I was not disappointed by my decision, travelling the world with the airborne regiment and seeing another operational deployment in Sierra Leone, where we arrived in Freetown to see to the safe withdrawal of British citizens in the face of a rebel advance. The advance soon stalled when the

Liberian-backed troops realized that paratroopers would not be deterred by gunfire, and would patrol deep into rebel areas, meeting force with force. On these jungle missions I found myself living the life I had dreamed of whilst reading Wilbur Smith in my parents' bookshop. Conducting operations with feathered tribal hunters armed with bows and antique rifles, I was the star of my own African adventure.

My next stop was Spain, where I was a staff officer at a NATO headquarters in Madrid. It was there in 2001 that I watched the TV screen open-mouthed as planes crashed into the Twin Towers. I had no idea what that attack would mean for the future, but I knew that things were about to change. The anger in the room was palpable, and the American officers present swore blind that someone would pay for the atrocity. The leaders of their country felt likewise, and that sense of vengeance was the catalyst for a war that is still being fought sixteen years later. There was no way I could have known then how long it would continue, but I was certain that, if Britain was to be drawn into any fight, I had the best chance of seeing it as a paratrooper.

That didn't prove true during the second invasion of Iraq. Like the first Gulf War in 1991, the occupation there was handled mostly by the army's heavier units equipped with their Warrior armoured fighting vehicles, or troop carriers with names like Bulldog and Mastiff. Para battalions did deploy to the theatre, but returned mostly disappointed with the action they had seen, the threat of IEDs making it almost suicidal for light-role units to operate within the cities. As a staff officer, I watched this action hungrily from the sidelines, looking for my own mission in what had become known as the Global War on Terror.

I found it in 2005, when 3 Para was warned to expect a deployment to Afghanistan the following summer. Our colleagues in 2 Para had already deployed there in the immediate aftermath of the Taliban's 'collapse' in 2001, when their forces had been smashed and sent retreating into the provinces that bordered Pakistan, but this was the first time that a formed unit would be sent as part of a deliberate and ongoing operation in the south of the country. Up until this point, much of the operations in Afghanistan had centred on Kabul, but now ISAF was looking to spread the central government's influence into the nation's more distant and rural provinces. Our role as soldiers would be to provide the security necessary to facilitate the civilian and military projects that would bring infrastructure and the rule of law to places where the roads were dirt and crime rampant. And so, during briefings, I heard for the first time the name of a province and its towns that would be spoken daily by news reporters and British civilians over the coming years: Helmand. Sangin. Gereshk. Now Zad. Lashkar Gah. Kajaki.

Musa Qala.

None of us understood the scale of the fight we were about to walk into, but there was a buzz in the air, and we knew that the coming operation would be 'tasty'. I did not want to miss the fight, and fate was on my side; it was my time to receive command of a company, and so I was able to transfer from my position in the Apache helicopter training teams, and back to 3 Para. The men I was to command had already left the UK for Camp Bastion – a runway and tented town in the Afghan desert – and I was keen to be on their heels. First there were the mandatory pre-deployment briefings and training exercises, and here we scoffed at the British defence secretary John Reid's words that the mission in Helmand could be completed 'without a shot being fired'. Those words will haunt the politician forever, but they would have haunted the Paras more had they been true. Like a dog on a leash, we were anxious to be let loose. Our flights to theatre could not come soon enough, but first, there was a reality of war that not many people are aware of: departure.

It wasn't that it wasn't difficult to say goodbye to loved

ones, including my wife, young son, and daughter. Of course those moments are hard, but they are also only a small part of saying goodbye, because when the soldier goes to war, life goes on without him. This meant busy days of organizing anything from direct debits for the electric bills to showing my wife where the MOT certificates were kept. It meant buying life insurance policies and asking a neighbour to check in on the place when my wife was staying with her parents. It meant finding a gardener, and giving my brother the letter that my family should read if I did not come home. It meant packing socks and buying sunscreen. It meant a hundred different things that made the days pass by in a blur that ended with hugging my family tightly before joining a few dozen other Paras for a bus journey to Brize Norton, where the RAF would take us on the next leg of our journey.

Civilian friends often ask me what passed through my mind as I waited for the aircraft to take off and deliver me to Afghanistan, expecting the answer that I was wondering what it would be like to kill someone. What it would be like to be hit by shrapnel, or gunfire. What it would be like to die. When I tell them that my mind was full of payment plans and car services, I expect they think it's my way of putting on a brave face, but it is the truth – I had deployed before, and I would deploy again. I was a soldier, and a soldier was all I had ever wanted to be. Those grimy, hard men of the Falklands War had smiled and waved as their ships had left the docks. I knew why, now. I was a paratrooper on my way to war, and I could not have been happier.

2

The flight to Kabul was not unlike any other long haul on a civilian airline, and by the time the RAF Tristar had hit the tarmac I was anxious to be free of the cramped seating, my back tight and eyes red from recycled air and a few hours of broken sleep. The heat of the country hit me before the doors had opened, and as we stepped into the Afghan sun men squinted and shielded their eyes, or hastily pulled out sunglasses from the daysacks on their shoulders. Instantly, patches of sweat began to show through the desert uniforms, noses assaulted with the perennial smell of an airbase at war – kerosene and wood smoke. RAF staff showed us to our billets. The base was sprawling, with the uniforms and flashes of dozens of nations present. The mountains beyond the airbase were harsh and daunting, and I thought about the nine bloody years the Russians had spent battling the mujahideen here before being driven from the country. As the sun set behind those distant peaks, I marvelled at the beauty of a country that seemed constantly ravaged by war.

That night, with a handful of other officers who were making their way to Helmand, I found myself in one of the airbase's bars. It was called the Toucan – a play on words as the limit of alcoholic beverages was supposedly two cans per person – and it was home to a mixture of nationalities and ranks, many of whom looked at our maroon berets and Para wings with envy. Kabul was quiet, and Helmand was showing itself as the place for a soldier to be. There was a handful of Special Forces at their own table, and I hoped for the chance to dig into the minds of these men, as they would know our enemy better than anyone. Before that was possible, however,

Brigadier Ed Butler, the commander of Task Force Helmand, arrived at the bar. As one of his company commanders, I joined him to get a better feel for the mission. At least it shored up in our minds that 'heading down south' was the thing to be doing.

The next morning, we flew by C-130 to Kandahar, the province that was the birthplace of the Taliban. Even the name was proof of the long history of war in the country – the word Kandahar was derived from Iskander, the Afghan name for Alexander the Great, who had founded the place after subduing the country in his most difficult and bloody campaign.

Our stay at Kandahar airfield was to be short, but we had heard of 'the boardwalk' and were keen to see this part of the camp that was already becoming famous in Afghanistan, particularly with the fighting troops who took pride in living on the bare essentials during operations. The boardwalk was a rectangular raised platform surrounded by shops that sold anything from ice cream to fur coats. There was even a Tim Hortons, which every man visited to pick up a reusable mug; the British soldier takes his brew drinking very seriously, and his mug is a treasured possession. A few of our group took the chance to visit the tailors, who could design and stitch custom patches for uniforms, showing anything from blood type to your name in Pashtun. I declined, having heard of a Para officer who could not understand why the locals hated him as soon as they set eyes on him. It was a giggling interpreter who had solved the mystery, pointing out that the officer's Pashtun name patch declared him to be an Israeli spy.

The boardwalk was more lavish than many of the rear areas I had seen during other operations, but I was not surprised by it. It's a minority of the army who are on the frontline, so to speak, and the logistical tail behind them sleep in real beds and have access to shops, Internet cafes, and restaurants. That's the way of war in the twenty-first century, but although I didn't resent anyone who wanted those kind of comforts, it wasn't my idea of soldiering, and I was glad that my time in Kandahar would be limited to an afternoon. By the time the C-130 took off again – doubtless made heavier by every man stuffing his kit with sweets, cigarettes, and Tim Horton mugs – I was itching to be on my way, and to 3 Para.

The excitement on the short flight to Helmand was palpable, men smiling beneath the helmets that we wore in case of an emergency landing. The Russians had lost a great many aircraft in their war here, and so the RAF adopted what was known as a Khe Sanh landing technique, where they dropped from altitude almost on the aircraft's nose, before pulling back sharply to land. It was an exhilarating experience, and a reminder that we were going against a real enemy, and not into a peacekeeping operation.

As the aircraft's tailgate lowered and the sunlight flooded in, men were almost bouncing onto the tarmac, keen to find their comrades and get going. Looking about me, I saw the beginnings of a desert city, rows of beige tents broken by a colourful mixture of shipping containers that had crossed in convoy from Pakistan. The airbase would become one of the busiest British-run airports, but in the summer of 2006 it was not much more than a runway watched over by a few parked C-130s and a smattering of helicopters, the ugly-nosed Apaches and burly twin-rotor Chinooks most conspicuous amongst them.

After claiming my Bergen and grip from the pallets of equipment unpacked and laid out on the dirt, I made my way directly to 3 Para Headquarters. As OC Support Company, I was nominally in command of specialists ranging from mortars to machine gunners, but owing to the nature of operations these elements had been split down to bolster the rifle companies, and so instead my role as the newly arrived major would be to run operations from the Joint Operations Centre (JOC). I hoped that, as much as possible, I would be able to break from this task in Bastion and visit the men of my company as and when they deployed onto the ground.

The tented cookhouse was full of the chatter of such deployments when I took my first meal there amongst the men I was joining. A Company had just been on their first op and had come across real resistance; its men were still full of swagger, knowing that they had been the ones to see the most 'tasty' moment of the tour so far.

In the battalion operations room, maps and pins gave me a better outlook on who was where, and what was developing across the battlespace. At the time of my arrival, the battlegroup was still mostly a fluid entity, carrying out strike missions rather than holding ground in fixed positions. Only C Company were involved in such a manner, holding the FOB at Gereshk, and already a low opinion of the Afghan native forces had permeated the British ranks. I truly believed that we were, man for man, the best soldiers on the planet, but I tried not to be too quick in dismissing the Afghan soldiers' capability. Foreign armies had come and gone, but they remained, for all intents and purposes, undefeated throughout history.

My first days in theatre were centred around the need to acclimatize both to the climate and to the operational environment. To this end I went running around the base before the day's heat became too intense, and participated in a slew of shooting practice. The empty desert around Bastion was our playground, and though it was far from a cowboy free-for-all, we were able to push the limits of the rulebook and engage in exercises that would have been impossible on the more restricted ranges in the UK. We practised reaction to effective enemy fire, breaking contact, casualty evacuations under fire – all things that would save lives out on the ground. When C Company were involved in a long-running contact following a meeting with tribal elders, it only pushed 3 Para's excitement levels higher, and every man was desperate to be the one with the best marksmanship and the slickest drills. The distant echo of bombs exploding from coalition air strikes only added to the sense of vicious anticipation – 3 Para was on notice to move, and I couldn't think of another unit I would rather be with. The battalion had a reputation for being grungy, with little regard for issued kit or regulation haircuts. It was acceptable for the Toms to deploy looking about as smart as a Botswanan border guard so long as their kit worked and their weapons were clean. There are many in the army who would rail against such flaunting of the rules, but as Paras we prided ourselves on individuality. After all, we were a rule apart in the army itself – it was only natural that such an attitude carried over into the ranks themselves, full of bravado that seemed beaten out of other infantry units. A paratrooper can live on nothing but pride.

Of course, the Paras had not come to Helmand alone. Though 3 Para made up the bulk of the battlegroup, it was supported by elements of engineers, signallers, logisticians, and air corps, as well as the RAF and some individuals from the navy. It truly was a team effort, and an international one at that – in Bastion's tented lines could be spotted Gurkha, Dane, Estonian, and Canadian. In the cookhouse, accents from every city and county of the British Isles could be made out. Just as I had felt a wave of patriotism to see the Union Flag carried across the Falklands, so too did I have an immense feeling of pride at being a countryman to the soldiers around me.

Not all were so sanguine in their feelings towards 'our team'. A couple of months after I arrived in Helmand, e-mails from a fellow officer were leaked to the press. In them he chastised the RAF – particularly their Harrier pilots – whom he described as 'utterly, utterly useless'. In the meantime, such reserve was expressed through grumblings at the cookhouse table, or with sneering looks towards those wearing the blue rank patches of the air force.

The first few days of my time in Helmand passed with

camp gossip and shooting on the ranges. I was happy to have made it to theatre, but I was frustrated – I had a toe in the water of the operation, but I wanted to jump in with both feet.

I soon got my chance. Called into the operations room, I was met by Lieutenant Colonel Stuart Tootal, his narrow eyes vital beneath a shock of grey hair.

'Adam,' he greeted me. 'How'd you like to get down to Sangin?'

'I'd like that a lot, sir,' I told him, smiling.

I was going out on the ground.

3

It was in the back of a thundering Chinook helicopter that I made my way from Bastion to Sangin, the twin rotors beating the air with their rhythmic 'wocka-wocka' cadence. Dusty portholes were embedded in the helicopter's side, and I watched through these as craggy mountain ranges began to grow out of a bleak desert. Then came the first signs of irrigation and fertile land, lush green broken by the mud brick of compound walls, which could be metres thick, built for privacy and security. These dwellings created a growing maze amongst the green as we neared the Helmand river. Sangin was one of the biggest of the population centres that clung to the river and, from the air, I could already see the enormity and difficulty of the task that A Company had in front of them; a single rifle company to maintain peace and stability in the town. The dense vegetation and blind streets made Sangin an insurgent's paradise. Amongst these compounds and in the surrounding corn-fields, I would see something in soldiering that I had not experienced before.

The Chinook landed on a patch of open ground beside the dry river bed, coloured smoke swirling from the flares used to mark the spot and enable the pilot to judge the winds. Shouldering my kit and with my weapon in one hand, I trotted off the ramp and jumped the last couple of feet to the dirt. It was not a hot LZ – one under fire – but that could change at any moment. Chinooks were precious few in Task Force Helmand, and the waiting A Company soldiers unloaded her supplies as quickly as possible, so that the ship could be away and back into the sheet of blue sky.

As the work party around me grabbed at ammunition containers and bags of mail, I sought out the company commander.

'Adam,' he greeted me, 'I'll show you around.'

'Jamie, good to see you,' I said. He was a rising star, bright and articulate, and I was pleased to be there with him.

I was led through a break in the hesco bastion – wired crates packed densely with dirt and sand – and got my first look at Sangin's district centre, as the seat of local government was known. The DC was built around a triple-storey building that looked like an angry porcupine, bristling as it was with antenna and machine-gun barrels, sandbags stacked tightly in windows and along the lips of the rooftops. Such a position would give a commanding view over the local area, and confirmed my initial feeling that the base was well placed, with almost half of its approaches backing onto empty land that could offer no cover for the enemy and provided the necessary space and relative security for bringing in vital supplies by helicopter. With something of a knot in my stomach, I realized that it could be vital for something far more precious – the extraction of wounded and dead. The battlegroup had just lost its first man to enemy fire, and the sense amongst the men was that he would not be the last of the soldiers to go home beneath a flag. Contacts were picking up, and though we trusted in our skill, everyone knew that there was luck involved in surviving enemy bullets – luck that could run out at any time.

'I've got my hands full here,' Jamie went on. 'Would be a big help if I could cut away a few of the tasks to you. Let me concentrate on securing the town.'

'What can I do?'

'We're starting to get some kind of contact on most patrols now. We're supposed to be setting up infrastructure for the locals, but we can't have the engineers come in and work whilst we're getting shot at, so my first priority is aggressively projecting our platoons out to try and push the Taliban away from the town. If we can get security here, we can get to work on the civil projects to bring the locals onside. Once we show them we're here to help, they should choose to keep the Taliban out themselves.'

I nodded at the idea. It was classic counter-insurgency doctrine, and had been proven to work. Having the security to implement the civil projects was key – nobody wanted a new well if using it meant running a gauntlet of death between our guns and the Taliban's.

He went on to tell me that all of his time was spent planning and implementing patrols. 'I need someone who can be a link to the Afghan Police,' he added. 'They're a fucking shambles, and we don't have the numbers to be able to do this without them.'

'Who's their commander?' I asked. 'I'll get with him and start working out the issues.'

'He is part of the issue.' Jamie smirked. 'And God knows where he is. Lash? Kabul? Apparently he's gone to a briefing from his commander, and that was weeks ago. No one can reach him.'

'He's dead?'

Jamie shook his head. 'Usual practice, apparently. The police commanders aren't here all that often, and since there's some fighting to be done, they're fucking off more than usual.'

'I'll see to the police,' I promised. 'Anything else?'

'Shuras,' he told me, using the Pashtun word for a meeting with local elders and religious heads. 'We've been having them, but the problem is, we keep getting contacted when we do. If you can handle the shura and the elders, I can command my platoons and keep the fuckers away long enough for you to actually have a conversation with them.'

I wasn't surprised to hear that the Taliban were making an effort to disrupt such meetings. It wasn't in their interest for us to have the opportunity to humanize ourselves with the locals. To establish relationships with them and to address needs that had not been met under the totalitarian rule of the Taliban.

'My Pashtun's not great.' I grinned. 'I hope you have good interpreters.'

'We do.' He nodded. 'And I've been trying to gen the guys up on as much of the culture as I can. I think it's making a difference.'

Jamie had served an Afghan deployment before with the American 82nd Airborne, and it was great to see him use that knowledge to try to endear us with the locals. After sharing a few cultural pointers with me to smooth over my introduction with the police, Jamie went on to brief me on the action they'd seen over the past few days, highlighting vulnerable areas and known enemy firing positions.

'The boys are loving it.' He smiled with pride, thinking of his soldiers. 'Anything else you need to get settled in?'

'I'm good. Thanks, mate,' I replied, a little envious that he was commanding a company of Paras with an enemy to face. 'I'll go and meet my police.'

In the army, underperforming and dishevelled troops are often referred to by such comically derogatory titles as Liberian Border Force, or Guatemalan Special Forces. Entering the police compound at Sangin DC, I thought the local law enforcement would need a whole new category of insult. They were certainly dishevelled, and kitted out in a combination of hand-me-downs from several world powers, but there was something about the men that I had not expected to find on the frontline of the fight against the Taliban.

They were high.

Red eyes and lazy smiles were the giveaway, a half-dozen police officers sprawled apathetically on the benches of their office.

'Are they always like this?' I asked my interpreter.

The man shrugged. I took that as a yes.

'My name's Major Jowett.' I spoke to the room, hearing my words translated into Pashtun. 'I'm here to work with you, and to assist you with enforcing the law in Sangin. There's a patrol leaving in an hour, and ten of you will be coming along as part of it.'

There was little enthusiasm – or dissent, to be fair – on the faces of the men who ranged in age from their teens to forties. All had the dark skin and features of the Pashtun. They were locals, which could be invaluable in some ways on patrol – they knew the town inside out, and could recognize those from other parts of the province, or country. It was incredibly difficult for British soldiers to tell Afghans apart by their looks, and impossible to do it by their dialect. A local from Sangin could identify the accent of a man from Musa Qala as easily as I could distinguish a cockney from a Scotsman.

Being local brought its disadvantages, too. The men were part of the tribal system that ruled Afghanistan with much greater power than a government in Kabul, a city that was as foreign to the locals as London or New York. If their tribal elder told them not to engage the Taliban, they would not. If they told them to avoid certain areas on patrol, or to persecute a certain family, they would. Underpaid and lacking leadership from their own commanders, the police had a high rate of desertion prior to the fighting. Now that the Taliban were flowing into the area, the rate had doubled – we were asking men to fight when they knew that their family might have their throats slit by Taliban fighters in reprisal. All things considered, it was hard to criticize them for using the plant that grew all around them.

'Get your gear together, gentlemen,' I said through the interpreter. 'I'll take you over to the main compound for briefing.'

There was no objection. With a few muttered words from the older men amongst them, the local police force began to stir.

I turned to the man behind me, one of A Company's sergeants who had worked with the ANP on several patrols. 'Are they always like this?'

'Pretty much, sir. Usually asleep or high from mid-afternoon. They find a bit of shade and then that's them. Siesta time.'

'What about their officers?'

'I've been here just over a week now, sir, and I still haven't seen them.'

I shook my head. How could a country expect its police force to function without leadership? More to the point, how did they expect them to function without pay? A Company's sergeant answered that question for me.

'When we got here, the only kind of patrolling they were doing was setting up checkpoints so they could shake down the locals.'

'How did that go down?'

The man shrugged his shoulders. 'Just a part of life in these shitholes, isn't it, sir?'

It was. It's hard to imagine when you're born and raised in Britain, but graft is a part of life in most of the world. Nothing got done in Afghanistan without bribes, and that was true from the lowliest farmer to the most powerful warlord in Kabul. It was as natural to these men as the almost constant state of war their country had been suffering for more than twenty years.

Thought of warlords and bribes brought my mind to Sher Mohammed Akhundzada – better known to the troops as SMA – and the recent briefing I had received on him. Until recently, SMA had been the governor of Helmand Province. He had attained that position by being one of the province's most powerful warlords, and so one of its most productive drug lords. Though he had been working alongside ISAF before the summer of 2006, SMA's drug running was seen as too unseemly for British high command, and despite the protestations of Kabul, he was stripped of his office. He went quietly, but his departure had caused violent ripples all the same – SMA had been keeping three to four hundred fighters on his payroll. Now without a wage, these men had flocked to the Taliban, swelling their ranks. Little wonder that the number of contacts was sharply on the rise.

I cast my eyes over the ANP men in front of me, conscious that we could be running into such trouble within the next few hours. Their appearance did little to inspire confidence, but I hoped the fact that these men were yet to desert meant they were solid.

'All ready?' I asked, the interpreter following in Pashtun from behind my shoulder.

A few men nodded. The rest looked at me in silence. I decided I would be the cheery Brit, and smiled.

'All right, then. Let's get out of here.'

The patrol was to Sangin's marketplace, an area of the town that was still thriving despite the presence of armed men and the never too far away threat of violence. I was informed that it was possible to purchase 'Osama bin Laden soap' at the market, which goes some way to explaining the political leanings of the local populace. Jamie had warned me that there was an 85 per cent chance of contact on each patrol, or an 85 per cent chance of steel rain, as the troops were mocking it. With expectations of such a downpour, Jamie had brought out a reinforced platoon to convey us to the planned shura – three rifle sections, snipers, machine guns, and an anti-tank team, whose javelin missiles could be used to pinpoint enemy firing positions at considerable distance. My force of Afghan Police formed up at the centre of the British troops in the position of 'least likely to suffer damage'. The front and rear of the patrol was most likely to be contacted first, but in counter-insurgency warfare, there is no such place as a 'safe spot'.

It felt great to be on patrol. I was a little green with envy that it was Jamie who had the honoured position of command-ing paratroopers on the ground, but I buzzed with pride and excitement just to be in the mix with them. It was what I had always wanted, and the weapon in my hands, and the kit on my back, felt light despite the beating sun and the dry heat reflected from the mud-brick walls of alleyways and com-pounds.

It was a different experience from patrolling in Kosovo. There, local kids had run to us. Adults had come from their homes to shake hands and pass the time of day. Here, locals avoided us as if we carried a plague. I suppose that, in effect, we did – Taliban informers could be anywhere, and to be seen to collude with us would most likely carry a beating at best, a death sentence at worst. The Taliban themselves could be watching down the barrel of their weapons, and a stray bullet is no less deadly than an aimed one. Nobody wanted to be in proximity to walking targets. More than that, I could see resentment shot from scowling faces and angry eyes. I had experienced a little of it in Northern Ireland, but the Pashtun scorn was heavier still – they knew that our presence was bringing a fight to their streets, and to their homes. They knew that, when the Taliban engaged us, we'd call bombs in from the sky, and those bombs were landing on their town. No, they were not too happy to see us, and who could blame them? In response, we would have to show them that the pain was temporary, and worth it. We would have to show them that we could bring security, stability, and better quality of life.

That day's shura was supposed to be a step in that process, where local elders could lay before us what projects their town needed most. Seeing the local traders hastily packing away their wares, and rolling down the shutters of their stores, it was obvious what was coming instead.

'All call signs, prepare to move back to the DC,' Jamie said over the radio.

What had been a bustling market was fast becoming a ghost town.

Jamie came back onto the net, relaying what his interpreters had heard by tuning into the Taliban's unsecured radio frequencies. 'ICOM chatter has them moving into position and preparing to attack. One Zero Alpha, move now, over.'

He began to coordinate his sections for the withdrawal. Now was not the time for us all to get up and walk, and so A Company's officers implemented the 'one foot on the ground' approach – no section would move unless there was another who had gone firm into over watch. It was as the final section's turn to withdraw came, that the Taliban made their move.

'Contact rear!' came the shout over radios and along the alleyways as the staccato sound of AK fire cracked from behind me.

'Contact rear! Contact rear!'

The attack had been expected, and the enemy fire was answered by the crackle of the rear section's rifle fire, and heavy bursts from a GPMG. The 'plop' sound of an underslung grenade launch was followed by the crash of its explosion. All about me came the shouted orders of NCOs as they pushed their men into positions and guided their fire onto enemy targets.

I took stock of my Afghan charges, surprised to see that they were already turned out to the flanks, poised and ready in the cover of the low walls, their faces showing no more sign of concern than they had at any point that day. A few began to fire bursts towards compounds, and through my interpreter I tried to distinguish if the bursts had been speculative, or if they had seen an enemy.

'Only fire if you can identify a fighter!' I urged them, not wanting the police to be cutting down civilians fleeing the fighting, though I expected that the locals were experienced enough to go to ground until the last bullet had flown.

I would be a liar if I claimed to know exactly what happened over the course of the next hour. There were around forty British soldiers involved in the fighting withdrawal, as well as the Afghan Police with me. For each individual, the memories of that hot afternoon will be different. Alleyways and compound walls see to that, and what one man saw may have been obscured to almost every other. What was consistent to all was the echoing crash of gunfire, the shouted orders, the difficulty of command and control in a rabbit warren of streets, and the stinging sweat and cordite that ran into excited eyes. At several points the contact fell silent, and it was possible to hear the gasping breaths of men as their heaving chests fought for space beneath their body armour. At those times it became quiet enough to hear chuckles between soldiers, and to see the white smiles in tanned faces. Untouched by the enemy fire, the paratroopers were living their dream. Who knows what thoughts occupied the Taliban fighters' minds, but they were dogged and determined, punishing us with fire whenever we broke cover. It was only when we came beneath the arcs of the support groups at the DC that Terry broke off his fight, heavy machine guns and grenade machine guns making a convincing argument that he should call it a day.

I was panting heavily when we ran back through the patrol base's gates. All around me, British soldiers were doing the same, but their smiles were intact, and some were clapping hands or high fiving. Salty veterans moved amongst them, ensuring that their young Toms had properly cleared their weapons, aware that the greatest moment of danger in combat is often at its conclusion, and at the soldier's own hand. It would be too cruel for a man to survive the enemy only to shoot a comrade because a safety catch was left off or a round in a chamber forgotten. It was a tragedy that adrenaline and the elation of coming through a fight unscathed made as predictable as it was avoidable. I had been proud to see A Company in action, and I was more proud still to see that their professionalism continued now that the firing had died away.

'Enjoy that?' Jamie asked me, pulling off his helmet and wiping a gloved hand at the sweat in his eyes.

'Loved it,' I answered truthfully. 'Shame about the shura, though.'

A Company's commander nodded in frustration. 'It's like this almost every time. Getting worse, really. Fuck knows how we're supposed to get anything done. We need a battalion here, not a company.'

His words were born of a desire to win, rather than any complaint. Jamie knew that his men could see off any fight, but he had the foresight to realize that our mission in Afghanistan would be won not in the contacts, but in the building of a fragile trust with the locals. Though that afternoon was a tactical success – a clean break from contact with no friendly casualties – it was a strategic loss, and a victory for the Taliban. They had set out to disrupt our shura, denying us a meeting with the local elders, and in that they had been totally successful. It did not paint a good long-term picture, but that was for men above our rank to decide. Jamie had done all that could be asked of a commander, moving his men back from an incredibly difficult situation with deft skill.

'I've got to get back to the ops room and debrief the battlegroup,' he told me, casting an eye over his men, the Paras gulping water as they hastily reloaded magazines and cleaned weapons. 'We'll be back out in a few hours.'

There would be no let up for A Company, and I was anxious that the Afghan Police be represented on every patrol – we were here to support them, after all, and local resentment would only increase if all the men on their streets were alien in looks and language.

Entering the police station, I found the Afghans as relaxed as they had been that morning. The contact seemed to have barely registered, and they sat calmly in the shade, cheap cigarettes dangling between their lips as they cleaned their weapons.

'Everything all right?' I asked them.

I got a few shrugs in reply. They may not have been presentable, nor did they follow the same code as Western soldiers, but Afghanistan bred warriors, and these men had lived up to that martial tradition.

4

I spent four weeks in Sangin with A Company, and they were amongst some of the best in my life. The tempo of operations was high, with daily patrols into the town that invariably ended in contact with the enemy. At times these firefights were simple shoot and scoots, and at others they were protracted battles that required the use of fast air and JDAM (Joint Direct Attack Munition) bombs to break contacts.

In many ways, Sangin DC seemed to me the ideal example of how a patrol base should be established, and run. As I've said, its excellent location afforded security for the men living within the compound, and also for its HLS, which allowed for a steady influx of supplies, and the rotation of men, of which there were plenty – an entire rifle company; support elements of snipers and anti-tanks; a mortar line; a detachment of Royal Engineers; a troop of the Household Cavalry and their Scimitar light armoured vehicles; the local force of Afghan National Police. Combined, it was a potent fighting force.

And yet . . .

Despite this number of men, and a variety of skillsets, it was not possible to project enough force onto the ground to deter Taliban attacks. The idea of implementing CIMIC (Civil Military Cooperation) projects had quickly become a pipe dream, and instead, the focus was shifting to killing enough of the enemy that security could be established, and CIMIC ideas could be identified. Unfortunately, more and more of these CIMIC projects would simply be a rebuilding of what we had already destroyed. Entire compounds had been turned to rubble. Power lines had been downed, and water pipes burst.

The Taliban were dying, but they were taking the town with them.

And the cost was not purely material. Sangin DC's doctor was noisily opposed to the practice of calling in air strikes. In an attempt to win 'hearts and minds', a regular clinic had been set up so that the town's locals could be treated by a Western doctor, but these patients were increasingly coming in with injuries caused by our own weapons. I saw one elderly woman stumble in following an air strike. It was only the stoop of her back that gave her age away – the majority of her face was missing.

It wasn't an easy thing to witness. Some soldiers, like the doctor, became vocal in their opposition to the policy that had us walking out into a certain contact, and the resulting casualties. Others amongst us, myself included, were unhappy with the results, but could see no other method, hoping that if we could fight the Taliban to a standstill, then the locals would be better off in the long run. Many of the Toms simply didn't care. They were enjoying the fighting and the awesome display of power of exploding bombs and strafing runs. They were too young, and too detached, to consider the bigger picture.

Task Force Helmand told us that we were in Sangin 'to have an effect' on the local populace, but increasingly, that effect seemed to be a detrimental one. 'Quick Impact Projects' was a term the army liked to use for CIMIC missions that could be turned around instantly, and I heard one officer remark that, 'The only Quick Impact Project in Sangin is a JDAM hitting the deck'. His words met with resigned chuckles, for what else was there to do? We were soldiers, and we had been given a mission. We could wish for more resources, we could ask for them, but in the end, there was no other choice for us but to crack on.

It was with mixed emotions that A Company received the news of their relief in Sangin. The men were shattered from five weeks of constant patrolling and contact, but they were also reluctant to leave. There was a sense that the tempo of operations and combat would be short-lived, and if they pulled out, then they might never fire another round. The soldiers of A Company had become addicted to the adrenaline of their mission, and wanted it to themselves, but it was clear that, physically and mentally, the troops were wearing down. Rotating them was for the best, as tired men make mistakes, and mistakes in war are often fatal.

I had grown to love A Company over the past weeks, but I would not be leaving with them – at least not directly. I was to be flown to Kandahar, where I would link up with a Canadian mechanized unit that would be taking part in the operation of A Company's relief in place (RIP) with B Company.

'I hope you've enjoyed your time here?' Jamie asked me as I waited for the Chinook, the sound of the beast's heavy rotors beating in the distance.

'Loved it. You've got a great company.'

'The boys are brilliant,' he agreed, heaping the praise onto his men and keeping none for himself. 'I'll see you in a couple of weeks.'

'Take care. Look after yourself.'

Conversation was killed as the Chinook descended onto the HLS. I ran to the tailgate, avoiding the bundles of mail and boxes of ammunition that the loadmaster threw into the arms of the waiting work party. Moments later we were in the air, and I craned to look at the town below me, noting the craters and destruction that had scarred the town since I had arrived a little over a month ago. If I had harboured doubts about the intensity of the operation in which I was involved, then the eagle's-eye view of the destruction dispelled it.

We were at war.

I met the Canadians somewhere between Kandahar and Sangin, dropped by Chinook at their vehicle laager in the desert. They made an imposing force against the bleak landscape, some thirty-odd light armoured vehicles (LAVs) with turret-mounted weapons that included fearsome automatic cannons. They reminded me of the British army's Warrior fighting vehicles, but with wheels rather than tracks. Like the Warriors, each vehicle had a troop compartment at its rear to hold infantry, allowing the squadron to conduct operations entirely by itself if needed. Their latest mission, however, was to be part of a combined effort to relieve A Company at Sangin, and it was for that reason that I had been dropped in their midst, with the brief from Colonel Tootal to act as liaison officer between the different nationalities of our forces. It seemed as though I was becoming 3 Para's Mr International, though there was no comparison between the Afghan Police of Sangin and the Canadians, who were some of the most squared-away and professional soldiers I have seen at work.

The desert is an empty place, but that doesn't mean that the enemy isn't present. Fleeting glimpses of motorbikes in the distance were often greeted by mortar rounds when the company came to a stop. Even a direct hit would struggle to cause casualties thanks to the armour, but the fire was intended to be harassing in nature. It was a classic part of guerrilla warfare: don't let your enemy rest; deny them freedom of movement; put the fear into them that the attack could come at any moment. And mortars are frightening. At least when you are under small-arms fire you can hit back. With mortars you simply have to get into cover, and hope that one doesn't drop in your lap.

The mortar attacks continued intermittently until we reached the green zone of the Helmand river. In the week of travel I had come to see the Canadians as funny and light-hearted, but now I was going to see them fight.

It all started when the squadron was ordered to proceed to the site of a drone strike on a compound and conduct a battle damage assessment. The fact that a drone strike had been launched here was telling – they were the weapon of choice in hitting Taliban leadership, and where there is Taliban leadership, there is Taliban support and fighters. The Canadians knew that they were driving into a fight. As such, their commanding officer placed the bulk of his squadron on a spur that overlooked the valley where the compound was sited. There was little damage to be observed through binoculars and weapon sights, but compound walls were so thick that they could be left standing after a nearby hit from a 1,000lb JDAM. However, the human body is not quite so sturdy, and inside those walls could be the vaporized or torn forms of its occupants. To find out, the Canadian squadron would need to dismount its infantry and push inside.

It was an unusual sensation for me, watching the half-dozen armoured vehicles push towards the gathering of compounds beneath the spur. I was with the Canadian unit as a liaison only, and had no role in its command. I was simply a spectator as the ground below us came alive with RPGs and small-arms fire, a huge ambush unleashed onto the approaching vehicles. Within moments, the vehicles on the spur were booming cannon fire into compounds in the valley, and my ears rang from the concussion. Below me, red and green tracer coiled and weaved across the terrain, clouds of smoke from RPG detonations drifting lazily as the Canadians fought hard to extract themselves from the enemy's killing ground. It was not a fast extraction, the Canadians methodical and no doubt wanting to punish the Taliban before they drove clear. I could only watch on, fascinated, marvelling that the enemy continued to engage despite the awesome weight of fire that poured down onto them from the spur. It was only the appearance of fast jets overhead that finally silenced the guns, the Taliban melting away before JDAMs could slam into their firing points.

I expected more of the same when we entered the green zone to form an armoured sleeve through which B Company, and a logistics convoy from Bastion, could push into Sangin DC. That sleeve would be held open as long as it would take for the loggies to drop their containers and collapse back through us, with A Coy following behind them, and I expected that the strung-out formation would be ripe for harassing fire from small arms and RPGs. 'Overmatch' was how the battle-group would counter this threat – effectively, deploying so much force on the ground that it would be suicide for the enemy to attack us. Though the Taliban were not afraid to die, they had shown that they were less willing to do so when there was no tactical or strategic victory to be gained. To that end, the relief of A Company saw two mechanized squadrons, three British rifle companies, and multiple units of ANP and Afghan army on the ground in and around the town, with Apache helicopters and fast jets buzzing overhead. The display of force did exactly as intended, and the enemy were unseen and unheard. It made me think about what could be achieved in the province if we could deploy a battlegroup to each town, rather than to have a single one spread across a province.

It was with some sadness that I left the Canadian force. I had enjoyed the experience of driving across the desert from task to task, and the Canadians themselves were great men, but when the squadron arrived in Bastion at the successful conclusion of A Company's RIP, I had my orders to stay behind. In fact, I had a lot more than that on my plate.

'Adam,' Colonel Tootal greeted me as I entered the operations room. 'I'm sending you up to Musa Qala.'

'Musa Qala?' I asked, a little surprised. To my knowledge, that town was being held by an armoured reconnaissance force of Danish soldiers. 'You want me to go as liaison with them?' I guessed.

Tootal shook his head.

'The Danes are pulling out. It's got too hot for them, and Copenhagen's pulled the chain before they lose any men. You'll be taking their place, Adam. We're forming a new company from scratch, and you'll be their OC. For the rest of the tour, you'll be the commander of Easy Company.'

5

I had been expecting a quick turnaround and a new assignment when I arrived at Bastion. What I had not expected was to be given a company – or the notion of a company at this point – in relief of an armoured force in Musa Qala.

Musa Qala – I knew of it, of course. It was one of the key towns in the province, a sprawling place of a hundred thousand people that sat aside the gravelly wadi of the Helmand river. Like everyone else in the battlegroup, I knew that the Pathfinders, a small elite of twenty-five men within the task force, had been dispatched there after a call for assistance from the local forces fighting to keep the district centre (a large compound) out of Taliban hands. The Pathfinders had expected they would insert quickly and beat back the enemy, as they had done with rebel forces in Sierra Leone. Instead the Taliban proved themselves dogged opponents, and PF were forced into close-quarter fighting so vicious that the enemy were often above or below them in the same building, as both sides manoeuvred to secure the compound. Only danger close air strikes had broken the Taliban assaults, and so PF had been relieved by an imposing squadron of Danish armour, Tiger Squadron, who were themselves bolstered by the addition of a rifle platoon from the Royal Irish. This force, I was now told, had been holding the district centre for several weeks, coming under daily attack.

Retaining control of the DC seemed to hold considerable political weight in both NATO and Afghan headquarters, particularly with the district governor, Daud, who – despite the fact that his own men were not holding it – saw the piece of land as a point of pride. Therefore, to abandon the position became inconceivable to our own chain of command, who believed that without the governor's staunch support, 3 Para's mission in Helmand could not succeed. Corporal McKinney, a section commander in Somme Platoon, was the first serious casualty of this policy, and the enemy's weight of fire made it impossible for the wounded man to be evacuated by Chinook. Instead, a smaller Lynx with no medical team had been forced into making a vertical drop into the compound itself. Thankfully, he had survived, but the incident had done enough to prove to the Danes that, without a secured HLS to evacuate the wounded, the situation was untenable. Their politicians were not willing to lose men holding the location, and informed ISAF that Tiger Squadron would be withdrawing to Bastion in forty-eight hours. This gave Colonel Tootal and his command two days to organize a relief force to take their place. But there was one slight problem.

There were no more companies to deploy.

B Company 3 Para were now in Sangin. C Company were in Gereshk; FSP Company were spread all over; the Gurkhas were in Now Zad; the Canadians were going back to Kandahar. A Company were now in Bastion, but to use them would rob the battlegroup of its last unit capable of manoeuvre, and would take away the ability to launch the most fundamental of missions, such as resupplies and reliefs. Without doubt, the battlegroup was overstretched, but we had been ordered to find a company for Musa Qala, and so that's what would be done.

'The Royal Irish platoon who are in play will be staying put,' Tootal told me. 'We're pulling another back from Gereshk, so you can have them.'

It's usual for rifle companies to be formed of three platoons, but as the CO moved on, I took it to mean that I was to make do with two – fifty-six riflemen instead of eighty-four.

'There's a mortar section there, and we'll take the snipers

that just came back with A Company. We're pulling in a couple of combat medics, too.'

I thought about Corporal McKinney, and how difficult it had been to extract him.

'Sir, I'd like a doctor. A surgeon.'

Tootal nodded. He'd foreseen the same need. 'We're getting one. We don't have anyone we can cut to you as a company 2IC, but we're getting an FST from the MOGs. They'll travel in by vehicle along with the police.'

'We're replacing the police?' I asked.

'Most of the local ones there have already deserted. The ones that are left are compromised. We'll get you standby police that aren't from the province.'

The Afghan National Standby Police were to the Afghan National Police what the feds are to the cops. They were also an admission that the local police could not be counted upon in any manner, and were a liability that was better cut loose.

'The only other blokes we can give you is a LEWT team.'

A LEWT team was a couple of signallers and interpreters who listened in to the Taliban's unsecured radio traffic, using it to build intelligence, and warn of attacks.

'Looks like getting blokes in and out isn't going to be a possibility?' I posed, and the CO nodded – the threat to the helicopters was too high. 'In that case, sir,' I went on, 'I'd like some real top tier terps that are tried and tested. Sounds like we'll need them, and we can't swap them out if they go shaky on us.'

'We'll get you those,' Tootal agreed. 'Come back here at 2000 hours, Adam. We'll have an insertion plan by then.'

Dismissed by the CO, I set out to find my company – at least, those men already in Bastion; my rifle platoon would not arrive from Gereshk until the early hours. The man who would be instrumental in organizing the ammunition and supplies that we would need was Paratrooper Sergeant Major Scrivener, the battlegroup's operations warrant officer. Like myself, he had also been tied to JOC, and was now relishing the opportunity to get out onto the ground. 'Scrivs' had a great physical presence, and had a reputation in 3 Para as being a cool head. Far from being the stereotypical shouting caricature of his rank, the sergeant major was measured, and a calming influence on others.

'Can't say I'm sorry to be getting out of the ops room,' the thirty-six-year-old confided to me as I briefed him on his new role. 'Hard being back here, when the lads are out on the ground.'

I knew exactly what he meant, and told him as much. Then I gave him his orders for that night; 'Beg, steal, and borrow what you can, Scrivs. We need to take as much eighty-one-mil and gimpy link as we can.'

'No worries, boss. I'll make sure the Chinook's struggling to get off the ground.'

Ammunition would be our lifeline, but if we were to take casualties, our medical team and supplies would be critical. With such a hazardous casevac procedure, what medical kit we took from Bastion could be the difference between life and death for a soldier, and so I followed our surgeon, Dr Mike Stacey, into the camp's well-equipped hospital, pilfering as much as we could, and learning more about the man whose skills I hoped we would never need. At over six foot and with a shaved head, 'Doc' cut a powerful and confident figure, though his quiet manner meant I could just as easily picture him as a GP in the Home Counties as I could a surgeon in a war zone.

It was on my return from the hospital to Battlegroup HQ that I ran into Abe Williams, an RAF Regiment gunner I'd met on a German Para exchange course the year before. He was also the best machine gunner I'd ever seen.

'What are you doing sitting around here with your thumb up your arse?' I prodded him.

'Bored as hell, to be honest,' he confessed. 'Would love to get out there.'

'You're a forward air controller, aren't you?' I asked him. 'Come with me to Musa Qala.'

'Why not?' He shrugged.

He likes to joke that he has never forgiven me.

I stood in the operations room as various officers took their turns at briefing for the upcoming operation, covering everything from intelligence to logistics. The Danish government were unwavering in their time frame of forty-eight hours, and this pressure had forced the development of a simple plan.

A Company, newly arrived from Sangin, would fly from Bastion in Chinooks to be inserted along the green zone at the edge of Musa Qala. An Estonian mechanized squadron operating in the desert would also join them, as well as units from the Afghan army. Just before dawn, Easy Company would insert into the town by Chinook.

A single Chinook.

I had to smile at the thought. Chinooks were big beasts, but to fit almost the entirety of my company onto the bird, not to mention the necessary ammunition and supplies we would be taking with us, went some way to showing how understrength our formation would be.

Well, I'd joined the army for a challenge, hadn't I? If this wasn't it, then it was time to retire.

'The rest of the battlegroup will move into place after dawn,' the officer continued. 'They'll hold down the route, and the Danes will extract in the early afternoon. The ANSP will insert at the same time, along with the FST.'

'Is it possible to get a shipping container of defensive stores with them?' I asked, thinking of the experiences of the Path-finders, and how we would need to fortify our position to the utmost.

The man shook his head. 'Wasn't possible, I'm afraid. The mobile units are already out in the desert. Wasn't possible to get anything out to them in time.'

He didn't have to say that there was no spare unit in Bastion that could have taken it to the operation themselves. We would have to do without the stores, at least for now. What we would have for our resupply was a system known as Eagle's lift. This consisted of pallets of ammunition and stores that would sit at the edge of Bastion's HLS. Captain Stu Russell, a Falklands veteran and now Battlegroup Logistics Officer, would manage all resupply. If there was a need for a Chinook to come into Musa Qala, it would carry those supplies in with it. Of course, we all knew the one reason why a helicopter mission to that exposed location would be sanctioned, and what would be going into the Chinook for the return leg.

Casualties.

I was so busy with the preparation for departure that I had no time to contemplate my own mortality, but as a commander it was my duty to consider the same question for my men. That was why I had pushed for as large a medical staff as possible, and why we had raided the hospital until our pockets and packs bulged with supplies. The ferocity of the fight against the Taliban was mounting across the province, and from what I could see, I was about to be dropped into one of the most volatile parts. Knowing that, I tried to harden myself to the truth that I could very soon lose men under my command. It would be folly to expect that we could come through the experience casualty free, but that is what I would aim for, doing whatever I could to see that Easy Company left the town intact, and together.

'Any questions, Adam?' Tootal asked me, the briefing done.

I had dozens, but they were not the kind that could be answered in the operations room; I knew how I would react under fire, but how would it be when the company was mine to command? How would I respond if my men were hurt? How would I make the decision to call a Chinook into the danger of a hot LS? How would I feel calling air strikes down onto people's homes?

'No questions, sir,' I told him.

It was time for actions.

Easy Company formed up on the concrete pan of the HLS, forty silhouettes chatting by torchlight. It was the first time the rifle platoon and HQ elements had come together – the whole company would not be formed until we were within Musa Qala itself. It was hardly textbook, but that gave the mission a sense of adventure that was palpable amongst the troops. No one was in any doubt about what we were going into, but that caused as many smiles as it did nerves.

'They scraped the barrel,' was a phrase I'd heard often from Easy Company mouths in the past twenty-four hours, but the words were more prideful than a condemnation. There was a sense that we were the posse being rounded up to relieve a fort surrounded by Indians. That we – the Dirty Dozen, pulled from the grubby corners of Helmand to form a unit – would perform a task no other would dare. Every soldier had his own Hollywood reference for who we were, and why we were doing it. Raised on action films and westerns as we were, it was impossible to think of our own war as anything but a reflection of our favourite books and movies.

I joined my sniper pair, Jared Cleary and Hugh Keir of 3 Para. They were D Company men and snipers at the top of their game. Now they were a key element of Easy Company.

'Looking forward to this?' I asked them.

Both men grinned, clutching the paraphernalia that marked them out as snipers.

'Can't wait, sir,' Cleary answered. 'Knights in shining armour, riding to the rescue.'

'Just be careful of saying that to Somme Platoon.' I smiled, referring to the Royal Irish men who had been in place for three weeks. 'I doubt they see it that way.'

'Will give them a good morale boost to know they've got the Reg with them, sir,' Keir put in. 'Probably worth a squadron of Danes each, me and Cleary.'

I laughed, and left the smiling men to it. They couldn't have been more eager to get to our destination if it had been the Playboy Mansion. This was what they had dreamed of and trained for, but it went deeper than that – soldiering was their reason for being.

'Mount up,' came the call, and all about me the silhouettes of Easy Company stirred in the darkness, NCOs ordering men into their place, the files steadily shuffling towards the Chinook's ramp beneath their burdens of weapons and ammunition.

'That's everyone, sir,' Sergeant Major Scrivener informed me, and I took a look at the crammed interior of the chopper, red light bathing the excited faces of my men.

'Let's go,' I told the loadmaster, and I stepped up onto the tail ramp, taking my place on the canvas benches. Seconds later, the rotors began to whine.

Easy Company was on its way to Musa Qala.

I could only pray that all of us would be coming back.

6

The Chinook was at bursting point, the cabin packed with men and equipment, so it was only by craning my neck that I could peer into the black sky through the helicopter's porthole. There was no light visible in the wasteland that surrounded Bastion, the so-called Desert of Death, and so I pulled my night-vision goggles into place, adjusting the dial until my world became one of green light. Through this eerie spectrum I saw the harsh mountain that grew angrily out of the desert floor, a flat bed of nothing.

Around me, my men chattered excitedly, their voices raised against the smacking of the rotor blades and the shaking of the bird's metal carcass. We knew what we were flying into – at least, we thought that we did – but there was no hesitation in their manner. There was only excitement, and anticipation. This was it. Soldiers lived for these moments. They dreamed of them. To fly into a town that was awash with enemies, and to link up with your friends, your brothers, and to stand beside them against the enemy. What more could a soldier wish for than that?

It was a thirty-minute flight from Bastion to Musa Qala, and that time was filled with laughter and banter. A few men slept, or at least tried to, drained from the hurried preparation of our departure. I saw their nodding heads through my night vision, and thought I should follow suit – sleep would be in short supply in the coming days – but there was no chance of dropping off whilst my body tingled with excitement, and my mind raced with a million questions.

Did I have enough ammunition? How would we charge the batteries if the generator broke? Could we get more medical kit from the Danes? What would I do if we were under fire when we landed? What if we were dropped in the wrong spot? What if we took a casualty? What if I became a casualty? What did my men want from me?

I answered that one easily enough – certainty. My men wanted certainty. We were going into a situation that promised little of that, but I could show it in my person and in my actions. No matter the hundreds of questions that echoed through a commander's mind in a necessary loop of checklists and problem-solving, my outward appearance to my men must always project absolute certainty.

In the darkness of the Chinook's cabin, I smiled.

My men.

I had joined the army for adventure and challenge. I had stayed because I wanted to lead. Now, here I was, taking command of a desert outpost on the other side of the planet from my childhood in sleepy Surrey. It had been a winding road to get here, but now I had what I had always wanted – the command of men at war.

'Five minutes' came over the intercom, and I turned my head back to the porthole. Desert was giving way to compounds and vegetation. We were drawing close to the Musa Qala wadi, a wide, dry, gravelly river bed that cut across the landscape like an ugly scar. Either side of it was the blanket of irrigation and irregular compounds. On its eastern bank was Musa Qala.

The size of the town took me by surprise. I had studied maps and aerial photos, but even so, the scale of the place snagged a little – it was huge, a sprawling labyrinth of compounds and alleyways bisected by roads, some of which were dual carriageways.

'Two minutes.'

As we shot low across the rooftops, I saw through the green haze of my goggles how much devastation had already been visited on the town – compound walls looked as if they'd been bitten by giants. Scree slopes of rubble cascaded into wide streets, or choked alleyways. Amongst this quiet ruin I saw no movement. Either the locals were gone, or they knew better than to raise their heads.

'One minute.'

I looked to the aircraft's open doors, seeing the two gunners straining forward into their harnesses, searching for danger. This was the moment when we were most vulnerable. The final approach. The minute where we must lose speed, the pilot flaring hard to bring a chugging beast to heel, and to land her on an area smaller than half a football pitch. Stealth had been lost the moment the twin rotors had been heard beating towards the city. If the enemy were ready, they'd see a hovering silhouette set against the inky gloom of a pre-dawn sky.

'Here we fucking go!' I heard an Irish voice pipe up, cracking with excitement and nerves.

I felt my stomach tighten as the aircraft's nose lifted, and we dropped towards the earth. This was the moment. This was Terry's best chance to kill us. If an RPG hit the bird, it would be a few seconds of screaming terror, and then we would be a smouldering wreck amongst the compounds, tomorrow's front-page news for our countrymen to read about as they chewed on a bacon sandwich and muttered about what a terrible thing war was.

The back wheels touched down first, and we rocked on the canvas benches as the laden Chinook settled, the pilot performing ballet with a bull.

'Go! Go!' the loadmaster called, and now all was activity, men scrambling for the ramp, cursing if their equipment snagged, or a mate sent an unwieldy weapon into a shin, or face.

'Off!' I urged my men. 'Off!'

I piled off the tailgate at the head of them. It was a blur around me as the Chinook's cabin continued to vomit ammunition crates and bundles of sandbags, the loadmaster throwing them clear even as the beast lifted itself from the ground. I knew what was coming next, and turned my back to the bird, crouching as I shielded my eyes from the blast of the engine's heat, and the churned dust that whipped across any inch of exposed skin.

Within moments the huge machine was gone, leaving the space around us feeling empty, despite the hive of activity as men filled their arms and piled their shoulders with kit, NCOs urging and organizing with hushed commands full of urgency.

I looked around me, seeing figures in the darkness. They were the men we had come to relieve, pushed outwards to protect the HLS, which I saw now was extremely exposed and overlooked by high ground and compounds. It was a terrible position to be in, but my men knew the same, and they were hasty in hoovering up all supplies thrown from the chopper, and carrying them inside the main compound through a gap in a partially collapsed wall, an early welcome to the situation that we were arriving into.

'Major Jowett?' a well-educated Dublin accent asked in the darkness. 'Captain Johnson.'

'Adam,' I told him as I shook his hand. Mark 'Johnno' Johnson was the commander of Somme Platoon, the Royal Irish soldiers that had been in place for three weeks, and who were now under my command. By rank and position, I took the man to be in his mid-twenties. Even in the darkness, I could feel the confidence of the energetic officer in both his manner, and movements.

'Can you show me around?' I asked. Dawn was threatening the horizon, and I wanted to take in as much of the location as I could before light tempted the enemy with the possibility of attack. Around us, Royal Irish soldiers were happily catching up with the comrades of their sister platoon. The lifting darkness was full of stories and laughter.

'Sergeant Brangan?' Captain Johnson asked a figure in the gloom, no doubt recognizing him from his silhouette, indistinguishable to a civilian, but as clear as a face to a soldier that knew him well. 'Can you show Barossa Platoon where to drop their kit, please? And where to centralize the ammo and stores they brought in?'

'Will do, sir.'

'It's a bit of a mad house this morning, isn't it?' the young officer spoke to me, unfazed by it all.

He wasn't wrong. As well as my incoming men, the centre of the compound was packed with light armoured vehicles and soldiers as the Danes prepared for their exfiltration later that day. I wondered at how we were to hold this position better than they had with a fleet of forty vehicles, and 140 men.

I pushed such thinking from my mind. We were here, and what we had was what we had. There was no other choice but to crack on.

'Show me the positions, Mark,' I asked.

'Just remember, sir,' he told me as we moved off, 'if it's open ground, you sprint. Even a lot of the cover is worth sprinting by, because it's not strong enough to stop rounds.'

'Sounds good,' I said, smiling wryly.

'And the rooftops are mostly belt-buckle.'

'You haven't had the chance to build up positions?' I asked him.

'Just not possible, sir,' he told me. 'We haven't got the stores, and even if we did, it wouldn't be possible. You'll see what I mean, sir.'

I did. We'd barely shown ourselves at a dash between buildings when rounds began to chew into the mud brick, spitting out chunks of clay. The crack and the thump of the incoming fire told me that it could not have come from further than a block or two away, and as I peered over a lip of the wall, and looked out at the town of Musa Qala in grey dawn, I understood why – the enemy were on top of us. Every side of the district centre was abutted by compounds and rubble. Every wall was overlooked. The enemy could approach unseen to within a grenade's distance of our walls, maybe closer, and every movement within our own 'sanctuary' could be spotted, and sniped at. As far as defensive positions went, I could not have imagined much worse.

'Not exactly textbook.' Johnno smiled, reading my mind.

'It's not.' I grinned back. 'Is that a sofa?' I asked, pointing to where a threadbare couch had been plugged into a gaping hole in the wall.

'Afraid so, sir. Rocket hit there, and it was the only thing we had left to try and fill the gap, and provide some cover from view. A lot of the cover is more sniper screen than fighting position.'

The light was growing, and by the sunlight I could make out the walls, which ranged in height from mid-thigh to above the head, every part of their length appearing like gnawed cheese. No part of the compound was unmolested. Where walls were overlooked by the enemy, there was a visible tidemark of impact damage to mark the limit of their angle of attack.

Now that the sun was rising, I could see Mark had the look of a man who was being worn thin through lack of sleep, and stress. I saw the same red eyes and hollow gaze in the men who held the fighting positions. It was the thousand-yard stare. The mark of the combat soldier.

'Been a long three weeks?' I asked the young officer.

'It has,' Mark admitted, and that was as far as his pride would allow him to complain. 'Boys have been great, though.' He added with feeling: 'My platoon won't let you down, sir.'

We continued the tour. Mark showed me where unexploded mortars had been covered with sandbags, and marked with brightly coloured tape for avoidance. Ordinarily, these unexploded shells would be cleared by engineers, but I was quickly coming to realize that there was little ordinary about Musa Qala DC.

'They tried to burrow in through the old Afghan ablution

block here,' Mark told me, pointing to a building that jutted onto the compound wall. 'Tried to climb in through the shit pipes, basically.' He smiled. 'So we've blocked it off and filled the place with trip flares and claymores.'

The claymore was a furious weapon – a strip of explosives packed over with metal ball bearings that would shred anything caught in front of it. It was possible to have them set off by tripwire, but Britain had signed an agreement that forbade us using them in such a manner. Instead, we could detonate them by use of a 'clacker', a paper-stapler-like object that was connected to the explosive with a command wire.

'Our own shitters are here,' the officer told me, pointing to the north-east wall, where two halves of an oil drum sat with a plank of wood above them as a seat. The smell of diesel and shit wafted thickly into my nostrils. Pity the soldier who drew the lot to burn his comrades' waste.

'We've got more claymores on the other vulnerable points,' he pointed out. 'We've marked the positions of the clackers with graffiti. If it looks like they're getting in, we've told the boys to let rip.'

'That works for me,' I told him, happy with what I was seeing, at least in the sense that Mark and his men were doing all they could with so little.

We came to a section of wall that butted onto a ruined building. Visible amongst the wreckage was a series of archways.

'This is the mosque?' I asked, recognizing it from aerial photography.

'Collapsed when PF called in some danger close air strikes,' Mark confirmed. 'Terry loves it now.'

There was little surprise to that. The ruined building provided a multitude of firing positions and covered approaches.

'We don't have the best position,' Mark offered, deliberately understating how terrible a defensive perimeter we were inheriting.

'The governor wants it held,' I told him honestly. 'If we have the governor onside, the job of bringing security to Helmand becomes a lot easier.' The words felt lame as I spoke them. The party line was severely undermined by the carnage that lay all about us.

'I'm sure there's a reason for it,' Johnson replied, like the good soldier that he was.

My tour concluded with an inspection of the two taller buildings in the compound, christened the Outpost and the Alamo.

'The Alamo?' I laughed.

'We've been using it for fire support, and it will be our fallback position if Terry gets inside the walls,' Mark said cheerfully.

The Alamo.

I looked again at the building, scarred by bullets and shrapnel, then at the impressive fighting force of Danes that would be leaving the compound within hours. Their heavy power had done little to deter the Taliban, and now those machine guns and grenade launchers would be leaving, as well as the steel that protected their gunners. In their place would remain eighty men, mostly riflemen, protected by little more than lightweight body armour, and their training.

My men.

We would not be falling back to the Alamo.

7

The Afghan sun continued to rise, and with it came the heat, our combat clothing soon becoming soaked and salt-stained whilst our throats dried to the texture of cardboard.

'It's just crept past fifty degrees,' Doc told me as we stood in what was now my centre of operations: a room of sandbag-filled windows and bright pink walls inside the single-storey building that sat in the northern sector of the compound, a scattered collection of plastic patio furniture serving as office desks and chairs.

There was a professional warning in the doctor's words. Fifty degrees was more than enough to fell a man if he was lounging on a beach, let alone bustling beneath body armour and helmet as we scurried to prepare for the Danes' departure. From the door of the ops room, the compound's yard looked like an overturned log, men rushing in every direction, the expressions on bearded faces of the Danes a mixture of relief to be leaving, and anger and shame at stepping away from a fight.

'They don't want to go,' Sergeant 'PJ' Brangan told me. 'Most of them, anyway. They're great lads. There's a lot of friendships back and forth between them and my boys.'

Sure enough, amongst the vehicles of the Danes I could see a peppering of Royal Irish soldiers. They had been born in different countries, spoke a different language, and served in different armies, but facing danger together was an experience that transcended all boundaries, and thick friendships had been forged on the anvil of combat. I saw that the Royal Irish men had their arms full of personal equipment and ammunition gifted by their departing friends.

'Got to feel shit for their blokes.' Sergeant Major Scrivener spoke up, knowing the mind of a soldier better than most. 'It's not like they have any choice over what their headshed does, especially at the ISAF HQ level.'

'What about your lads, Mark?' I asked the platoon commander. 'Do they want to leave?'

Mark smiled. He knew that his men were confined to these walls whatever their personal wishes.

'They're knackered, but they're good. They would never leave now that Barossa Platoon are here,' he told me, and I could hear he believed every word of that. I had no reason to doubt him. In the short time since our arrival I had seen the strong bonds of camaraderie between the men of the Royal Irish platoons. Without a doubt, they would fight for each other.

'I want to put the Afghan Police here.' I spoke to my ops room at large, pointing to our sketch map of the compound. 'There's forty of them coming in as the Danes go, and I think this stretch of western wall north of the gate gives them their own section of perimeter to control, so that they don't feel insulted, but it's close enough to these other positions of ours that we can stop a breakthrough there if they decide to run.'

No one commented on the fact that I was taking such a possibility into account. We had all seen that the national forces could range from reliable to shambolic. The entire reason that the ANSP were replacing the ANP already in the compound was due to the latter's reluctance to fight, and their high rate of desertion.

'If we get good Afghans, we'll integrate them more as we go along,' I concluded. 'But to begin with, let's keep a tight lid on them. I don't want the reason we end up in the shit to be because someone got high or slept on watch.'

'Very good, sir.' Scrivs nodded. Discipline was the responsibility of every soldier but, as sergeant major, he would see that every man stuck to those standards, and would punish any who failed to do so.

'I'm going to take another look around,' I told the room, once talk of provisioning and administrating the incoming Afghan Police had concluded.

'Want me to come with you, sir?' Mark offered.

I declined. The compound was small enough that I already knew my way. 'Get some rest, if you can,' I told him, knowing that when the Danes left, respite would be at a premium.

I pulled my helmet onto my head, fastening the chin strap. Eyes squinting, I stepped out of the open doorway and into the full force of the Afghan sun.

If I were the Taliban, how would I try to kill me? That's what I asked myself as I moved around the compound, trying to ignore the hive of Danish activity as I sought out weaknesses in our defences. *How would I kill me? How would I kill my men?*

Putting yourself in your enemy's shoes was key in both attack and defence, and well trained in Western militaries. The Danes had asked themselves the same questions I was now asking. So had Somme, and so had the Pathfinders before them. I doubted very much that Helmand's governor and his local militia had, or they would never have chosen this site to be their district centre, and the prime target for their Taliban enemies.

It was a shocking choice for a defensive position. Truly shocking. If I had chosen this as part of a planning exercise, I would have rightly been torn to strips by my instructors. The compound was overlooked at almost every angle. Rubble and rat runs gave cover directly to our walls. Only sangar three in the north-east corner of the compound had overhead cover, where loopholes had been dug out of the walls of an outbuilding, and I hated to think what a direct hit from a mortar, or an air burst from an RPG, would do to my men in the other positions. That dark but necessary thought brought me to the helicopter landing site, a totally exposed and overlooked scrap of dirt that abutted our compound. It was a lethal trap, and I had already discounted the possibility of helicopter resupply – I could not risk a helicopter and her crew even for the defensive stores we so badly needed. But for a casualty evacuation? My stomach knotted as I considered how I would make that call. Could I risk the helicopter for walking wounded? Probably not. What about the more seriously injured? What about critical? What if I had a soldier who was so badly hurt that his chances of survival were limited even if he made it to the surgeon's table at Bastion? Should he be left to die, to guarantee the safety of the helicopter's crew?

I looked again at the pathetic positioning of the HLS. There was nothing I could do to change it, and I could only pray that I would not be pushed into a situation that required making those kind of decisions. The army promised its men that they would be taken care of if hurt. It was a basic principle of the contract that allowed men to put themselves in danger. As their commander, I was one of those responsible for ensuring that the promise was upheld.

I shook my head, realizing that there was little to be gained by dwelling on these facts. There were a thousand variables, and any decision would have to be made in the moment. I could only plan so much, and so I moved away from the HLS to find areas that I *could* control.

One was the Alamo. It was made up of two storeys, but both were tall, giving it the height of three, requiring two ladders to gain access to its rooftop, where sandbags perched atop the low walls. The Alamo had been built as a local jail, its first-floor cells medieval in their barren nature. The inside of the building had been daubed with Taliban graffiti, the language lost on me, but not so the childlike paintings – stickmen with RPGs destroyed tanks, whilst burning helicopters fell from the sky. Though crude, there was something eerie to the scribbles.

I wondered where the artists were now. Were they outside my walls, picturing that exposed HLS, and how they could bring their art to life?

I moved away from the paintings. At the centre of the Alamo was an open courtyard. I wondered if it was where the inmates had taken their exercise. The frantic sounds of the compound were dulled in the space, and it was almost serene. Not a bad place to contemplate a prison break. I grinned to myself. Funny, now, how the Taliban were trying to break *into* a place they had been so desperate to get out of. What was a good place for my enemy's musings was a good place for my own, and I saw quickly that Mark Johnson had been right – regardless of any Taliban break-in, due to its height and fields of fire the Alamo would be instrumental in any small-arms contact, an excellent position for our fire support such as the GPMGs, light mortars, and snipers. I got on my personal-role radio and asked the sergeant major to see that the building was well stocked with a reserve of ammunition. Little point of a last stand position if our ammunition was beyond reach.

The sunshine hit me with a slap as I emerged onto the Alamo's rooftop. I kept my body low, and an anxious sentry was glad to see that the new arrival had more sense than to strut about the rooftop as if he were on a parade square.

'I'm the new OC,' I greeted the sentry.

'Ranger McConnell, sir,' the man replied.

'Somme Platoon?' I asked, knowing it from his tired, red eyes.

'Yes, sir.'

I looked around at the fighting position. Empty shell cases had been swept by hand into large piles in the corner. Sand-bags had been chewed open by enemy rounds.

'Ready to show Barossa Platoon how it's done?' I asked him.

'Yes, sir.' The young soldier couldn't have been older than nineteen. 'Nice of them to turn up,' he added, grinning.

I grinned back, glad of the friendly rivalry – competition

between soldiers was a great thing. When the chips were down, the will to not fail before the other man was a powerful driving force. Pride was as vital in combat as gun oil and ammunition.

I looked into the compound, where the Danes were making final checks on their mechanical steeds and heavy weapons. From the absence of mortar and gunfire, I guessed that the Taliban did not expect them to be replaced, and were happy enough to sit back and watch their enemy roll out. I wondered what their reaction would be when they discovered there was a skeleton British company left in the wake of the Danish armour.

8

The time had come. The Danes were leaving.

It was early afternoon, the sun high and angry. Beneath its gaze, bearded soldiers took final looks at a place they would remember forever. As the entanglement of the front gate was cleared of wire and stacked bed frames, they mounted their vehicles and prepared for the order to move.

I stepped into the operations room. The Danish departure was not as simple a matter as them battening down their hatches and driving away into the desert. It was a battlegroup-level operation, involving elements of air and land: 3 Para; Estonian army; Afghan Police; American jets; British Apaches; the Danes themselves – the extraction was a concert, and the orchestra's players were many and international.

I was not the conductor. That role fell to Battlegroup HQ, but I was responsible for seeing that my company's part in the symphony was played without a wrong note. In order to achieve this, the proceeding hours had been spent in planning, going over the commander's questions of how and what if? As Somme Platoon were familiar with the enemy's likely firing points, they would man the compound's sangars whilst fresh Barossa pushed out into the streets, securing a couple of vital junctions that the Danish beasts could lumber through before cutting loose onto the wider roads. Once in the more open ground, their turret-mounted heavy weapons should see them safely through any ambush.

I looked around the ops room at my headquarters team; Sergeant Major Scrivener; Freddie the IO; Staff Sergeant Wornham and his three signallers; my JTACs. All were engrossed in their tasks, talking into radios or marking maps.

They were too busy to be worried about what would happen when the Danes left. Not so the men in the fighting positions. They had to watch, and wait. Waiting is when you worry about what *could* happen. Once the first round cracks overhead, then the time for worry is over, and that's when a soldier is in his element.

Waiting is the hard part.

I heard the scream of a fast jet cutting through the sky. It was a reassuring sound to my ears, but there would be others in the town who would hear the burning engines with dread, knowing that the payloads of bombs were meant for them. Already the town had been smashed with munitions. From what I'd heard, it was the only thing that saved the Pathfinders from the danger of being overrun. The jets were untouchable in the sky, and circled our heads like vengeful guardians. I knew I could call on them if we needed it, and the knowledge that such firepower was within my grasp was both reassuring and terrifying – nobody wanted to be the person that ordered an attack that left a family of innocents dead. No one was stupid enough to think that you could simply term flesh and blood 'collateral damage' and shake off the guilt. We were here to help the Afghan nation and the people of this town. If I called in air, it had to be for good reason – taking life from some to save that of others – my men. Above all else, my men were my concern.

'Battlegroup net, sir,' Lee Simmons, one of the signallers informed me, handing me a radio handset.

'Cobalt Six,' I spoke into it, then received the news that we had been waiting for – the wadi and its banks had been secured by A Company and the Estonians. There was no enemy contact. It was time for the Danes to leave.

I heard their engines rev in the compound's yard as drivers and vehicle commanders received the same message over their own radios and intercoms.

I turned to Barossa Platoon's commander, Paul Martin. 'Paul, Push your platoon out.'

'Will do, sir,' he replied, and I could see a wolfish look of anticipation on his face. The young captain knew that, as soon as he and his men stepped foot outside of the gates, he could be thrown into the biggest test of his life.

'See you later,' I told him, and he walked out into the sun, calling for his platoon to prepare to move, and to clear the final obstacles from the gate.

'How long for them to get into position, do you think, sir?' Scrivs asked me, the veteran checking the fit of the magazines in his chest rig.

'Couple of minutes,' I answered, gesturing for a radio handset from my signallers, and informing the battlegroup that Barossa were now pushing out onto the ground. I pictured the faces of the soldiers as they chambered a round, and moved through the gate. I knew that they would be sharing winks and smiles. They were setting foot onto a two-way shooting range, and there would be no doubt in their minds as to who were the best and most skilled soldiers in the town. From the expression on Scrivs' face, the old soldier was picturing the same. We were both a little jealous that we were not the ones stepping beyond the walls and into trouble, but that was not my place. I was in the district centre to lead, to command, and to control, and that was why I tuned my ear into the chattering of several radio networks, and watched the adjustments made to maps and boards as the battlegroup's units manoeuvred to support the Danish extraction.

Accented English cut onto the battlegroup net. It was the Danish squadron commander.

'Moving now. Out.' He spoke to a host of men waiting on his action from the gate of our compound, to NATO headquarters, and the corridors of power in Copenhagen.

'They're off,' Doc Stacey spoke from the doorway. His medical centre established, he had come to watch the show. I said a quick prayer to myself that he could remain in the ops room for the duration, his services not needed by my men, or by our allies.

'What did you make of their medical wagons?' I asked him. With our men in position, there was little to do now but wait for the Danish armour to uncoil and snake into the town's rubbled streets.

'Fantastic,' he told me. 'Not sure what it would be like working in them when they're bouncing around, but the kit was great. Shame we couldn't hold on to one of them.' He shrugged.

'Shame we couldn't hold on to all of them, sir,' Scrivs noted. 'Nice to have a few armoured pillboxes.'

'What's wrong with two sandbags and a poncho, Sergeant Major?' I joked.

'Oh, that's more than enough, sir. Could see a Russian armoured division off with that.'

'All quiet so far, sir.' One of the signallers spoke. 'No contact anywhere.'

'They know it's not a fair fight,' Scrivs offered, and I nodded in agreement. As the relief of A Company at Sangin had also demonstrated, the Taliban could be quietened if it was possible to bring in an overwhelming show of force. The presence of the Danish squadron alone was impressive, but that had not been enough to deter attacks. Coupled with two rifle companies, however, as well as the Estonian mechanized squadron, Afghan forces, and an airspace buzzing with attack helicopters and fast jets, it was enough to keep Terry in his hole. Once again I wondered at what could be achieved in Helmand if we could bring this kind of force protection to bear on a daily basis, providing the necessary security for the CIMIC projects we were promising, but had yet to deliver upon. At the very least, we could keep the Taliban at bay without having to resort to using close air support. Alas, there was no such force that could be held on the ground for longer than the relief operations. And so, when the battlegroup withdrew to Bastion and their other bases, I feared that the Taliban would emerge from their holes like dark spiders, creeping through alleyways and rubble to inspect what had been left in their web.

I moved to the doorway. The movement of the Danish vehicles kicked up dry dirt that obscured their final waves to their British friends in the fighting positions. Then the masked faces were gone as they ducked down into hatches pulled tight against the threat of small-arms fire. Only a few of the Danish vehicles were lightly armoured, and in these nimble frames rested the descendants of Vikings, beards dusty beneath helmet and goggles as they made final checks to the fit of ammunition belts in machine-gun feed trays.

'They look bloody hard,' Scrivs spoke up behind me, with a Para's grudging respect. 'Wouldn't want them turning up at your monastery, would you?'

We laughed.

'We're going to be here a few weeks at least, Sergeant Major,' I told him. 'I'm sure you can sculpt a fine face-warmer in that time.'

The man snorted, and rubbed at his face. 'Don't know if I want to, sir. Worried it might come in white.'

We chuckled again.

'That's not such a bad thing,' I told him. 'The Afghans respect beards as a sign of maturity, so if you can get a thick white one going, they'll probably elect you as a tribal elder.'

'Perfect, sir. I'm sure the missus would be happy to relocate out here.'

I grinned at the jest as the radio continued to chatter against my left ear. To a novice, the entanglement of different units and voices could be mind-boggling, but with experience came the ability to tune into the net as effortlessly as breathing, distilling what was relevant, what was not, and replying with voice procedure that was as ingrained as a first language.

'Zero Alpha, send over,' I spoke into my headset on the

company net, the voice of Barossa Platoon's commander having offered up a sitrep.

'Zero Alpha, Two Zero Alpha. All quiet at my location. No movement seen. Total ghost town, over.'

'Zero Alpha, roger. Hold your position but prepare to collapse,' I told my subordinate, looking at the dwindling number of vehicles in the district centre. 'Seven vehicles remaining in the compound. I'll bring you in as soon as the last one passes. Any eyes on the Afghan Police, over?'

'Two Zero Alpha, roger. Just picked them up now. Making good speed and passing the Danish wagons. Four Hiluxes, each packed out with about ten pax per vehicle, over.'

'Zero Alpha, roger, out to you. Charlie Charlie One this is Zero Alpha. Be aware we have four Afghan Police vehicles en route to our location from the west, on the same road as the Danish vehicles. Pass this information down to every man in your sections. We do not want a blue on blue. Zero Alpha, out.'

'I'll go man to man,' Sergeant Major Scrivener offered, meaning that he would move along the fighting positions to ensure that no soldier with an itchy trigger finger or a lazy eye mistook our police reinforcements for Taliban and opened fire. I assented with a nod, and he disappeared towards the nearest firing step.

The Barossa Platoon commander's voice buzzed in my ear. 'Zero Alpha, Two Zero Alpha.'

'Zero Alpha, send, over.'

'Two Zero Alpha, Afghan Police are now at my position. Have held them short waiting for your command, over.'

'Zero Alpha, good stuff. Send them in now. Out.' I switched to my personal role radio. 'Sergeant Major. Police are coming in now.'

'Roger, sir,' I heard on my headset, then the man's voice calling out across the compound. 'Afghan Police coming in. Don't brass them up for fuck's sake, lads, or it's more stag for you!'

I turned into the yard. The last of the Danish vehicles was leaving. Through the dust, the tail-end Charlie machine gunner offered a wave. I didn't know if it was directed towards me or anyone in particular, or was just a farewell to the place they had called home, and fought for. The tired gesture seemed almost apologetic.

And then the Danes were gone.

The Afghan National Standby Police arrived moments later, and were waved through by two of Barossa Platoon positioned at the gate.

'Park 'em up over there!' I heard one of the young soldiers ordering the new arrivals. It wasn't easy to make them out through the dust, but it was clear enough that these Afghans were a breed apart from the local police they had replaced – their eyes were narrow and Asiatic, and many were clean-shaven. These were not Pashtun men but the Tajiks and Hazaris from the north of Afghanistan, an area that had been at war with the Taliban since the strict religious movement's birth in the mid-1990s.

'Two Zero Alpha, Zero Alpha,' I spoke to my men on the ground. 'Afghan Police are in the compound. Collapse now. Slow and steady. Out.'

I saw the sergeant major return from his rounds of the fighting positions.

'All quiet up there, sir,' he reported. 'Absolute ghost town,' he added, repeating Barossa Platoon's observations.

'I'm going up top to take a look,' I told him, not trusting that the calm would hold now that the tail of the Danish convoy was rattling clear. 'Can you see to the police? Get them dug in quickly along their section of wall?'

'Can do, sir,' Scrivs spoke, already breaking into a run, in the same mind as I that the Taliban could break out towards us at any moment.

'I'm going up onto the Alamo,' I called quickly into the ops room. After a short run and climb, I was poking my head up onto the rooftop. The sun was still fierce, and I saw the sentries sheltering beneath a pathetic construction of sandbags and camo netting. I made a mental note to have the sergeant major distribute sunscreen – undermanned as we now were, a badly burned soldier would have to take his duties with the rest, but I was under no illusions that he would operate as efficiently, and so I would have to do what I could to prevent avoidable injuries.

'Anything going on up here, lads?' I asked the pair of young soldiers nestled behind a gimpy.

They were slow in answering, and I saw a quick look of confusion between the friends.

'I'm the OC.' I smiled, embarrassed that I hadn't yet had the time to visit each man under my command and introduce myself.

'Oh!' One of the men grinned back. 'All right, sir? Nah, nothing going on up here today, sir. They don't like to come out when the Apaches are about.'

I followed the man's nod to the horizon, where a pair of Apaches prowled, low and menacing.

'Can't say I blame them,' I replied, remembering the helicopter's awesome destructive power from my time on the Apache training team. 'What are your names, lads? I'm Adam Jowett.'

They gave me their names, Rangers Russell and Manoa, and I asked them to point out a few of the enemy's favourite firing points that sat within their arcs. Invariably, these positions were elevated. Often windows.

'One of them will pop up, and when he goes back down his mate will just jump up,' one of the men informed me, grinning a little. 'Don't know much about changing fire position, sir. Dunno if they did any pre-deployment training.'

I chuckled, along with his friend.

'Keep sharp, boys. The Danes are gone now, so expect them to try and probe.'

'Yeah, no bother, sir,' they told me, as if expecting RPGs and a zealous enemy was as commonplace as tea and football.

I made my way back to the ops room. On my way, I listened to the radio as the battlegroup units peeled away from the town and began their moves back to Bastion. The backs of the units were what the Taliban had waited to see, and the crackle of small-arms fire teased in the distance. I heard the contact reports filter up to battlegroup level. The enemy fire had been short and desultory.

'Not much of a contact,' Scrivs shrugged as I arrived in the ops room.

'Not much of a contact,' I agreed, thinking of my men, and their survival.

Barossa Platoon's commander arrived at the door. 'All my lads are back in, sir.'

'Good job. Get the gate piled up again, and then have your lads get water and scoff. Last light isn't far off, and I want the whole company stood to.'

He quickly took his leave to see that the scrap iron, metal sheeting, and razor wire – anything that could be found to form an obstacle – was moved into place

'Time for a brew, I think, sir,' Scrivs offered, dispatching a signaller to the task. A few minutes later we were passing steaming mugs around. It was tradition to share a brew with your comrades, and the liquid tasted all the sweeter for the Danish extraction having come off without incident at our own end.

'It's quiet. Too quiet,' is a phrase every soldier and civilian is familiar with, and despite being somewhat of a humourless cliché, there was a lot of truth in the statement. And so, despite the lack of contact so far, I was not prepared to relax. Not until every single one of my soldiers was out of this town and back in Bastion.

'Anything on the ICOM?' I asked my LEWT team.

'Usual bollocks, sir,' Staff Sergeant Ian Wornham spoke up,

the jovial NCO known to me from his days at 1 Para, where he had built a reputation as a 'good bloke'. 'God is Great,' he explained of the Taliban's radio chatter. 'The enemy are retreating.'

I took a seat on the bench beside the men. The battlegroup had broken their hold on the town's outskirts, and I expected that Taliban curiosity would not be far behind the fading silhouettes of the Danish column striking out into the desert.

We heard the first indication of it not long later. Choppy voices, translated by two of our interpreters.

'I think this is a commander,' said Naz, a wiry Hazari with intelligent eyes. 'They're thanking Allah that the infidels have left.'

Not all of them, but the Taliban seemed oblivious to that.

'They think it's only the Afghan Police here,' Fardin added, speaking to me. 'They think all of ISAF is gone, and there is only the police.'

I went to question him further, but another burst of talk on the radio made me hold my tongue. I recognized only Allah Akbar – God is great.

Naz and Fardin shared a look before translating.

'They say that, in the morning, they will attack. They will attack, and by tomorrow night, they will be drinking tea in the governor's buildings.'

I looked over the faces of my interpreters and signals team. They were grim. The time had been set, and there could now be no more doubt.

The Taliban were coming.

9

I left the LEWT team and made my way back to the ops room – Battlegroup HQ needed to know that we had confirmed visitors in the morning, not that they were any less surprised than I was. No one had expected that the enemy would be content to walk away from the town's DC when the Danes did, and I was pleased that my commanders then assigned a pair of American A-10s to us for the morning. Usually, air assets were allocated as and when a unit came into contact. By pre-allocating these in-demand aircraft – the Warthogs were the favoured close air support of all in theatre – Battlegroup HQ were acknowledging not only that contact was inevitable, but also that the fight would be intense and on top of our heads from the get-go.

Knowing exactly what aircraft we had assigned to us, I went in search of my JTACs. The sun had yet to set, and so I crouched and bobbed my way up onto the rooftop of the Outpost. Following me on their hands and knees, antennas protruding from their radios, the artillery and forward air controllers had the look of militant porcupines. I told them the good news.

'That's fucking bang on, sir,' Bombardier Ray Anderton smiled. The young soldier was from 7 Para, the brigade's artillery regiment, and would be the man who directed the aircraft on to their targets, a highly pressurized job for anyone, at any time, let alone when someone was shooting at you. 'Best to only bring them on task just before we need them, boss,' the expert offered. 'So we don't lose them for refuelling when things go noisy.'

'Get them here at first light minus ten,' I agreed, 'but hold them out of sight and sound.'

I had considered the possibility of using the aircraft as a show of force in the morning, but had decided that it would only delay the enemy's attack and make its timing less predictable, meaning that my men would either have to remain stood to, baking and tiring on the walls, or rush for the positions when the enemy attacked, handing that momentary opening of the battle to them. Neither situation worked in our favour, and so we would leave the enemy to think that they had the element of surprise, and when they attacked, we would smash them.

'How long before calling them in and the shells hitting the enemy?' I asked.

'If we keep them out of sight and sound, two minutes, boss,' Ray answered.

I saw a helmeted head pop up through the opening in the Outpost's floor.

'Hi, Mark,' I greeted the platoon commander I'd sent for. 'I was hoping we could use your expertise. We've got a pair of A-10s for the morning, so we're working out strafing runs and pre-designating anything that may need a bomb in it.'

'A pair of A-10s?' Mark said happily. 'My favourite.' He shuffled across the roof to come alongside us.

'Western side's your best bet for the strafing runs. They use that whole line of buildings as firing points. It's a danger close target, but so is pretty much all of it around here. The rounds will be close to our boys, but the road gives a very clear demarcation line for the pilots.'

I looked at the aerial photo in my hands, trying to put myself in the pilot's seat. Surely enough, the road outside the western wall was not only straight, but wide in places. The enemy would be close to us, but distinctly separated.

'That's perfect,' I agreed. 'Let's cue that one up, please, gents.'

And so the JTAC went to work on building the mission; what direction should the pilot approach from? What markers should he look for as he came onto his target? What direction should he break away? If the JTACs could build a comprehensive picture, and the pilot was confident he had his target, then he could unleash his payload on the first pass, without needing a confirmation, and deny the enemy a chance of escape.

Once the likely targets for our air support had been planned, we turned our attention to where the artillery fire of I Battery, 7 RHA could be employed. These gunners were operating from a gun line in the desert, and the FOO was their eyes and ears on the ground. With him, and using Johnno's localized experience, we began to plot the enemy's favourite firing points so that the FOO could relay them to the gunners in the desert. Each point would then be given a reference, meaning that, in contact, we could call for artillery on a given position quickly, rather than having to relay the entire fire mission of grid references, distance from friendly troops, and other such factors. In times of conventional war, these pre-designated targets would be confirmed by the artillery firing a spotting round, so that they could be adjusted and accurate from the moment their fire was needed in battle, but we did not want to create unnecessary destruction in the town, and permission for such test fires would have been unlikely to have been received from Battlegroup HQ in any case.

'Anything else, sir?' Ray asked me.

I looked at my map and aerial photos. 'No. I think we can comprehensively smash them if they misbehave. Just stand by that, if we require a casevac, then we will probably need a lot of air to quiet things down enough to bring a Chinook in.'

'No dramas, sir.'

'You guys go get some scoff and some rest,' I told the artillerymen. 'I'm going to stay up here for a bit.'

The 7 Para men moved away. Johnno remained.

'Going to be a bit tasty in the morning, boss, I think,' the

Irishman offered. He didn't seem fazed by the thought, but nor was he smiling.

'Would look like it's shaping up that way. How are your boys?'

'They're good. Cutting around Barossa, trying to pass on anything helpful. What the lads should be taking with them into the sangar, and that kind of thing.'

We lapsed into silence. The sky was darkening now, the sun having dipped behind the western mountains in the desert. A band of red light was all that was left of the day. It gripped the horizon, fighting a losing battle with the night. Eventually, it slipped away. I expected that by the time it returned with the dawn, we would be engaged in our own struggle for survival.

Now that darkness had fallen, I asked Johnno to quiz me on the positions of our sangars, med centre, and ops room. There was no place for ego with the enemy at hand, and I needed to be able to move about in pitch darkness at night, still able to avoid the areas that opened me up as a juicy target in daylight.

'Let's go back to the ops room,' I told the shadow beside me once I was satisfied I knew the compound as well as I knew my own home.

Inside the ops room, Sergeant Major Scrivener was busy preparing for dawn with the attention to detail so common to and vital of men in his station. Senior NCOs really were the backbone of the army, and I took a moment to be thankful that I had been gifted with the presence of one of the best that the regiment had to offer. I knew without doubt that, when the bullets did begin to fly, my job would be made infinitely easier by having Scrivs in my command.

'Brew, boss?' one of the signallers asked me, bright-eyed and eager, not a sign of fatigue or trepidation in his face.

'Thanks, Jones. How's the battle prep going, Sergeant Major?' I asked. Whilst planning and overall command lay with me, the minutia of battle preparation lay with the CSM and his platoon sergeants.

'All good, sir,' he replied. Then, with a quick check about him for privacy, added, 'Platoon sergeants seem like good blokes. They're on top of it.'

That was a relief to hear. Undermanned as we were, I was heartened to know that these men would not require being watched over and closely scrutinized by Company HQ.

The sergeant major then handed me a piece of paper, and I looked at the items checked off from the list of battle preparations: weapons cleaned and oiled; all magazines loaded; claymores positioned; extra ammunition taken to each sangar; clean water in the med centre; quad bike fully fuelled and checked for service, with trailer attached; parachute flares in sangars in case of pre-dawn attack; Afghan Police briefed on casevac plan; mortar stores split to separate locations in case of direct hit; all water bottles filled; extra food and ammo moved to Outpost and Alamo.

The final note brought me up. No man had made light of the fact that we were stocking those buildings with the stores necessary to make our last stand there should the wall be breached. The men of Somme especially knew the possibility that the Taliban could breach the defence – where there had been armour and heavy weapons, now there were a few riflemen – and had been quiet and concentrated as they carried their burdens to the buildings that could be the site of their final battle.

'What time do you want to do orders, sir?' the CSM asked me.

I looked to my watch. It was close to ten at night. Dawn, and the enemy, were eight hours away. Earlier in the evening the platoon commanders had been quickly briefed by myself to provide work parties for the sergeant major, and to prepare for the following day, but I had yet to deliver the briefing that would outline how we would conduct the engagement in the morning. The men needed little insight from me as to how to best fight from their positions, but eventualities such as casevac and enemy infiltration needed to be covered in depth. To neglect them, or to pay such matters lip service, could result in the death of my men.

'Let's do it at 2300. Give them time to finish their prep, and get some scoff.'

With the brew provided by Signaller Jones, a slightly scruffy-looking soldier from the Valleys, I sat down at the table and flipped open my notebook, preparing my orders. It was a process I had done thousands of times in my career, most often with offensive actions in mind. The British army is built to be mobile, and on the offensive – the only way to win battles and wars with a smaller force – and so I felt slightly neutered to be sitting back and allowing the enemy to dictate the time of our engagement. The place of battle had been set by the ego of the district governor, and so my planning was mostly limited to how I would mitigate both those imposed factors and turn them to my advantage. You want to fight at dawn? Fine. I know when to have my men ready, and when they can rest. You want to put us in a shitty compound? Fine. I know where I can pre-designate targets and strafing runs. Regardless of the situation we had been put in, we would be ready for the enemy.

I felt a hand on my shoulder. It was the sergeant major.

'It's 2255, sir.'

I gave him a nod of thanks and finished my tea, kept lukewarm by the Afghan summer.

And then, on the eve of battle, I briefed my men.

The small ops room was crammed. My usual team was in attendance, plus both platoon commanders, their sergeants, the JTAC, medics, snipers, and mortar detachment commander. I kept my orders short and simple. The Taliban were coming to capture the district centre, and it was our job to kill them when they tried. There was no reason or need to overcomplicate it, but there was a good reason to plan for eventualities.

'If you take a casualty, get him down onto ground level as quickly as you can,' I told my assembled commanders. 'Get the word out over the telephone lines, the radios, and by mouth. The medics will come to you with the quad bike and take it from there. Once the handover's done, the guys need to be straight back up and fighting.'

I saw heads nodding at this. The quickest way to get wounded to the doctor would be by using the quad bike, and the quickest way to lose the firefight would be if our men forgot that and began to carry their wounded to the aid post. Noble as that was, we had to plan that we would be so stretched that we could ill afford to lose a few men from a section, even if just for a few minutes.

'Anything to add on the med side of things, Doc?' I asked. The man shook his head. 'Sergeant Major?'

The veteran turned to look at the assembly. 'Gents, make sure every one of your blokes has his field dressing, tourniquet, and morphine in his left trouser side pocket. Keep it standard for the company.'

Med plan in place, I went on to cover how and when we would withdraw to the Outpost and Alamo if necessary, the criteria being that the Taliban had breached the compound and that fighting from the walls was untenable due to exposed backs and flanks.

'Every man needs to know this plan intimately,' I stressed. 'If we fall back into the Outpost and Alamo, we can provide mutual support for each position, and call down artillery and air on the rest of the compound. We can't do that unless we've accounted for every single one of our men.'

I looked at the faces of the soldiers in the room, and saw a grim acknowledgement of that fact. No one wanted to be the soldier who was taken alive by the enemy. No one wanted to see an air strike smash apart a building, and wonder whether or not his friend was still inside.

'We'll centralize everything sensitive in the ops room tonight. Sergeant Major's going to place two phos grenades next to it. If we do have to fight back into the compound, last man out phosses the room to deny it to the enemy.' I then went on to detail the fallback procedure to the inner buildings, at pains to make clear who should blow the claymores, and when.

'Any questions?'

There were none. The company knew its task, and it knew the stakes.

'Are you sure?'

A hand went up. It was the mortar section commander, Corporal Groves, his Brummie accent surprising for a Royal Irish soldier.

'Sir, is it true they're saying they'll be drinking tea here tomorrow night?'

The room blurted out a laugh.

'That's right.' I smiled, glad that the enemy's intention had made its way around the troops. Their backs would be up at the thought that the enemy would think them so easily swept aside.

I dismissed the assembly, the heads of platoons and sections moving away to disseminate the orders to their own men so that the plan trickled downwards, making it to even the most junior soldier. I would give it an hour to do so and then move about the sangars and rooms myself, talking to the men and answering questions if they had them, ensuring that the plan was as clear in their minds as their daydreams of girl-friends and families.

'You should get some rest, sir,' the sergeant major offered me kindly once the room had emptied. I thought on it for a moment, and realized that my plate was about as empty as it would get for the foreseeable future. I had done all I could, and when the enemy came, I would need to be sharp.

'I'll watch the ops room,' he pushed.

'Thank you, Sergeant Major,' I accepted. 'Wake me up in an hour, please. I'm going to pass around the blokes, make sure they're all happy with what's going on.'

They were, every soldier eager for what the dawn would bring. Satisfied that Easy Company was prepared, I knew I should snatch what sleep I could. And so, with my body armour as a pillow, I stretched out on the floor of the dark room next door to our ops room. There were camp beds scattered throughout the company, but I wanted to be close to the ground in case of mortar attack, an example set by the men who had been living here under attack for weeks. I closed my eyes, and tried to push out of my mind a thousand thoughts. Surprising myself, I was asleep within moments.

I was woken by a shake of my shoulders. I was alert instantly, having been in that kind of rest known to any soldier – the shallow kind, senses tuned and ready to shout out at the slightest disturbance.

'Two a.m., boss.'

I thanked the faceless shadow and got to my feet, pulling on the body armour that had been my pillow.

'Everything all right?' I asked as I walked into the ops room.

'All quiet, sir,' Sergeant Major Scrivener answered.

'Go get some sleep, Sergeant Major.'

The veteran made no attempt at resistance. We all knew how long tomorrow would be.

Dawn crept closer over ticking clock faces and a black horizon. I busied myself in plans, and walking the fighting positions. I had yet to meet every soldier in my company, and was haunted by the thought that I could have a man killed or wounded, and he with no idea under whose orders he had suffered.

'What's your name?' I asked a silhouette in a sangar, after having introduced myself.

'Johnston, sir.'

'Where are you from?'

'Belfast, sir.'

We talked a little about the Ranger's hometown. Twenty one years old, this was his second deployment.

'Are you happy to be here?' I asked the youngster.

'Couldn't be happier, sir. This is why you join up, isn't it?'

I wouldn't expect a soldier to give any other kind of answer to his company commander, but there was an edge of excitement in his voice, and I believed the man. That same buzz was present in the conversation and bearing of all within the compounds, professionals recognizing that they were about to face the ultimate test of their craft and manhood.

I heard the approach of the relieving sentry, and cleared the way so that they could complete the handover without my interference.

As the hours crept by, activity in the darkness began to build, tired men raised by a friendly prod of their NCO's boots. Farts echoed from the rooms set aside for quarters, light flickering as stoves were lit to heat rations and make brews. Soon, the stale smell of cigarettes was growing thick in the air. Though most of the industry was hidden in the night, it was possible to sense the bustle all around. It occurred to me that the thought was clichéd, but there really was something in the air, a feeling of excitement that was almost tangible. Though still dark, the threat of dawn was beginning to lighten the sky one shade at a time. I heard the voices of the platoon sergeants as they made final inspections of their men, ensuring all were fed and watered.

'Don't forget to shit, too,' I heard one say. 'It's gon'ae be a long fucking day.'

I looked at my watch – four a.m. Time to move into position.

'I'm going onto the roof,' I told my men in the ops room, and made my way up onto the undulating surface of the headquarters building that seemed more like a ploughed field than a roof. I stayed low, the wall about me thigh high at best. There were black shapes lying in the darkness, men who had been even keener than myself to get into position.

'Morning, boss,' Ray Anderton greeted me. With his A-10s only twenty minutes from being on station, the JTAC was bright and cheerful.

'How's it going, Ray?'

'All good, boss. Ready to make some widows.'

I looked to the horizon. The dawn was chipping at it, a band of pale grey light beginning to break through. I pulled my night-vision monocle over my eye, seeing men moving in the green as they hustled into position, the shapes of the Afghan Police distinguishable from Brits – not only were they without helmets, but their uniforms were dark. Our own desert pattern reflected light at night, and was easier to pick up through the sights.

I looked to the front gate, thinking again how it was our most vulnerable point. Though well defended by men with small arms, I didn't like to think of the effect a suicide truck bomb could have on it – at best, we'd have a huge hole torn into our defences.

I felt the presence of more men on the rooftop. Counting through the monocle, I saw that we were fully present now – joining myself and the JTAC were the off-duty signallers, the company runner, and a fire team from Somme Platoon. More cover would have been nice, but we had great arcs to the west, and I was confident that this was the best position for me to oversee the battle, and from which to launch the reserve section, who waited tucked away in cover close by. There was nothing to do now but wait, and watch the band of grey light grow thicker and thicker into the sky, taking away the night, and bringing the Taliban in its wake. As the darkness gave way to the wan light of a new day, the enemy came for their tea.

'Contact!'

10

The Taliban's opening salvo was a crashing barrage of six RPGs fired almost simultaneously, the whoosh of their rockets followed almost instantly by the slamming explosions as the deadly projectiles detonated against the main gate and west wall. Within a rapid heartbeat, it sounded as if every piece of small arms in Afghanistan was firing.

'Rapid fire! Rapid fire!' NCOs tried to shout above the din, and I forgot the big picture for a moment, instead seeing the world through the sight of my weapon, knowing that every round counted in this initial clash – the struggle to win the firefight, and to gain the dominance that would allow for freedom of movement on the battlefield.

I looked to the low buildings separated from our western wall by the dual carriageway, fifty metres from my own position, and twenty from our wall. There was no glass in the windows, the spaces full of the flash of muzzles. The enemy had moved into position unseen, protected by the town's labyrinth, and now their bullets zipped and cracked the air above me like deadly insects, dust blossoming from walls where they bit.

I drew my sight onto a burst of muzzle flash, and fired two double taps, watching one fighter collapse; then I crouched down behind the thin wall, using my left hand to help manoeuvre me to a new position, not wishing to present an easy pop-up target for the enemy. I ignored the instinct that told me that the air above me was full of death, and came up onto my knee, searching for more flash – I had dozens of targets to choose from. I engaged, hot cases from a GPMG beside me bouncing onto my thigh as the Royal Irish gun ripped bursts into the Taliban positions.

Perhaps ten seconds had gone by since the opening salvo. Already the calls of 'Magazine!' rang out as men dropped into cover to replace empty cartridges. Target indications came thick and fast, the enemy numerous, firing points given away by the flash of their weapons. It was time for me to pull back and assess. I looked around the compound.

Not one part was without contact. Every wall, every sangar, was engaged. Unseen forces kicked up dust and tore open sandbags. Far more visible was the red and green tracer that played against the dawn sky like deadly fireworks, ricochets shooting into the air at almost vertical angles. It was a sight to behold.

'Want me to call the A-10s?' Ray Anderton shouted to me across the din.

'Not yet.' It wasn't the time. The A-10s were our trump card, and the time to play it would be when the enemy showed his hand, and made a push to break into the compound. For now there was no movement to be seen. I expected that the weight of fire they'd received had stunned them – they'd been thinking that there were a few dozen Afghan Police in the compound. They hadn't been expecting the concentrated weight of fire and marksmanship of two platoons of Royal Irish Rangers and their nine GPMGs.

Clicking on my safety catch, I made a conscious effort to detach from the battle around me. That is easier said than done when you can see the bullets churning plaster from the walls behind you, but it was essential. I had to know what the enemy was planning. I had to consider their next moves. I had to consider where their attack was weakest, and strongest. By observing the actions of my men – their rate of fire; the speed with which they changed magazines; the amount of dust kicked up by enemy bullets – I began to build up a picture of where the Taliban were pressing hardest. As I observed, I dreaded the moment I would see one of my men hit; dreaded hearing that agonized call of 'Man down!' With so much lead in the air, I knew it was only a matter of time before that happened. Easy Company's Rangers and Paras were handling the fight like pros, moving from cover to cover after every few shots, offering no easy targets, but the sheer weight of fire must tell eventually. I had no concern for myself in that moment – my fear was entirely for my men, and the sickening thought of knowing there was no way a helicopter could fly into this maelstrom to evacuate the wounded.

'Magazine!' a Ranger called beside me. I moved to the low wall and pulled my rifle into my shoulder, picking up the slack as the youngster changed magazines. The western buildings were still thick with muzzle flash. There were PKMs amongst the AKs, the enemy's equivalent of our gimpy.

'Back in!' the young soldier called, and began firing.

I moved from the wall and made one more sweep of the compound, concluding that the western side was most hard-pressed. I needed to show myself there.

'I'm going to the western wall,' I told the JTAC. 'Runner, come with me.'

The young soldier, one of the Irish, nodded back. We kept as low as we could whilst moving from the rooftop, and then I was at the ops room door.

'Sergeant Major,' I called within. 'I'm going to the western wall. Looks like they're thickest there.' Scrivs would take over from me if I went down, and so it was important we stayed separated during the contact. 'Anything I should know?'

'ICOM started going crazy once they opened up, sir, but not much useful. They're micromanaging their guys, but doesn't seem like they're making any efforts to move onto us, yet.'

'OK. Good. Let me know on the PRR if that changes.'

'Will do, sir.'

The runner behind me, I ran for the Afghan Police positions on the western wall. The air above our heads was still thick with zips and cracks, the sky beginning to turn a bright blue now that dawn was becoming day.

The Afghan Police were having rare fun in their sector, I quickly saw. They were smiling, fighting to be the ones in the firing positions. One of their men had an RPG, and he sent a rocket crashing across the street into the enemy-held buildings.

'Everything OK here?' I asked one of their lieutenants. I had left the interpreters to the more important work of the ICOM, but the Afghan officer easily guessed my meaning.

'Very good, Adam Khan! Very good! Many Taliban!' He grinned.

You couldn't help but smile at the attitude. These men were born warriors, and nothing less.

'Keep it up!' I clapped him on the shoulder, then made for the Outpost. Working my way through the rat runs that led to the raised fighting position, I could hear the ferocity of the firing above. The sound of the fifty-cal machine guns was conspicuously absent from the symphony.

'What's up with the fifties?' I yelled to the soldiers who were field-stripping them.

'It's the fucking ammo, sir,' one of the Irish answered me. 'Fucking gun keeps jamming after every fucking round, sir. They're fucked, sir.'

I'd seen the same in Sangin. We had travelled a long way with a crappy batch of ammo. The fifty cals were a battle winner, able to punch through walls and terrify the enemy, but now the poor quality of the ammunition was rendering the weapons useless.

'Do what you can,' I told them.

Thank God for the gimpy. Those guns were ringing true, streams of 7.62 pouring from the Outpost and into enemy firing points. I watched the men change belts skilfully and quickly, the weight of fire barely letting up for a moment.

'Go for it, go for it!' an NCO extolled his fire team. 'Get those fuckers!'

I put my head above the parapet but pulled back quickly as a chunk of wall evaporated alongside me, grit stinging my face. I ducked and popped up a second time – there seemed no let up to the west, but in other sectors the weight of fire was beginning to slacken. Like the momentum in a football game, I could see that, in those areas where we had weathered the storm, we now dictated the pace of the firefight. It was we who were pinning down the enemy, and not the other way round. Any movement of theirs between buildings and firing points was quickly picked up by our sangars, and men called out to claim kills as dark shapes dropped out of sight behind walls and window ledges.

'Bit fooking mad this, sir, isn't it?' A Royal Irish lance corporal beamed at me. His face was red from heat and adrenaline, eyes white, lips pulled back in an almost maniacal grin – he was enjoying this as much as our Afghans. There was more than one place on the planet that bred warriors, it seemed.

The battle was a madness that continued for almost an hour, during which time neither side let up. The enemy made no attempt to storm forward, and so we stood like two boxers with leaden feet, swinging wildly at one another. For the Paras in the company, we had taken milling to a new level.

I had been reluctant to call in an air strike – we were here to help build a town, not flatten it – but the Taliban's doggedness forced my hand. With so much lead in the air, it was only a matter of time until it found a victim. When a trio of enemy mortar rounds crashed in and around the compound, I made the decision.

'Ray, I'm coming back to your location,' I warned the JTAC over the radio. 'Get the A-10s ready to go.'

I joined the JTAC on the ops room rooftop. We huddled together with our maps and radios as the others fought on.

'Where do you want it, boss?' Ray asked.

'They're strongest on the west,' I told him. 'That's the tip-ping point. I think that if we can break up the attack there, then the others will fall off.'

Ray got on his radio and began speaking to the pilots. They were men of the Texan Air National Guard, and Ray smiled whenever he heard their drawl.

Using the company net, I ordered our mortars to cease fire. They had been throwing bombs into the air since the begin-ning of the contact, the enemy so close that the barrels were pointing almost vertically, but now we would need them silent – we couldn't risk a collision between mortar and aircraft. Once the tubes fell silent, Ray sent confirmation to the pilots.

'They're on their way.' He grinned.

I sent the word out over the company net. NCOs began to relay it by mouth. I could imagine the nervous excitement of the soldiers as they waited for the American jets to swoop in. I could imagine it well, because I was feeling it myself.

'Thirty seconds!' Ray shouted to everyone within earshot, fighting to be heard over the rattle of gunfire.

I looked into the distance, hoping to pick out the brute, but the first I knew of its presence was a long ripple of explosions that churned dust and dirt into the air across the western flank, the aircraft's nose cannon carving into the buildings with a deathly patter of explosives. Seconds after the explo-sions came the report of the cannon itself, a mighty roar that sounded like a giant buzz saw. There was a flash across the sky as the aircraft cleared the area, leaving stained into my sight the picture of a blockish creature, a snarling mouth painted onto its serpentine head.

'That was fucking awesome!' a soldier called, others whooping with glee. Within an instant the Taliban fire from the western side had dropped to nothing. The fire on the other flanks had reduced to a trickle.

'That's given them something to think about.' Ray grinned. 'Another one, boss?'

'Again,' I ordered. The enemy were hidden, but those rounds had been designed to punch through Soviet tanks, and so they would easily pass through roofs and ceilings. Now that the enemy were pinned down, it was time to punish them.

The A-10 pair came in again. And again. And again. They came in until their guns were empty, and the enemy firing points were riddled and smouldering. Being so close to the gun run had been terrifying. I hated to think what it would be like to have those shells come down on top of you. What mess of bodies would be inside those buildings now? But my own men were intact, and that was all that mattered to me. The enemy dead had made a choice in coming to attack us, and though I did not revel in the carnage, neither did I pity them.

The contact was broken. Where the air had been alive with buzzing bullets, now there was the lone crack or burst as the sangars engaged the enemy survivors as they skittered away between buildings, Irish curses and taunts chasing after them.

'Hey, Terry, where you going? You forgot your tea, you wanker!'

It was eight o'clock in the morning. We had come through our first attack.

It would not be our last.

11

I crouched low as I made my way off the rooftop. Not all of the enemy had melted away, and any exposed movement drew single shots, or bursts of AK fire.

'Stand down,' I ordered over the company net. 'Sangars to minimum manning. Platoon commanders to the ops room. Out.'

Standing down didn't mean that the men relieved of duty would be free to flop onto their body armour and sleep – weapons needed to be cleaned; magazines needed refilling; ammunition needed to be taken to the fighting positions; defences hit by machine-gun and RPG fire needed shoring up. Whilst the main body of men saw to those tasks, others would be preparing food and refilling water bottles. In a blink of an eye, the men would find it was their turn to man the sangars. There would be no rest for anyone, at least not until darkness. As I dropped into the courtyard, I heard platoon sergeants and section 2ICs calling for ammo states, section commanders repositioning their men to cover arcs now that the numbers in the fighting positions were thinning.

I pulled off my helmet as I stepped inside the ops room, my hair a thick tangle from dust, sweat, and cordite. Sergeant Major Scrivener had anticipated my arrival, and pushed a brew into my hand.

'I'm waiting on the platoon sergeants, and then I'll redistribute the ammo,' the Para told me, allowing me to cross off one thing from my mental list.

'Those A-10s sounded close,' he added, then grinned.

'Fucking close.' I smiled. 'Smashed them, though. They've got great cover on that flank, but at least the road makes it easy to mark them.'

Mark Johnson and Paul Martin appeared in the doorway together, both platoon commanders drenched with sweat, eyes alive with still-dissipating adrenaline.

'Well that was something,' Paul said, wiping a hand through his hair. 'Anybody else's ears ringing?'

We laughed. They were.

'It's a miracle no one got hit,' Johnno added.

There was no laughter at this. No smiles, even. We knew how lucky we'd been.

'We can't expect that we can keep taking that much fire without sustaining casualties,' I told my subordinates. 'First thing I want to go over now is to reiterate the med plan. I think it's pretty clear that we won't be able to bring a casevac in during an attack – the Chinook would get shot out of the sky – so it's imperative that we get any casualties to Doc Stacey and under his care immediately. Let's go over it.'

After that first attack, we now had a better idea where casualties could be lowered from rooftops. Where the medics had the most cover to extract them. Where they could be placed out of sight of the enemy if their triage placed them at the bottom of the list for treatment and the medics had their hands full.

A burst of fire crackled outside. We waited for more, but when there was none we continued with our debriefing – time was precious.

'Our Afghans look like they're more than capable of holding their own,' I told the others. 'So no need to bolster them. Reserve section worked well, too.'

The reserve section had been thrown to where the fighting was thickest, adding their weight to the fire to gain the upper hand in that sector, before pulling back to be retasked.

'I'm going to tell the Afghans that I want one of their RPGs for the reserve,' I explained. 'That's a great bit of firepower we just can't match ourselves.

'Freddie. Ian. Anything useful from the ICOM?'

The two men shared a look, our intelligence officer Sergeant Freddie Kruyer gesturing for the signaller to speak.

'The terps are starting to get an idea of who's who on the Taliban's net. Once we have voices we can start working out their chain of command. Then, from the instructions they give, we can begin to piece together where they're giving the orders from.'

'Once we get that,' Freddie added, 'we can smash them with the mortars.'

'Great stuff,' I said, relishing the opportunity to be on the offensive in any way. 'Speaking of mortars, mark down on this map any firing points you came across this morning. If they were heavily used we'll pre-designate them for our mortars.'

'Shame we can't hit their forming-up points,' Paul Martin spoke up. 'There's no way of seeing them until they're almost on top of us.'

He was right. The town's maze of alleyways and buildings gave the enemy the cover they needed to sneak into position, and denied us the chance to smash them when they were at their most vulnerable – grouped together in their forming-up points. By looking at maps and aerial photos we could put ourselves in the enemy's shoes, and make educated guesses at where these positions would be, but it was against the rules of engagement to throw shells at random onto locations that we could not observe. However, it seemed as though Freddie had come up with a possible solution.

'We can't shell where we can't see unless we have some intelligence that the enemy are there,' the cunning man confirmed. 'But we can see certain open areas that Terry has to cross. Moving laterally, across a road, for instance. If we hit them in these spots when they're moving, maybe they'll slip up on the ICOM, and give away their position.'

'Would they do that?' Paul Martin asked.

Ian Wornham nodded. 'They'll say things like, "No. That didn't hit us. It was a hundred yards away." They give us clues, because they have no idea we're listening and trying to piece together a puzzle.'

'That's a brilliant idea, Freddie,' I told him earnestly. 'Get to work on that. Anyone have anything else? I've got to call into Battlegroup HQ.'

There was nothing. The platoon commanders returned to see to their men. Freddie and Ian turned back to their radios, and the puzzle of finding the enemy.

I called through to battlegroup on the secure satellite phone, briefing them on that first attack. They had been given the usual contact reports during the fight, but on the phone there was no need for voice procedure, and we could talk openly in a normal conversation.

'We're going to be going through mortar and gimpy ammunition like crazy,' I told them. 'So prioritize that on any lift. The fifty cals are useless with the ammo we have, so don't waste space on a lift for fifty ammo unless it's a new batch.'

'Got it. Anything else?'

I had no time to reply. Outside, the air erupted once more.

'Got to go. Contact,' I said.

We were back at it.

The second contact was as heavy as the first, small-arms fire belting into the compound from all sides. Men rushed from their admin areas, some almost naked but for their helmets and body armour. I had been explicit when I told my soldiers that – body armour and helmet aside – I didn't care how they were dressed when the enemy attacked, and we needed to stand to. Better a man on the firing step in shorts than a fully dressed soldier pulling on his boots and out of the fight.

The rhythm of the battle was similar to the first attack. The enemy had the ability to initiate it, and did so from the same firing positions as they had at dawn. Within minutes of our men filling our own firing positions, we had wrested the fire-fight from the enemy, taking control of it through superior individual skill and marksmanship. Our mortars began to boom, and the enemy answered with indirect fire of their own, a 107mm rocket screaming in with fury to tear chunks from the courtyard, lumps of dirt and burning shrapnel thrown over the fighting positions.

'Incoming!' men screamed, hitting the deck as a second shell shrieked in to bury itself in the Outpost, where it failed to explode.

The launching of the shells was always accompanied by a loud bang, and we waited with trepidation for another. Doubtless they were using the spire outside the compound as a sighting point to achieve such accuracy. There was nothing to be done about it but win the firefight we were engaged in, and take out the enemy that we could see – the fleeting black shapes that ghosted between windows and buildings.

'Fuck this,' I grumbled to myself, anxious at the carnage a 107 would do with a direct hit to a wall or fighting position. 'Ray, what air do we have?'

'Pair of F-18s.'

'Let's find them something to smash, and get this broken up,' I told him, referring to the contact, then pointing out two three-storey buildings that the enemy were using to swipe at us with PKM belt-fed machine guns and RPGs, essentially acting as the enemy's FSG. I was certain that, if we could take them out, the rest of the attack would wither and die as the first had done.

High in the sky, the pair of F-18s began to circle like vultures. The Taliban continued to fight on, regardless of their presence.

'They're making their run now,' Ray warned me. 'Keep your mouth open and ears covered for when the pressure and the blast wave hits. It's danger close.'

Danger close meant that the target was within 150 metres of our position. I passed the message over the net and by voice. Easy Company's fire dwindled to nothing as men relayed the shout to take cover. I wondered if the enemy knew what was coming. Their continued fire suggested either that they did not or that they didn't care. Confined in their buildings, the first that they knew of it was probably the hideous shriek of the 1,000lb bomb falling to earth. The apocalyptic explosion tore through the streets, the blast wave shaking our guts like a hard right hook, dust forced into our open mouths, our ears, and our noses. Such was the power of the blast that it rocked some off their feet, one soldier tumbling from his rooftop position into the dirt below. He rose, unharmed, as the column of smoke and debris pillared towards the sky.

The sound of the enemy fire was gone, but we were not done.

Another shriek. Another blast wave. Another column of destruction towering towards an azure sky.

'Wow,' was all that Ray could say.

Contact was broken.

The enemy came another four times that day. Each time they were ferocious, and we seized control of the battle from them only with a staggering amount of small arms, mortar fire, and close air support, the jets needed at every engagement to convince the enemy it was time to go home, if only temporarily. Expecting a final push at dusk, I had the company fully stood to and ready. The enemy showed up on time, thick streams of tracer dancing across a pink sky. It was chaotic, and it was wonderful. The day closed when a B-1 – an American bomber designed to nuke Russia – dropped a 2,000lb bomb onto a building used as an enemy firing point, reducing mud brick to dust.

As the final attack died in the twilight, and I stood the men down, I took stock of the state of my body. My ears were ringing, dehydration had a grip on me, and my guts churned from the slap of so many blast waves, but I was happy. Dog tired, but happy. What we had gone through this day was every soldier's dream. We had withstood attack after attack, we had punished the enemy, and we had done it all without a single casualty.

'How many do you think we killed, sir?' one of the young signallers asked me within the ops room.

'Dozens,' I guessed.

'We got confirmation for a lot of them over the ICOM,' Staff Wornham added. 'Wounded, too. They were reporting back to their commanders on casualties.'

'They sounded terrified,' the young signaller added.

'I was scared enough myself when those bombs hit.' The staff sergeant laughed. 'Blast wave knocked half the stuff off the desk.'

His light-hearted, nervous laughter spoke for the company as a whole – we could barely believe that we had come through such a fight without a scratch.

I made my way amongst the platoons, checking in on the soldiers who were stripping weapons and replenishing magazines. No one was in any doubt that the enemy would reappear with the dawn. I felt an enormous amount of pride as I observed these young men. Many were teenagers, and yet they had stared down one of the most savage enemies on the planet – a cadre of men who had known war all their lives, and who were committed to die for their cause. Through their actions, my men had shown they possessed the will to die, though it was an outcome none sought. The will to kill, on the other hand, was something that they brandished with glee, arguing over who had shot whom, and which amongst them had amassed the greatest tally.

'Did you fuck get him, yer bollox!' One lance jack laughed at a private soldier. 'He was mine. I got him with the gimpy.'

'He was already dead when you hit him.' The other youngster grinned. 'You just made him dance around a bit.'

I left the men to their discussion. It was a reflection on the tempo and proximity of the fighting, understandable when you have spent a day in a fighting position with the enemy metres away. An enemy that you know will show you no mercy if you surrender. An enemy that you know will fight on until you, and all your kind, have been wiped clean from the earth.

'Looking forward to tomorrow?' I asked a knot of soldiers.

'Oh aye, sir,' they answered as they scrubbed at the dirty working parts of their weapons. 'Can't wait to get stuck back in on the bastards.'

'You reckon they'll come again?' a skinny soldier asked his comrades.

The leader amongst them scoffed. 'Fuck aye they will. Fucking mad cunts, they are. What time's kick-off, sir?' he asked me.

'Same as today, lads,' I answered, then took my leave of the young Rangers. There was work to be done, a day's fighting not finished until reports and logs had been completed.

'All the ammo's replenned to the fighting positions, sir,' the sergeant major told me. 'Here's the ammo state.'

He handed me a piece of paper. On it was scrawled the amount of ammunition remaining for each type; .50 cal for the heavy machine guns; 7.62mm link for the GPMG; .338 for the snipers; 5.56mm ball for rifles; 5.56mm link for light machine guns; 9mm for pistols; 51mm mortar, smoke; 51mm mortar, high explosive; 81mm mortar, smoke; 81mm mortar, high explosive; claymores; grenades. Knowing how much ammo was left allowed us to work out how many minutes of fire we had for each weapon's system.

'We're OK for a few days of this,' the sergeant major summarized. After that, it would be sticks and stones.

'Thanks, Sergeant Major. Get some rest. I've got to back brief the JOC.'

The veteran gave me a nod and left the room. I put my call through to Battlegroup HQ, apprising them briefly on everything from the enemy tactics to our ammo state.

'You expect they'll attack again in the morning?' the ops officer asked.

'I do.'

'We'll cut some air to you. A-10s?'

'That would be great.'

'No problem. Good luck.'

I hung up the phone and looked at my watch – six hours to first light.

I wondered if I'd sleep.

12

I was woken by one of the signallers at 0300. I had ninety minutes of sleep in the tank, and with dawn an hour away, it would have to do. I poured some water from a bottle onto my toothbrush and scrubbed my teeth. The stale smell of dehydrated cigarette breath was thick in the rooms, overlaid by the ration-induced stench of farts.

I made my way into the ops room, taking a gulp of the sweet brew that was passing from hand to hand.

'All quiet?' I asked the sergeant major.

'All quiet, sir.'

'I'm going to take a quick look round.'

Ducking back into the darkness, I made my way about the courtyard, keeping to the shadows and hard cover, not wanting to be the kill who announced that the enemy had night vision for their weapon systems. All about me, some seen but most felt, was the presence of my men preparing themselves to fight, then making their way into the fighting positions. There was little talk, and many yawns. Most had not had eight hours' sleep in the last four days combined, let alone in a night, and their actions were becoming automatic, a product of countless nights on exercise. Musa Qala was not the Brecon Beacons, but the soldiers had received some inoculation against bone-weariness from exposure to fatigue since their first days as recruits. Some well-meaning politicians and 'do-gooders' rail at the rigours of the army's training regimen, but I was seeing the effect that hard, realistic training was having on preserving the lives of my men.

I looked at the sky. Night was giving way, the stars were fading. It was time to get into my position on the ops room roof. The previous day, it had proven itself to be the most advantageous position to observe the district centre as a whole, and so I would continue to use it as my place of command and control.

'Morning, boss.' A bristling mass of antennas greeted me as I appeared on the rooftop.

'Morning, Ray,' I greeted the JTAC. 'You made comms with the air?'

'Roger. A pair of A-10s again. Boar Two-Three, and Boar Two-Four.' 'Boar' was a reference to the A-10's nickname, the Warthogs.

'They've got such ally names.' I smiled, picturing the pilots who were circling out of sight, ready to visit violence on the enemy I was certain were not two hundred metres away, pushed into position and preparing for their attack.

As the band of pathetic light on the horizon grew from a thin line to a smudge, we anticipated that moment. We waited in near silence but for the scratch against the rooftop as a soldier shifted his weight or scraped a boot. The near silence where coughs were caught in a man's throat, and ammunition belts clinked softly against the metal of machine guns as men checked, rechecked, then checked again the position of cocking handles and sights. On the ops room rooftop, I heard the gentle splash of piss into a bottle as a soldier took a last chance to relieve himself before battle.

'Who wants Lucozade?' I heard an Irish voice whisper to his comrades.

I looked out over the town. Black shapes of compounds and buildings were not revealing detail, their windows like black teeth in rotting mouths. I expected those dark chasms to fill with muzzle flash at any moment, and felt my finger anxiously nudging the safety catch of my rifle. My stomach felt empty, the same kind of energetic nerves that I had experienced as a child on cross-country race day. The inevitable fight was a challenge – a competition – and one where the stakes could not be higher. There was no second place to be taken from the battlefield. There were only winners and losers. The living and the dead.

Five RPGs launched almost in unison. The rockets were barely out of the tube before cries of 'RPG!' came from a score of throats, the warning redundant as the warheads slammed into the mud-brick walls, sending debris in every direction. Within a moment, the air had gone from the stillness of dawn to the cacophony of battle. The dark maw of the town came alive with hundreds of muzzle flashes. Tracer raked and bounced above our heads. Ricochets whined and near misses cracked the air like a whip. With my men, I threw my fire into this chaos, my finger pulling gratefully on the trigger now that the waiting was over, and I was free to double tap at the flashes of light that marked an enemy seeking to kill my men – the soldiers of Easy Company who now fell upon the defence of their comrades with skill and aggression, calling fire control orders, directing fire, clearing obstructions to their weapons with practised motions, whooping as they saw an enemy fall in their sights.

My magazine almost empty, I pulled back from the wall, reloaded, and looked about me. Thirty seconds into the fight, it was time for me to assess where the enemy was strongest. What was their intention? Where was the pinch point?

Already it was clear that the enemy's concentration was thickest in the west again, a heavy weight of fire coming from the two- and three-storey buildings that were separated from our western wall by the mere twenty-metre break of the road.

'Same run as yesterday?' Ray asked me, the man reading my mind – we had A-10s in the air, and yet again it seemed that their service would be needed in smashing the enemy on our western flank.

'Hold off on them for now,' I instructed the JTAC as rounds cracked close by our heads. 'Let's see how this develops.'

It 'developed' by the enemy holding their circle about the

district centre, a ring of fire that poured rounds into our positions. Miraculously, not a man was hit by this storm, whilst our own men cheered and excitedly claimed kills as the enemy dropped in their firing positions.

I looked to the bazaar, a long row of shops on the western flank, seeing the flash of fire but only the vaguest sense of movement. The rooms were deep in shadow, but there was a remedy for that.

'Send the ANP's RPG gunners up to the Outpost,' I ordered over my personal radio to the sergeant major. 'Have them hit the shops. Try and blow the backs out of them so we can silhouette targets.'

I saw the shape of the veteran weave his way to the Afghan Police's position. After a few moments for explanation, they followed in his wake to the Outpost. Within minutes, the boom and bang of their launch and explosions was added to the riot of noise that enveloped the compound. The ANP gunners' aim was true but the enemy's fire showed no sign of slacking.

'Ray, with me,' I ordered the JTAC, and we dropped from the roof, running as fast as we could whilst crouched and bent at the waist like Italian grandmothers. The air above us was clipped with tracer, but we made it to the western wall intact. I was unwilling to call in a danger close mission unless I was in the same position as my men. If I or Ray made a mistake, we would pay for it along with the soldiers fighting on the wall.

'North–south run like yesterday,' I confirmed to the JTAC.

'Release the hounds.' Ray grinned, then set about bringing the pilots onto task. As JTAC, Ray would now coordinate the intricacies of the pilots' approach, but the decision to execute the fire mission, and the heavy price of failure, were mine to bear alone.

'Clear hot,' I said, and at that point the dogs were let free from their leash, screaming in from their holding pattern to rain uranium-tipped shells into the enemy.

'Five seconds!' Ray called, and I echoed his warning, pulling men down behind the meagre safety of the wall. Most came reluctantly, wanting to see the spectacle of an A-10's cannon carving apart air and land, and a spectacle it was – high-explosive fire ripped apart buildings as if they were made of paper as milk bottle-sized shells gouged their way into firing points. It was a huge right hook to the enemy's temple, but though staggered, he was not beaten.

'Again,' I told Ray. And they came again.

And again.

And again.

The Taliban had come for a heavyweight slugging match, and they took the hits until they were driven mercilessly into the ground by the sheer brutality of the A-10s' fire, the air choked by the carnage of dust and debris, the rising sun blocked by a thick cloud of dirt.

How can anything survive that? I asked myself, but despite the firepower, the enemy lived on. We saw the shadows of them as they moved to pull their dead and wounded from the blistered streets.

'Back to the ops room rooftop,' I told Ray.

About us, the contact was petering out. The repeated blows from the A-10 pair had put our opponent on the canvas. For now, at least, he was out. I spoke into my radio, and issued the order.

'Stand down.'

I was in the ops room when Freddie called to me. The intelligence officer was with the LEWT team, and animated. They all were. Something had gotten them excited.

'Lots of ICOM chatter,' Freddie explained. 'Sounds like lots of new fighters moving into the area.'

This seemed like a strange thing to be excited by, and I told him so.

'The commander's talking them in,' he said. 'The groups are

coming in from all over, and there's one voice that's guiding them in to the meeting place.'

'Can we find it?' I asked, quickly catching his enthusiasm.

'Maybe.' He nodded viciously.

And so we set to work with maps and aerial photos. As the interpreters translated the intercepted radio messages, Freddie and I did our best to correspond words to features on the paper in front of us – wadis, compounds, colour of buildings. All could be used to help us triangulate the enemy's position.

'These new voices,' Staff Wornham informed me, 'are all out-of-area fighters. Terps reckon some are Pakistani.'

So far, the accents on the radio had been identified by our interpreters as Afghan and Pashtun. Now it seemed as though members of a wider insurgency were converging on our position. I made a note to relay this development to Battlegroup HQ.

'Bring the JTAC here, please,' I asked Lee Simmons, and soon we were joined by Ray.

'Can we talk to some air?' I asked him. 'I think we're starting to get a rough idea of where they are. If we get someone up in the air, I reckon we can confirm.'

Minutes later, Ray announced that an RAF Harrier GR7 had been cut to us. Freddie began to point out features on the map.

'So we've got the red desert here, MSQ wadi here, and green zone here. Based off what we're hearing, I think that one of their incoming convoys is here.' He pointed to the map with a sharpened pencil.

'I'll have the pilot check it out,' Ray replied, and passed the coordinates on to the pilot. Soon after, the pilot confirmed that he could see a convoy of twelve pickup trucks. I was not the only one in the room to feel a tremor of excitement.

'What's the latest on the ICOM?' I asked Ian Wornham.

'More of the same, boss. There's three different call signs

saying that they're coming with their fighters. They all keep referencing a blue building in a compound.'

'Pass that on to the pilot,' Freddie instructed Ray. Moments later, the pilot replied that he was going into a high and lazy holding pattern to better observe the convoy of trucks.

'We need positive identification to smash them,' I told Freddie, meaning that we had to be sure the trucks were full of enemy fighters, and not civilians.

'Are we sure they're not green forces?' I then asked my HQ group.

'Task Force Helmand have confirmed there's none in that area, sir,' a signaller answered me. I hadn't expected friendly Afghan forces to be operating in our battlespace without us having been informed, but it was one more thing that needed checking off before we could sanction an attack.

'Pilot, sir,' Ray said. 'He says that he can see weapons amongst the men on the trucks. He also says that their poise is military like. They have sentries out, and seem to be on a defensive footing.'

I took it all in. We had the radio intercepts, and we had the pilot's visuals, but they came from a man travelling at hundreds of miles an hour, and thousands of feet in the air. The final word to attack the convoy had to come from me, as we had instigated the mission, and nightmare scenarios flashed into my mind – I did not want to be the man who gave the OK and destroyed a wedding party. Easy Company were not in contact, and this decision would not save the lives of my men – at least not in the immediate moment. If they were Taliban reinforcements, however, then the chance to strike them now could save the lives of my men in the days to come . . .

'Clear hot,' I told Ray, the military behaviour of the men in the vehicles convincing me that this was the enemy, and no innocent party. 'Let's smash them.'

Ray passed me the handset so I could give the pilot my initials and confirm the mission with my final, definitive authority to strike. The pilot read it back and confirmed. The room was silent but for the chatter of the enemy on the ICOM. Then the shrill report of rocket launches echoed across the town.

I held my breath. My heart stopped in my chest.

Nothing on the radio. It was as if the enemy were oblivious to the attack, and if that were the case . . .

'We're under attack!' The interpreters translated in unison as the enemy burst onto the ICOM – there was no translation needed for the tone of the Taliban commander's voice; it was high-pitched with fear.

As the sound of explosions rumbled in the distance, the ICOM came alive with the desperate cries of the men on the end of a deadly strike.

'I've got wounded!'

'My commander is down!'

'They're strafing us! My men are dead!'

So it went on. The pilot reported that eight of the eleven vehicles were destroyed through a blazing salvo of rockets, and 500lb bombs. Three of the vehicles had turned on their heels, and these the harrier pilot turned over to a pair of A-10s that had come to join the feast of targets – I expect that the enemy did not make it far before the tank-busters devoured them.

I slapped Freddie on the shoulder. 'Great job,' I told him, repeating my praise to all the others in the room.

Every man was smiling, buzzed to have been able to wrestle the advantage from the enemy and to take offensive action against them. The ICOM was enough to tell us that the Taliban had been mauled, and in that carnage, we had turned the tables a little more in our favour.

'Maybe we'll have a quiet night?' one of the signallers ventured. There were grounds for his optimism, the reports of enemy dead and wounded still rolling across the ICOM, but the Taliban were dogged. Despite their casualties – or perhaps because of them – they came again at us in the afternoon, small arms and RPGs beaten back with our own fire and close air support. They made their last attack in the twilight, the contact broken through a punishing barrage of mortars dropped just outside our perimeters. So close was the fire that our mortar barrels were pointed almost vertically upwards.

'They're tough bastards,' Freddie acknowledged as the smoke cleared, fine debris from the mortar strikes hanging against the carpet of red sky.

'They are,' I agreed, wondering at our enemy, and how they continued to break themselves against our positions. Even an air strike on their gathering reinforcements seemed to have done little to take the wind from their sails. The ICOM was thick with announcements that 'such and such has gone to paradise', but those deaths seemed to have no impact on the enemy's resolve. Why would they, when they viewed death at our hands as the surest pathway to heaven?

'Good work today, Freddie,' I told the man again, meaning it. 'Now get some rest. They'll be back in the morning.'

13

Once darkness had settled, I returned to the ops room, preparing to deliver my round-up of the day's activities to Zero back in Camp Bastion.

'More ICOM, boss,' Staff Wornham greeted me. 'The local commanders are encouraged by their new numbers. Say they're going to put on a big push in the morning.'

We'd smashed them from the air and from the sangars, and still they were encouraged?

'Any luck distinguishing commanders?' I asked, it not being the place to voice my concerns.

'Getting there, boss. They keep referencing the Harrier strike as the big bombing. They're complaining they have no way of taking down our jets.' He smiled.

I dreaded to think what our situation would be if the enemy did have such a capability, but that was a thought for the Taliban commanders to ponder. I had other plans.

'Wake me up in an hour.'

The short rest passed in a heartbeat. Then, bleary-eyed, I took the soldier's medicine of a brew and cigarette as I went over the morning's defence plan and fires with Ray and Freddie.

'What's that you've been working on, Freddie?' I asked the IO, seeing a complex matrix of numbers written on a piece of card.

'Trying to crack the enigma code?' Ray snorted.

'Nah, I've been plotting the times of day the enemy are most likely to attack, and where.' Freddie showed us the card enthusiastically. 'First and last light, guaranteed contact. About eight a.m., good chance of contact. Eleven a.m., we haven't had any contacts.'

'You trying to be a weatherman or Mystic Meg?' Ray poked, laying on a mocking accent. 'This morning, at eight a.m., there is a 60 per cent chance of steel rain.'

Freddie waved away the banter. 'I'll hang this on the ops room door,' he said earnestly. 'Lads can take a look, and figure out when's the safest time to pop out for a wash, or shit.'

Like Ray, I struggled not to spit out my tea.

'You've made a shit forecast?' I asked him.

'I thought it would be useful,' he answered defensively. 'I've built a shower and nobody's used it.'

'I wonder why.' Ray giggled, then added, 'No one wants to be the man who got fragged washing his balls.'

'Put it up on the door,' I told Freddie, not wanting him to be put out. 'But next time you're bored, get some sleep.'

'Will do, boss.'

Freddie's matrix went up onto the door. Throughout the night, newcomers to the ops room questioned it, laughed, and thanked Freddie for his efforts, especially his consideration for their shit schedules.

'Thirty minutes to first light,' I announced to the men in the ops room, reaching for my gear and rifle.

They knew the drill. Already outside could be heard the yawns and stifled curses as men were roused for the stand to.

'Another day, another dollar,' one soldier shrugged between drags on a cupped cigarette.

Steadily and without fanfare, the men of Easy Company made their way to walls and sangars. Weapons were oiled, checked, and checked again. Belts of ammunition were laid out delicately atop bullet-riddled sandbags. Last-minute jokes and encouragement were shared between mates. Dry tongues worked to push down a few more spoonfuls of ration-pack breakfasts, lips left bright red from bean juice, spoons licked clean and then replaced into the soldiers' favoured pockets.

Dawn crept closer, revealing the faces of men barely into their twenties, youthful looks dried out from the heat, tired red eyes sunken beneath the rim of helmets. The look of a combat soldier pushed to extremes of the body and mind, his exhausted figure roused from a snatched moment of sleep to stand and face the enemy once more, for what other choice was there?

It was 0450 on Easy Company's third morning in Musa Qala when the RPGs fired again, and the ops room sent its ritual warning to Bastion.

'Contact. Wait out.'

The morning's first contact developed in the usual manner – RPGs and small arms answered by our own small-arms fire and mortars, contact finally being broken when our pair of assigned A-10s swooped down and poured hell onto the heads of our enemies. The air strikes seemed to be the only way we could deter enemy attacks, and I made a vow that those pilots would never have to buy a drink so long as I was at the bar.

There was little time to relax after the first attack. Weapons needed attention. Ammunition needed to be redistributed. Reports had to be compiled and sent up the chain of command. Our bodies needed to be fed and watered, critical if we were to continue standing and fighting in the soaring Afghan heat. To touch exposed metal without gloves was an unpleasant experience, to say the least.

'Lots of ICOM, boss,' Staff Wornham informed me. 'Talking about making a big push today.'

'Another one?' I grinned. 'Any specifics?'

'Sounds like the new commanders that arrived yesterday. At least six commanders, and some are Iranian and Pakistani. We're starting to get a good idea of who's who, now.'

'Great job. Let me know if the chatter starts building.'

I left the ops room. It was midday, and I wanted to make a tour of the fighting positions, looking for weaknesses and vulnerabilities that we could patch up before the enemy spotted them. As I moved from cover to cover, my boots crunched on the hundreds of empty cases and broken pieces of link that littered the walls. All around me, pieces of wall had been gnawed away by enemy fire. Sandbags lay split and torn apart. In the heat of contact, I had marvelled that we escaped the enemy's weight of fire with no casualties. Seeing the destruction about me now, I thanked God again that our luck was holding. But I was under no illusion that it would last forever. The enemy were putting thousands of rounds into the air, and it would take only one to bring about the moment that every soldier dreads most – not his own death or wounding, but that of one of his comrades.

As if reading my mind, the enemy attacked.

One moment there had been the quiet of the Afghan summer, broken by the clink of weapon cleaning and the light banter of soldiers. Now, there was the cracking whip of lead in the sky, green tracer streaking over the heads of Easy Company's men as they rushed from their accommodation, helmets and body armour pulled on with one hand, weapon and webbing cradled in the other. The men of the company came in all states of dress – shorts and boots; sandals and underwear – but this was not the time to stand on ceremony. This was the time to get into a fighting position and kill the enemy.

I ran for the ops room wall, flinching as rounds hit a row of sandbags above my head, their contents sent spilling down into the space between body armour and flesh, rubbing raw patches against my sweating skin.

'Ray!' I called to the JTAC, seeing him sprinting in the same direction as I was heading. 'What air do we have?'

'Waiting on the request now!' Unlike first light, we did not have pre-assigned call signs to call on. These would be allocated to us now that we were under contact.

I crouched and crawled my way onto the ops room rooftop, joining a half-dozen men already there, rifles popping and LMGs rattling. They looked like the motley crew of a pirate ship, half-clothed and with stubbled faces.

'Watch my tracer!' one of the Royal Irish soldiers called, letting rip a burst of fire into a nearby building to the north. I followed his target indication, pumping rounds into the windows, fleeting black shapes dashing from cover to cover as the enemy sought to engage us. Suddenly, I realized that this was not the enemy's standard tactic of encircling the compound and pouring fire into us from all around – they were fire-and-manoeuvring their way forward; trying to close the distance, and reach the walls. In doing so, they presented the men of Easy Company with the kind of target that every soldier dreams of.

I double tapped a figure in the lee of an awning. Bodies began to fall in the streets. Not for the first time, we saw the enemy drop as we fired. They lay in exposed alleyways and roads. They lay on rooftops, and in doorways.

'Fucking smash them!' an Irish NCO called, and the nearest gimpy gunner tore through bursts that ripped a pair of fighters from their feet, and left them as husks on the sun-baked tarmac of the western road.

As the rounds hit mud brick around me, I pulled back from the fight to make my assessment. The enemy had changed tactics, and I could only think that the attempt to close with us was due to the accuracy of the strafing runs we had been bringing in on top of them. They were dying as they tried to advance, but perhaps they saw this as preferable to the inevitable end of their attacks, as our aircraft's rockets and cannons pummelled them into submission – at least for a time.

There was no chance of bringing those strikes in closer now. We had already been danger close, and calling in air onto our own position was to be considered only if we were in danger of being overrun entirely. If the Taliban made it to the walls, they would have to be weeded out and killed the old way – by an infantryman and his bayonet.

'Vehicle west! Vehicle west!' a half-dozen voices began to shout in unison.

I looked to where the men were indicating, seeing a pickup truck moving at speed towards our location.

Suicide bomber, was the first thought that entered my mind. If it were packed with explosives, the pickup could easily tear a hole through the makeshift barrier that was our front gate.

The soldiers on the western wall didn't wait to find out, and bullets began to tear into the vehicle. Enemy fighters in the truck bed began to fire back, whilst beside them, more Taliban advanced along the rows of buildings, scuttling in and out of cover as they attempted to fire-and-manoeuvre onto our position. Within seconds of the vehicle making a line for the gate, its windows were shot out and it slewed to the side of the road, crashing into a building. The enemy advancing behind it stalled as the soldiers on the western wall turned their attention from the pickup to the dismounted fighters, and these men now fell back, dragging their wounded with them.

The Taliban's forward movement had been halted, but still fire poured in from every direction. I called the mortars, requesting that they blast the pre-designated target to our north-west. Moments later, that sector of the battlefield was a sea of churning explosions, smoke, and debris. As if someone were turning off a tap, the enemy fire gradually closed to a few pot shots and agitated bursts of machine-gun fire.

Careful to keep my head down, I looked out to the streets. Black-robed bodies lay where they had fallen. There was no sign of the wounded, the Taliban fighting forward to either recover their comrades or die in the attempt. Though I hated what they stood for, there was a part of me that admired their bravery.

The pickup truck changed that.

'Major Jowett! Major Jowett!'

It was one of the Afghan Police lieutenants calling me. The man was agitated, which was not an emotion I was used to

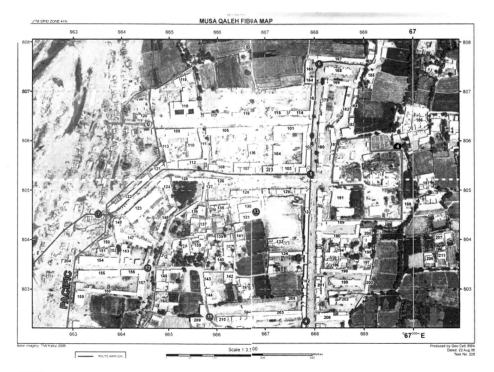

Aerial reconnaissance photos of Musa Qala. The district centre perimeter is in red.

Some of the thirty Danish Tiger Squadron armoured vehicles that left Musa Qala on our arrival. The Outpost is in the background.

The view to the west of the district centre. The enemy held these buildings. Awnings mark the bakery in the foreground.

Looking in towards the western wall, the front gate that was rushed but never breached. A small sangar position is to the left, with a jeep and the ops room in the background.

Looking west, the Needle and enemy-held buildings dominate our compound. A destroyed Gaz-66 jeep is in the foreground.

Popular and courageous, LCpl Jon Hetherington, twenty-two years old, from 14 Signal Regiment (Electronic Warfare). Killed in action 27 August 2006.

North of the Outpost, every angle was fought over with rifles, GPMGs, and grenades. 'Mount Doom' is in the background.

The Outpost, looking north-west, with one of our two HMGs destroyed in place by enemy fire, its mount lying empty. GPMG and HMG barrel to the left.

Lt Paul Martin briefs Barossa Platoon inside the clinic. Left to right: Rgr 'Ozzy' Osborne, Rgr 'Livo' Livingstone, Lt Martin, Sgt 'Gillie' Gillespie, Rgr Steven Rice, Rgr Kris Bradshaw, and Rgr John Purdy.

The mosque – the scene of bitter grenade and small arms fighting – viewed from the south-west sangar. The Needle in the background is opposite the main gate.

Rgr 'Livo' Livingstone mans the GPMG, hard at it on the Outpost.

The western wall looking south into the mosque. There was intense fighting from the stairwell where fighters repeatedly attempted to break through.

Snipers Hugh Keir and Jared Cleary on the Alamo's eastern wall.

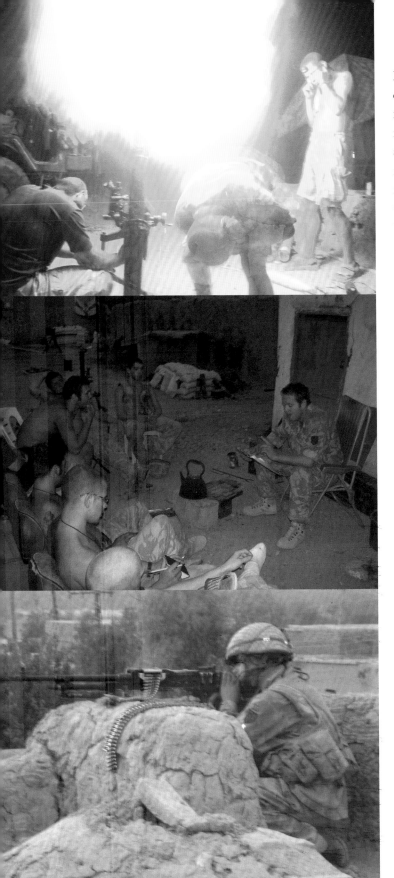

Indispensible: one of our two mortars firing near vertical for a danger close mission. Left to right: Rgr Robert Crockard, Rgr Thomas Smith, and LCpl David McFarlane.

Cpl Danny Groves briefs the mortars. Anti-clockwise from Danny: Rangers Adam Dunlop, Jason Mooney, Robert Crockard, Thomas Smith, LCpl Rab McLurg, LCpl David McFarlane and Rgr Douglas McLaughlin.

Paratrooper Adam Scozzi with GPMG shooting to the south from the Alamo.

Sharpshooter on the left with L96 sniper rifle, paratrooper on the right. Taken from the Alamo looking east.

'Don't get that radio shot!' Bdr Ray Anderton, me, and Cpl Abe Williams. Our ability to call fast air and artillery strikes was key to the defence during the siege.

A time to think. Between attacks, Rangers Joe Ward and Norman Russell on the Outpost.

One of the six casevac missions powers away from the northern HLS. Sangar three is to the right.

Call sign 'Widow 76' ('We put Warheads on Foreheads') Ray and me next to the tally wall. A Danish Maskingevær M/62 (MG 42) destroyed by shrapnel adorns the wall.

The Outpost looking south-east across the southern edge of the HLS. Sangar three is in the foreground with the perimeter dog legging it back to the ops room building. The Alamo is in the background.

seeing from him. In every contact he had been unflinching and steadfast.

'What is it?'

He pointed in the direction of the truck. His English was poor, and my knowledge of his language almost non-existent, but I got the gist of it well enough – those were his people in the truck.

I moved with him to the front gate, where Afghan Police were already frantically trying to pull apart the barricade. I got onto my radio, telling the company to remain stood to, and to lay suppressing fire if needed. I didn't sense a trap, the lieutenant's conviction enough to persuade me that he and his men had cause to move out to the stricken vehicle. The absence of the Taliban moving forward further confirmed the idea – if it were their wounded fighters in the truck, they would want to recover them. So if not the Taliban, who were they?

I felt sickened as the obvious answer to that question presented itself. When the Afghan Police pushed the vehicle through the gates and into the courtyard, my heart sank to see it confirmed.

We had shot civilians.

There was a family inside the cab of the truck. As the police began to pull them free of the wreck, it was clear that three were dead. There is no purpose in describing their wounds, gender, or sex. None of that will bring them back. I would rather say simply that they were innocent, and they died at our hands.

There were two survivors from the family, and both had gunshot wounds. One was the patriarch, the other a young man. Joined by an interpreter, I attempted to talk to him. Shocked and in grief, the man was terrified of me. It was the only time I had seen that reaction from an Afghan, and it struck me forcefully that we were here to help these people, and yet the man regarded me with abject fear. I have no doubt he thought that I would kill him. Instead, I asked him how his family had come to be driving towards our compound. Musa Qala was a deserted war zone. These were the first civilians we had seen. What had compelled him to drive into the middle of a battleground?

The Taliban. As the family were driving to Gereshk, they had been stopped by a group of fighters. Two of the Taliban climbed onto the truck and directed it into the town. The man had been too scared to disobey, and now half his family lay dead. He was wounded himself, but there was no way a Chinook and its crew could be risked to recover him to Bastion, given our precarious position. I was sick and ashamed to admit as much, but that was war. However angry and empty I felt, there was no changing the facts.

In any case, the man had no desire to leave the bodies of his family. In accordance with Islamic tradition, they needed to be buried before dusk. The Afghan Police helped to wash and dress the bodies, whilst the more mechanically minded in Easy Company repaired the tyres and radiator of the shot-up truck. It was silent work, every man wondering if his rounds had done the damage.

'We couldn't have seen this coming,' I told both platoon commanders. 'There's no civilian pattern of life here. It was during an attack, and there were fighters on the truck. This is nobody's fault.'

They nodded, accepting the truth, but sickened by the waste of life. Like the other men of Easy Company, they had smiled and patted backs when the enemy had fallen, but those fighters had made a choice. They had come to a battleground to kill us, and they had died in turn. There was no remorse for the death of those enemies, but for this family, there was a collective feeling of sadness and loss.

'It's shit,' a young soldier spoke as he eyed the wrapped bodies being loaded onto the pickup's bed. 'Fucking shit.'

I considered talking to him, but decided against it. This was a matter to be discussed amongst comrades. I was still a stranger to most of these men, and they did not need my patronizing words. They knew that it had been a mistake, but they also knew that it had been an unavoidable one. As the young soldier had said, it was shit. Fucking shit.

14

The Taliban were not idle as our own Afghans prepared the civilian dead and wounded for their departure. In the mid-afternoon they launched another two attacks, again using the tactics of fire-and-manoeuvre in an attempt to close the short distance to our walls. Following the enemy's use of civilians as a ploy, Easy Company's soldiers fought with more tenacity than they had at any point in the combat so far. There was no whooping and cheering when a man dropped a fighter, simply drawn faces and angry snarls. The enemy had shown their true colours, and any growing sense of respect for their bravery had been replaced with cold contempt. The Taliban's use of civilians to screen their attack had consolidated in our minds the reasons why we were in Afghanistan. Life had no meaning to these people other than to use it for furthering their religious and political aims. 'Well,' as some of the soldiers began to say, 'if they want to die for it, I'm happy to help them.'

Both afternoon attacks were broken by our own small arms and mortars. I found it telling that, following the civilians' deaths, we had not needed fast air to end the Taliban's assault – that had come through the sheer ferocity of our own fire. At one point I had even witnessed a soldier so determined to engage an enemy in the alleyway beneath him that he was leaning clear over a wall, a comrade holding him by the webbing so that he didn't pitch forward. So secured, the young soldier hosed down the fighters that had been creeping in towards his position.

In those afternoon attacks we saw the enemy's willingness to die in a fashion that was near suicidal. Many of the two- and three-storey shop buildings that overlooked our compound were flat-roofed, with not even a hint of cover. Onto these bare surfaces the Taliban deployed their PKM gun teams. It was an attempt at creating a fire-support group, but it provided Easy Company with targets far easier than they would ever see on the ranges of Sennybridge back in Wales. No sooner had the gun teams arrived than the fighters would be picked off. The enemy's machine guns would remain where they were, and moments later a second pair of fighters would rush onto the roof to take the place of their fallen comrades. Soon they too would be dead . . . And then the third pair . . . And then the fourth. One gun in particular stuck in my mind, a never-ending stream of individuals who were dead the moment they placed their hands on the weapon.

'Are they stupid? Are they trying to recover it? Why don't they wait until dark to go and get it?' men asked. The fight was becoming a slaughter. There wasn't quite a sense of guilt at the killing, but if anything is ingrained in a Brit it is a sense of fair play, and this skewed balance between our training and tactics led some soldiers to feel as though they were putting down animals rather than engaging skilled fighters.

'They must be new,' Freddie opined as we discussed the matter later in the ops room. 'Totally green. No training. Nor their commanders.'

'Well, they won't be getting any better now,' Sergeant Major Scrivener put in. 'Not the place to be learning tactics.'

'I couldn't believe what I was seeing,' I admitted. 'If they had started making loopholes, or firing from some kind of cover, they could really give us a headache with those machine guns.'

'Fucking idiots.' Freddie shook his head, delivering the enemy their epitaph. 'I'm going to go up to the Outpost, boss. Count the bodies.'

I expected he'd be outside for some time. The black-cloaked enemy dead littered the streets. They reminded me of bundled rubbish bags, awaiting the bin man.

'Any word on the ICOM about them recovering their dead?' I asked the duty signaller.

'No, sir.' Lance Corporal Hetherington shook his head. 'Since that last attack it's gone quiet.'

The young soldier passed me the log book containing the transcribed enemy intercepts. It was clear to see when we had been in contact, a steady stream of enemy messages extolling their men to push forward, whilst others reported casualties.

'I like this one,' Sergeant Major Scrivener announced, pointing out a particular exchange. It involved an irate commander bollocking his subordinate for failing to take out one of our machine guns. The subordinate had promised that he would try again, and then there was a long period of the angry commander demanding updates before a new voice answered him, informing the commander that his subordinate had died trying to carry out his orders, and that the majority of their group were now dead and wounded.

'That is a good one.' I smiled at the soldiers around me. That was my men that they were talking about killing, and they had themselves been ended in their attempt. There was nothing else for me to feel but the satisfaction of my own soldiers' survival. Whilst we remained in the district centre, nothing else mattered.

Dusk was approaching. With helmet and body armour on, rifle in my lap, I reclined in one of the ops room's plastic chairs. There was a fag dangling between my lips, a thick covering of stubble on my face.

'What?' I asked, feeling Hetherington's amused look.

'Nothing, boss.' He grinned.

I expected I knew what. I was a good fifteen or more years older than most of the men in my company, and the beard was only ageing me further. I remembered stories about how, in the Second World War bomber crews, a man in his late twenties was in danger of being nicknamed 'Grandad' by his comrades.

To many of these soldiers, born into young families across Ireland and Britain, I was their father's age, or very close to it. Of course, there was the strong possibility that many of my men did not know their fathers. The infantry have always drawn heavily on boys from broken homes and hard backgrounds, and that was as true now as it had been at the battles of the Somme and Barossa, two bloodbaths fought by the ancestors of the Royal Irish men in these sangars, the battle names adopted by the regiment's platoons so that the sacrifice of those who had gone before them would always be remembered and honoured. Some might scoff at such notions, but the lineage of a soldier is a real thing, and has tangible effect. A soldier fights harder when he knows that he is upholding tradition. A soldier will endure when he knows that men from his own town, his own family, fought under the same cap badge and colours, often dying for them.

I had seen some of the Royal Irish fighting from the outposts in their green regimental headdresses, known as caubeens, and so long as the instance of it happening was the exception and not the rule, then I had no intention of stopping that occasional practice. Sometimes, men need a reason to fight, and to fight hard. Regimental pride gives them that. It was the reason that my maroon beret was in my pocket at all times, a connection to the past deeds of my own regiment. How could I bemoan my own position when legendary commanders like Colonel John Frost had held out for so long against a German SS Panzer Division? How could I complain about the dust and heat when Paras had been frostbitten and frozen in the wet snows of the Falklands?

If anyone doubts the strength of this belonging, make your way to your nearest football club. Watch the passion, the camaraderie, and the pain of defeat. Listen to England fans talk about Sixty-Six as though it was their birthday, wedding day, and a lottery win, all rolled into one. Now magnify that a thousand-fold under the intense microscope that is battle and war, and you will come close to knowing why a soldier takes pride from an emblem or flag. You may not understand it, but you will *know*.

'I'm going up onto the roof,' I announced. About me, the men of the ops room pulled on their fighting gear. Only a skeleton crew was left to man the radios and maps during a contact. All others, regardless of trade, were expected to fight. I had not once needed to enforce this point. It was expected by the men, and accepted eagerly. They were soldiers first, tradesmen second. They wanted to fight.

Up on the roof, I saw the outline of helmets set against the incoming dusk as men crawled and shimmied into position. This day had been longer than most, the emotional moment of the civilians' deaths doing as much to drain my men as heat and the enemy had been doing for days now. It was a marvel that no man had succumbed to heatstroke in the temperatures that soared above 40 degrees, and I gave my NCOs thanks for this. They were the men who ensured the youngest, most inexperienced soldier was hydrated. They were the ones who shoved a packet of rations in his hand when all the soldier wanted to do was sleep. They were the ones who lit the fires, pouring dozens of sachets of sugar into the section brew until a man could feel his teeth falling out as he drank it, but dentistry problems could wait – first, we had to survive, and my men were doing that through perseverance and dogged professionalism.

It was exactly 1900 hours when we were hit again.

'RPG!'

The rounds crashed into the Outpost, brick and debris showering down from the detonations. Within one shallow breath, the Afghan dusk had been transformed from a time of tranquillity to a devil's playground. Thick ropes of tracer weaved overhead. Rifles spat, machine guns barked, and men shouted commands as they attempted to bring order to the chaos.

It was the heaviest weight of fire yet. The enemy had several machine guns to the north, and these PKs unloaded upon us in long, menacing bursts. Black shapes appeared on the rooftops, and though our own machine gunners and snipers swept these teams away quickly, there was yet again a fanatical supply of replacement gunners and other teams that were emplaced within the recesses of buildings and rat runs. Despite all that we had endured so far, I caught the knowing look between the soldiers about me – a little exhalation of breath, and exaggerated wide eyes that said: 'That was tasty. That was the biggest and the baddest of the assaults so far.'

For the first time since we arrived in Musa Qala, I felt real fear at putting my head above cover. The air was so thick with bullets that it seemed impossible I would not get hit, but my men were braving the storm, and there was no way that I would stay in cover whilst they took those risks. I came up from my relative shelter, and began to double tap at the shadowy shapes that darted forward from cover to cover.

Hit . . . Hit . . . Hit . . . Miss.

We had to win the firefight and suppress the enemy's fire. *We* had to be the ones that beat *them* down. If the enemy could gain the upper hand, and keep us pinned in position with our heads below the parapet, then they would be free to manoeuvre onto us and into the compound. If we lost the walls, and were forced to retreat within the Alamo, I knew that our casualties would be grievous. You do not turn your back on an enemy without him mauling you.

'What's in the air?' I asked Ray.

'Boar.'

I thanked God and the Air Operations Centre for that mercy. Boar were the A-10 call signs. If we had needed them at any time, it was now.

'Cue them up east to west,' I told the JTAC. 'Most of their machine guns seem to be up there.'

'Roger.'

The word was barely out of his mouth when we both flattened ourselves to the rooftop.

'Incoming!'

Mortar rounds screamed in over our heads, the explosions echoing out from the compound, dirt and debris dropping onto us from the strikes.

'Back up! Back up!' I shouted, hearing the same call going out from my NCOs. We could not afford to lose a split second in the small-arms battle, and men scrabbled back to their knees and feet, exposing themselves bravely to the indirect fire.

I looked to the western wall. There was a commotion amongst the Afghan Police, a few of them milling about a prone body. From their manner, it was clear that their comrade was dead. Two of them carried him away whilst the others rejoined the fight.

'Need you to give the OK, boss,' Ray told me. 'Danger close, as always.'

'Clear hot. Go.'

'Strafing run to the north!' Ray announced to the men, the message being relayed from mouth to mouth above the din of the fight. 'Thirty seconds!'

I caught sight of the dark shape across the rooftops – a murderous shark powering its way towards its prey.

'Five seconds!' Ray called, but men were already taking a knee or flattening themselves against rooftops. They had developed a sixth sense for when to take cover during air strikes. The Taliban, their eyes on us, had not. Their fire continued until it was drowned out by the maelstrom of the A-10s' cannon fire, machine-gun teams on rooftops wiped away as if they had been nothing but a bad dream. The destruction caused a respite from the north, but on all other sides the Taliban kept pushing. They kept pushing, and, through a reckless regard for their own lives, they got closer.

'They're in the mosque, boss,' one of the Royal Irish beside me pointed out, and sure enough, I could see darting figures and muzzle flash amongst the rubble that led all the way up to, and into, our compound. So close that a strafing run on that position would churn our own sangars into dust. There was only one way to dislodge the enemy there.

I ran down into the ops room. 'Sergeant Major!'

'Sir?'

'There's enemy in the mosque. I'm going to take the reserve section and clear them out.'

'Let me go, sir,' Scrivs replied, calmly. 'You don't want to get tangled up in it.'

'You're right,' I said reluctantly. I hated to admit it. 'I'm going to get over to the western wall, and get a gun run north to south.'

'All right, sir. The police have a KIA.'

'I saw him. I'll get over to them after this gun run.'

And with that we went our own ways, Ray on my heels as we dashed between cover to the western wall. The fight about us showed no signs of letting up and I began to think on what our next move would be if the A-10s could not dissuade the enemy.

The north–south gun run arrived within minutes, the high-explosive shells crackling as they bit into buildings. The dusk, already on its way, seemed hurried in as the carpet of smoke choked the air.

I looked back across the compound, seeing the sergeant major and the reserve section lobbing grenades into the rubble of the mosque. More came back from the enemy, exploding against the nearest sangar. The enemy were close enough that I could hear their cheers of 'Allah Akbar', and the answering insults from Irish voices. There was no way that I could pull the reserve back from that position. We were fully stretched now, every man but Doc Stacey and a single radio operator engaged with the enemy. As a commander, it pained me to have no reserve, but there was no other choice. The enemy fire was too strong, and they showed no sign of letting up in their attempts to worm their way closer.

'Another gun run,' I told Ray.

We brought it in. Then another. And another. Sergeant Major Scrivener beat the enemy back with grenades and insults. On the other sectors, the A-10 Boar call signs struck the enemy again and again, until the ICOM was full of messages detailing their dead and dying. They hated the shark-faced planes with a passion, and once again, they had to melt away rather than be cut to ribbons by the American machines.

Eventually, quiet settled over the battlefield. There was only the sound of machine gunners reloading belts of ammunition. The clink of empty cases kicked by a boot as a soldier changed firing position.

I checked in with the police. They had lost a man to a mortar round, and now, for the fourth time that day, they would prepare a body for burial. They took the death of their comrade with the same stoicism we'd heard on the captured radio intercepts of our enemy; 'He is gone to God. God is great.'

I met with the sergeant major in the ops room. 'Enjoy that?' I greeted him.

'Never thought I'd be throwing grenades on this tour,' the old sweat admitted.

'I'm not going to lie.' I smiled. 'I'm a little jealous. That looked ally.'

'Felt ally, boss.' He grinned.

'I'm going to take a section and do a clearance patrol out there,' I informed my right hand. 'Make sure there are none of them skulking around, and then we'll reset claymores and trip wires.'

'No worries, boss.'

I found my section and led them to the mosque. The rubble mounds closest to our position needed to be free of enemy before nightfall, as they could simply clamber over a low piece of wall to gain access to the compound. Our only defence against this was a series of trip flares, and the vigilance of the men in the sangars.

Clambering through the rubble was eerie. I didn't expect to find any Taliban but there was a chance some had remained, and so my finger rested anxiously on my rifle's trigger as we moved around the destroyed building. Signs of the enemy were everywhere; tail fins of RPGs; dropped ammunition; pieces of link; empty cases; grenade pins; discarded field dressings; blood trails.

Looking back towards the compound, the nearest sangars were only metres away. The enemy really were under our noses. It was a marvel that Easy Company had yet to take a casualty. This close, how could the enemy possibly miss?

With the trip flares and claymores set, we returned inside the compound. I was not the only one shocked that we had come through such a storm unscathed, and that night for the first time the men talked of their mortality. It was in every corner and sangar. The whispered fear and the shrugged questions – would I get hit? Would I live through this? How would it feel? What would happen to me if I died?

That final question was the only one I could answer. If any man of Easy Company paid the ultimate price, then he would be taken home to be buried by his family. When it came to death, that was the only promise I could make.

I made my way up onto the Outpost. Darkness was not far away now, the streets deserted but for the dead and the dogs. These big, brutish hounds appeared from the destruction smelling blood, and dinner. One began to tug on the arm of a dead Taliban fighter that lay in the street.

'Looks like he's waving,' one of the Outpost's sentries giggled. 'Goodbye, mate, thanks for coming!'

His comrade picked up the joke, and took it further. James Blunt was popular that year, and soon the pair of Irishmen were singing, 'Goodbye my lover, goodbye my friend . . .'

Perhaps it was the feared desecration by dogs that pushed the Taliban into action, but soon, unarmed men began appearing from the growing shadows. They made themselves known, walking in the open, their hands visible and manner unthreatening. Sentries settled in behind their guns, but I made no move to stand the company to. Everything about the men's demeanour spoke to their intention – they had come to recover their dead. I did not even have to speak the order that my men should hold their fire. Every one of them understood that, and I expect they felt some grudging respect that a man would risk himself so brazenly to recover a body of a friend.

It was strange to see the enemy up close, and at length. I could see fear in their faces – the knowledge that they could be cut down at any moment – but also a willingness to accept that fate in order to perform their solemn tasks. The fighters were young, as soldiers always are, dark beards beneath chestnut eyes. They were of Pashtun origin, but whether from Afghanistan or Pakistan, I could not tell. I only knew that they were the enemy, and when they returned with weapons, then we would kill them.

As darkness fell on our hardest day, the Afghan hound was shooed away, the waving body lifted onto the shoulders of his comrade and carried off.

Goodbye my adversary.

I'll see you in the morning.

15

In the early hours of 27 August 2006, my fourth day in Musa Qala, I was roused from a ninety-minute sleep to take my turn monitoring our battlegroup net in the ops room. In the day, this net was a rolling commentary of contacts from across the battlegroup. If we were not engaged ourselves, we'd listen in to the sitreps with interest or excitement. When we heard the nine-liner reports that marked a casualty, we'd listen in with dread, men from that regiment trying to work out who the unlucky person was by their zap number. At the end of each day, battlegroup would send out an intelligence report that was essentially a wrap-up of that day's activities. It read like a Saturday afternoon's football scores; 'In Sangin, ACM engaged a foot patrol with small arms and RPG. One ANA soldier KIA, two WIA. Four ACM killed. Engagement broken with two 1000lb JDAM from F-18s. Gereshk, IDF attack, three mortars. No casualties. Now Zad, small-arms engagement on the DC, broken by gun and missile runs from Apache.' And so on it went. There was more than a little soldier's pride that our daily tallies ran longer than those of the other elements of the battlegroup. Dog tired and threadbare though we were, we *wanted* to be in the thickest of it. We knew that we were a part of something that not many soldiers since the Falklands had experienced – going toe to toe with the enemy. Real, intense combat.

Perhaps one of Somme's corporals summed it up best: 'I hope they don't run out of blokes, boss. I fucking love it here.'

I didn't ever say that we were normal.

I thought over the events of the previous day. There was little doubt that the enemy were upping the intensity of the attacks, and the memory of what happened to the Afghan family was an open wound. Still, there was no point in replaying that incident in my head, and I told myself that I had to stop thinking about it. Though the result was tragic, there was not a shadow of doubt in my mind that our actions had not been anything but necessary and lawful. That would be little comfort to the survivors, but what else was there to do? Turning back time was not a weapon in our arsenal. We were making do with what we had, and no doubt that moment would visit me again for years to come, but for now, I had the survival of my own men to consider.

Through Naz, I learned that the family were keen to leave the compound so that their dead could be buried in their own town as soon as possible, and I told them that we would help them on their way as soon as the inevitable dawn attack had been beaten back – to do anything earlier would likely push what remained of the family into yet another crossfire. Until then, they would have to remain inside the district centre.

'Game of shithead, boss?' Lance Corporal Hetherington, the duty signaller, asked me.

'Why not.'

Shithead was a staple card game in the ops room, beloved by the troops because it allowed the winner to call his defeated opponent 'a fucking shithead' regardless of rank. There was practically a line of men waiting to play when either I or the sergeant major shuffled the deck. I wasn't the best at the game, and many a giggling soldier got the rare opportunity to insult a major. There was only mirth in the words – I hope! – but it allowed the soldiers to vent a bit of their spleen. Better through cards and words than losing their cool on a wall. Combat is a pressure cooker, and humour and humility are ways to ease that stress before it causes an explosion.

'You're a shithead!' Hetherington declared, adding 'boss' a moment later, unable to resist the army formalities that are drilled into us from day one of training.

'I am shit at this. How about backgammon?' I asked, knowing my strengths.

'Yeah, all right, boss.'

We were only halfway through the game when the ops room began to fill with red-eyed soldiers – dawn was approaching.

'We'll just call this one a draw.' I smiled.

'I've almost beat you, boss,' Hetherington pointed out. This was true.

'All right then,' I laughed. 'Nobody touch the board.'

We got to our feet, joining a cluster of men who were sharing out cigarettes and lights. Soon, the ops room ceiling appeared to be floating on a cloud. With our smoking, plus the amount of dust in the air from air strikes and mortar rounds, none of us would be leaving Musa Qala with healthy lungs.

I joined Ray on the far side of the ops room. He was looking with some pride at the tally marks of the strikes he had masterfully called in so far. It was an impressive array of firepower: thirty-two gun runs from Apache, A-10, and Harrier; thirty-three rocket runs from Apache and Harrier; fourteen 500 lb bombs; four 1,000 lb JDAMs; six 2,000 lb JDAMs; eight Hellfire missiles; I didn't attempt to read the amount of strikes from 7 Para's 105mm guns in the desert, or our own mortars. Above this tally was scrawled the JTAC's slogan; 'We put warheads on foreheads.'

'Bloody hell.' I shook my head. 'Have we really been that busy?'

'That's just the first two days, boss,' Ray laughed. 'I haven't had chance to update it yet.'

'Well, keep up the good work, mate. You're doing an amazing job, honestly.'

And he was. Every attack had been on the nose. Not a bomb had been dropped without careful consideration and planning under the most intense pressure and danger. Every man in Easy Company was doing his job, and doing it well, but

Ray and Abe were the incredible goalkeepers who were keeping the Taliban from putting one in our net. Having met them only days before, I was now certain that there was not a better JTAC anywhere in the battlegroup.

I looked at my watch. 'It's 0430. Let's get up to the roof.'

In the fading darkness I made my way with Ray up the uneven steps onto the ops room rooftop. Other black shapes followed us, men taking up positions on the hard surface, bruised and scraped knees aching without the adrenaline of combat to mask the wear and tear.

'I feel like I'm a hundred years old,' Ray whispered as he took up position beside me. I smiled to myself at that – he couldn't have been more than twenty-six – but I understood the sentiment. Our bodies were battered and bruised from crawling and hurling ourselves around on the unforgiving Afghan dirt and mud brick. Hands were nicked and burned from hot barrels and razor wire. Our bodies were dehydrated, baked in the sun and starved of sleep. When roused by attacks throughout the day, we looked like a militia of homeless self-harmers – but looks were deceiving, and I had yet to see an NCO have to grip one of his men for slacking on drills. Aching and exhausted we may have been, but as dawn showed its hand on the horizon, we were ready.

'RPG!'

That the Taliban's opening salvo was expected did not make it any less daunting, the enemy's rockets ploughing into the compound as the optimistic birdsong of the early morning was eclipsed by a racket of small arms. Even by the standards of the fights so far, the enemy's fire was relentless, a tide of steel that broke over our positions, sending adrenaline into our veins, and our balls and stomachs tight within our bodies. The fire was furious, the air all around alive with the concussion and crack of shots as they travelled faster than sound.

'Rapid fire! Rapid fire!' I called out, alongside my NCOs. There was no other kind for this moment. The weight of fire was so heavy that we were in danger of being pinned down. If that happened, the enemy would close the short distance and be at our walls. There was no choice but to brave the onslaught, and fear gave way to pride as I saw that my men were doing exactly that.

I pulled my NVGs down onto my eyes. It was still dark enough for them to be of use, and light green splashes danced across my vision from dozens of muzzle flashes, and bursts of tracer round. The attack seemed strongest in the north, at the Outpost. I considered moving there to call in the fires, but the ops room roof itself offered great arcs of fire in that direction. Given the weight of lead in the air, I decided against making the open dash – we could call in the strike from here. I was not about to wait any longer to use our air support.

'Ray. Get the A-10s. West to east strike on the north.'

'Roger.'

Ray flattened himself against the rooftop and began to talk to the pilots. I began snapping shots to the north, and that was when I heard the shout – the call that I had been dreading since the moment our Chinook touched down days ago.

'Medic! Medic!'

It froze my blood.

'Medic!'

The cry came from metres away – it was on our rooftop.

I turned, and saw Ranger Diamond shooting as he stood protectively above a prone soldier. I ran to him, pushing the NVGs up and away from my face. Arriving at the pair I quickly pulled Diamond into cover – there was no way he'd stay untouched with so many bullets in the air.

'He's been shot, sir!' the frantic Ranger told me.

I rolled the stricken man onto his back and saw with raw horror that it was Lance Corporal Jon Hetherington.

I felt for a pulse.

I couldn't feel one.

'Get on the landline! Tell the medics to bring the quad here! Now!'

First light had yet to fully set in, and as I looked for a wound, I felt with my hands – there was little to suggest what had caused the damage, only the blood left in its wake.

'You two!' I pointed at the nearest soldiers. 'Come here! Stay low!' The fire was only feet above our heads. There was nothing we could do for our casualty here on the rooftop. Alerted over the landline, I knew that Corporal Mick 'Frenchie' French, from Mike Stacey's medical team, would be on his way.

'We've got to get him down!' I told the soldiers around me. There was nothing delicate about it and, staying as low as we could, we manhandled Hetherington to the stairs, struggling to carry him across the uneven steps. Rounds thumped into the walls around us, and I worried that at any moment another of us would go down – it didn't seem possible that the enemy could miss.

Miraculously, we made it to the last step just as Frenchie raced to us on his quad bike. He was still pulling a U-turn as we loaded Hetherington onto the bike and passed him into the medic's charge.

'Gunshot wound to the chest! No pulse! Go!'

From hearing the call for a medic to putting Hetherington into Frenchie's care had taken less than thirty seconds. There wasn't another moment now to pause and take stock – I sent the men back into the fight on the rooftops, and headed myself to the ops room. I stopped just inside the door, and caught the eye of the soldier manning the battlegroup net.

'Send a warning order for a nine liner,' I told the man. 'Gun-shot wound to the chest. T1.'

T1 – critically injured. Deep down I knew that he was dead, but it was the doctor's job to pronounce him, not mine. Until I had that word, we would go through the process and cling to hope.

I clambered back onto the rooftop. There was no sign of

the enemy fire letting up. Black shapes darted in the alleyways as they began to press forward.

'Stoppage!' the soldier closest to me called, ducking into cover. I moved up to the wall and began to engage the nearest building, picking up the slack as the soldier cleared the obstruction of his rifle's ejection port.

'Back in!' he shouted, and I crouched down into cover, changing magazines. As I raised my head, I looked over the compound – where was the pinch point? Where should I throw the reserves?

The incoming fire from the rubble of the mosque was intense, but now I heard over the company net that the south-eastern sangar was taking grenades from the alleyways and buildings that jutted onto it. That was where I needed to go.

'Reserve section on me!' I called, and we began the mad dash between buildings, crouched double, sweat trickling into our eyes as rounds tore up the air. Somehow, we made it unscathed.

The sangar ahead of us was under siege, Taliban grenades exploding against its sandbags. Cries of 'Allah Akbar!' were only metres away. The Royal Irishmen in the sangar answered with long bursts of gimpy fire.

'Grenades!' I ordered the eight men of reserve section. 'On my count, we lob them over this wall!'

'For fuck's sake don't throw short!' the section's commander pressed his troops. 'Don't want one of these fuckers bouncing back at us!'

I took a grenade from my pouch. It was a Danish type, one of dozens that the men of Easy had begged from the departing Vikings.

'On my command!' I called, pulling my pin. 'Three, two, one, GRENADE!'

Nine grenades went sailing over the wall that we now pressed ourselves into for cover. Two seconds later, the explosions ripped through the alleyways. There were screams, the gimpy in the sangar following the detonations with hammering fire.

'Stay here,' I told the section's commander. 'If they start to move back up, give them more grenades.'

'Aye, no bother, boss,' the soldier said, grinning.

I was in the southern part of the compound, and so I ran towards the med centre. I only had to look inside to have my worst fears confirmed.

Jon Hetherington's body lay quietly aside. Mike Stacey was preparing the gurney for the next casualty. 'Sorry, Adam. Round went through one armpit and out the other. Even with a hospital right here, there was no surviving that injury. He would have been killed instantly.'

I wanted to swear. I wanted to punch the walls. I wanted to throw my helmet across the room. But what would any of that have achieved?

'Thank you, Mike,' I said.

And then I left him. Questions, anger, and sadness could wait. We were still under heavy attack, and I had a company to look out for.

I ran to the west wall, and the JTAC.

It was time to break the contact.

It took gun runs, rocket runs, and a 1,000 lb bomb to deter the enemy's dawn attack. Dozens of grenades were thrown back and forth in the area of the mosque, and the south-eastern corner. Taliban dead were scattered through the buildings and streets. Our own fallen soldier, Lance Corporal Jon Hetherington, lay in the med centre. He was twenty-two years old.

There was little time to mourn him. Barely had the first contact been broken that the second began, ushering in the heaviest day of fighting so far.

At 0813 we saw the enemy moving into position and engaged. They attacked with small arms and RPG.

At 1005, as soon as our air cover left the area, the Taliban attacked again with small arms and RPG; they came with the same medicine at 1300.

At 1530 they followed their usual attack, but also threw in mortars for good measure, the attack ending only when a huge 2,000lb bomb was dropped by a Rockwell B-1B, the blast wave so strong that it knocked men from their feet, the debris causing a momentary eclipse of the blistering sun.

Undeterred, they came again at 1715 with mortars, small arms, and RPG.

At 2020 the enemy were spotted moving into position, and it was time for us to give them their own taste of mortars.

Every one of these engagements was broken only by danger close fire missions from aircraft, mortars, and 7 Para's artillery pieces in the desert. Throughout the day, Ray and Abe called down fire as close as twenty metres from our own positions. The enemy were unfaltering, and came again and again no matter what punishment we had inflicted on their previous attacks. ICOM told us that, in the final push, one group had lost thirteen fighters, and yet, somehow, the enemy were still unsure if there were coalition forces inside the compound.

Despite the exhaustion and the tragedy of the day – or as likely, because of this – the men of Easy Company laughed at this revelation: 'We're here, you fuckers.'

And we were. The day was a blur of RPGs, tracer, and air strikes, but the enemy had been beaten back time and again, often from as close as a few metres away. Their bodies lay in front of the main gate and in the alleyways. There were no wounded in the open. If they came that close to a sangar, a burst from a GPMG was not doing anything else but taking life.

As darkness began to fall, we looked to our own casualty. Hetherington had been placed in a body bag, and positioned within the cooler confines of one of the camp's cellars, there to join the Afghan policeman who had died from a mortar strike the previous day.

What happened next may seem callous, but it was an action that any fallen soldier would want his comrades to take; they split up Hetherington's kit, dividing out ammunition, cigarettes, and toiletries, whilst handling the young soldier's most intimate items with delicate care, letters and photos of his family that would accompany his body back to Bastion. Of that repatriation, there was little talk. Given the weight of the enemy's attacks, and the vulnerability of the HLS, there was no way that either Battlegroup HQ or myself could in good conscience demand that a helicopter crew be put at risk to retrieve him. Jon Hetherington was gone, and the last thing that he would have wanted was to have a crew fly into a hot LZ to recover his body. He would have understood the decision, as did every other man in Easy.

But what if he hadn't been killed? I was forced to ask myself. What if he had been critical, but alive? What then? How could we have brought a Chinook into that maelstrom? Without doubt it would have been shot from the sky. It would have been carnage, and yet, what were the other options? To wait until darkness? Hetherington was shot in the enemy's dawn attack. Could Mike Stacey keep a critically injured man alive for over twelve hours? I had no doubt as to the man's skill, but he was one surgeon in a makeshift med centre. There was no escaping the horrible truth that, should we sustain critical casualties, then they might die waiting for their evacuation.

That was not acceptable.

It has long been expected in the British army that, in return for a soldier being willing to fight and put himself at risk, he can be assured of speedy evacuation from the point of his injury to proper medical care. We call this the 'golden hour', and it is as good as law in the mind of a soldier. Should a man be hit, then he expects to be on a surgeon's table, in a hospital, within an hour. At Musa Qala DC, it was clear that there was no way we could uphold that decree.

I called Battlegroup HQ from the ops room. The unfinished game of backgammon sat lonely; Hetherington would not be returning to finish it with me.

'What was a signaller doing on a rooftop?' they asked me.

I didn't dignify the question with a response. Doubtless it had come from the top. A desk who assumed only the infantry fight, and had no idea that every man bar the doctor was fighting from the walls and rooftops.

Instead I pointed out – and not for the first time – that the positioning of our compound not only made it difficult to defend, but also made casevac from it near impossible. I recommended other locations in the vicinity that we could secure – by ourselves if needed – and to continue our operation of providing security for the citizens of Musa Qala from there. Of course, that very mission had shown itself to be an illusion – there were no civilians in the town. It was simply a shooting range occupied by ourselves and the Taliban. I also put that argument forward to Battlegroup HQ, but their answer was always the same – that we would hold our current position. There would be no relocation, and the situation of casevac was a bridge to be crossed when it happened. Battlegroup were no happier about this than I, and I expected that the order came from far higher than 3 Para's command. Perhaps not even at brigade level, but higher again, in the strategic strata.

I kept trying, because if the near sacred rule of the 'golden hour' was to be stretched thanks to our commanders' apparent unwillingness to risk offending the governor, then I had to admit to myself that there was the very real chance that my soldiers would die when they could have been saved.

'It's a matter of when, not if,' I told 3 Para's staff over the satphone. 'We're not going to get hit like this every day and leave with one casualty.'

'We understand,' they told me.

And perhaps they did, but it made no difference. Those who *truly* understood without any doubt were my men. With Hetherington's death, the feeling of invincibility had vanished. Now was the time to confront one's own mortality. To recognize that you – or worse, your close friends – could die or be horribly wounded. Easy Company's men recognized too that, should they be wounded, then they might die waiting on a stretcher beside a hot HLS. I was not the only man dreading such a scenario, but I was the only one responsible for it. I was not proud of the sense of relief I felt that Hetherington had died quickly, and been spared suffering. As it was, the men had taken his death as well as soldiers could – no one had expected that the company could come through such a storm intact – but had he died when he could have been saved, then the company's morale would have died with him.

Lance Corporal Hetherington's death *did* raise questions from the ranks. Some younger soldiers wondered aloud why the doctor had not worked on him for longer, unwilling to admit that there was such a thing as an unsurvivable injury, terrifying thought that it was. Others questioned the JTAC, though not with hostility. The men wished to know if fires could be brought in closer. Ray and Abe explained that the strikes were as near as they could be – danger close – and that to take a step up from that would involve calling artillery and air onto our own heads – a real possibility, should the Taliban break into the compound and force us to fight back to a final position in the Alamo or Outpost. During this questioning and search for assurance, it was the place of the experienced NCOs within the company to explain to the youngest soldiers that war was war, and that the nature of that endeavour meant that, at times, soldiers would die. Friends would die. There was no getting past that most basic and brutal of facts, but even having seen it played out in front of their eyes, it was a lesson many of the men could not yet grasp, as if it had all been a terrible, lucid dream.

I could only hope that there would be no more of them.

'That was some fucking day, sir,' Sergeant Major Scrivener shook his head as we shared a brew outside the ops room, the man's eyes red from dust and cordite. 'Ammo's all redistributed. We're going through it like no one's business but we've got stacks of five five six. Running low on the eighty-ones, though.'

The 81mm ammunition was for our mortars, and was proving instrumental in breaking contacts. I made a mental note to prioritize it on the Eagle's lift.

'We'll start using the 105s more, and save the mortars for the eastern flank,' I told him, the reason for that geographical separation being that to put 105 rounds onto our eastern flank would involve them coming over our own heads as they were fired from the desert. Should they drop short . . .

I pulled my dog tags from out of my shirt, and began to affix the Danish grenade pin to it – the first I had thrown that day. Other men were doing the same. It was a small bit of morale boosting, living in the axiom that 'allyness saves lives.'

'I went back onto the roof to see where Jon Hetherington got hit,' I told the sergeant major, the scene replaying in front of my eyes, a series of events that seemed almost imaginary. 'Just bad luck.' I shrugged, picturing it. 'He was changing firing positions and it caught him in the armpit. There isn't any body armour out there that would have made a difference.'

'Still, I'll make sure the Osprey stays in the most exposed sangars,' Scrivs agreed, referring to the heavy duty armour, the plates covering most of the torso rather than just a direct placement over the heart.

'Have you noticed how the men are saying "piss" during the contacts?' He smiled in an attempt to lighten the mood.

I had. Just as they shouted 'Magazine!' or 'Stoppage!', men

were shouting out 'Piss!' when they needed to roll away from their fighting position to relieve themselves.

'The blokes gave it everything today,' I told Scrivs, and that was true. 'I really couldn't be more proud of them.'

'They're mega blokes,' he agreed.

'You seen anybody taking it hard?' I asked him.

He shook his head. 'They're too fucked. It won't hit them properly until we're out of here, or things calm down.'

The sergeant major spoke from experience. I sensed that he was right – we were all knackered. Sleep deprivation alone was enough to dull our usual senses and emotions, never mind the unrelenting stress of combat. Time and time again we had been pushed to the limits of our training and courage, and there was no end in sight. As an army, we were taught to be on the offensive, always on the attack and with clear goals in mind: seize this objective; clear the enemy from these woods; take that building. To be sitting back, with the battle rhythm dictated to us by the enemy, left us all feeling adrift. Would these attacks last for days, or weeks? Would we be relieved, or would we slog on alone? There were no answers to be had, only questions, and uncertainty is often filled with negativity – the worst-case scenarios.

It was a bleak night. The usual banter of the troops was gone, replaced by muttered conversations about mortality. 'If I die, see that my brother gets this letter.' 'If I get brassed up, play this song at my funeral.' The little details that young men think about when they know that it's all to come again in the morning. Once weapons were cleaned and mouths were fed, eyes were shut for an hour or two if a man was lucky, and then it would be time to rouse bruised limbs, pour a brew down a parched throat, and drag a cigarette's smoke into scarred lungs. All too soon he would be crawling and clambering onto the firing step, slipping off a safety catch, and awaiting the enemy, who would creep forward with the dawn. Those final moments before light allow space for a soldier's prayers and fears. Time to ask for deliverance, and to worry about what happens if it's not forthcoming. A moment to wonder how you, an eighteen-year-old from Armagh, found yourself behind a machine gun on the other side of the planet, a few minutes away from giving death, and perhaps, receiving it.

What were my own thoughts that night? They were of the Afghan family who left with their dead during a lull in the battle. They were of a young lance corporal from Wales who had died fighting for his mates. They were of Easy Company, who stood defiant and ready to face the enemy that had killed their friend, an enemy that would not rest until every one of my men was dead.

Unstoppable and unrelenting, the spectre of dawn appeared over Musa Qala.

There was no escaping it.

'Contact!'

16

Anything in life can become routine. As human beings we adapt quickly to our environments, and combat is no different in that way from any other experience. Picture a seasoned skydiver – do they feel the same kind of rush on their hundredth jump as they did on their first? The stakes are as high, but the skydiver's threshold for adrenaline has been raised. They may be more experienced, and so better placed to deal with emergencies than the novice, but such familiarity can also breed complacency. If such a feeling had been creeping into the soldiers of Easy Company, then it had died with our comrade Jon Hetherington. Our mortality had been brought sharply into focus, but, exhausted as we were, the enemy's attacks began to blur and merge into one rolling battle. Often times a soldier's tour of duty is devoid of contact, and then even the smallest of the attacks that befell Easy Company would have been recorded in detail, men playing back every second of their personal war movie. Over the three days that followed Lance Corporal Hetherington's death, Easy Company came under a sustained attack that was as ferocious as anything we had experienced since our arrival in Musa Qala. However, through a combination of fatigue and battle hardiness, these individual assaults and days merged to form the story of our defence of the district centre, pushed tight between the tragic bookends that were the loss of our comrades' lives.

At dawn on the 28th, the enemy came behind their usual barrage of small-arms and RPG fire. It was as heavy an attack as the previous day, and my red-eyed men beat it back by standing up into the storm of steel, picking off enemy gun teams and fighters until the air cover swooped in, gun runs and bombs breaking that first contact.

As the dust settled, ICOM chatter announced that a mortar team had arrived in Musa Qala. We had no more information than that, and at 0756 we were stood to again as two RPGs smashed into the HQ building, shaking the guts of the men on the rooftop as we beat back the assault. We brought in the air power onto the usual targets. The attack fizzled out, but the enemy did not let us rest.

Later that morning, two mortar rounds tore chunks from the HQ building. Miraculously, no one was hurt by the whining shells. Our chance to hit back came when the snipers ID'd armed men on motorbikes, and the JTAC vectored in air to pulverize the fighters. The next move, as was so often the case, belonged to the enemy. At 1608 they battered the compound with an opening salvo of seven RPGs. Two hit the main gate sangar, blowing the men out of the back. The enemy failed to change firing position, and were killed by the Royal Irish, who had dusted themselves off and returned quickly to their guns. During that contact, two more mortar rounds whined through the air, but fell short, exploding just outside of the compound's walls.

Following strafing runs, silence fell over the town. We laughed when we heard claims from a Taliban commander over the ICOM that coalition forces had quit the district centre via support helicopter. Considering there had been no Chinooks in sight, we wondered who this commander was, and if he was making use of the country's heaving opium trade.

The ICOM had been busy that day, commanders urging their men on to make sacrifices, and to never let the foreigners leave Afghanistan alive. It was eerie to hear our deaths wished for by the enemy outside our walls, but we dealt with it as soldiers deal with any emotion – with piss-taking and laughter. Later that night, one enemy commander requested an English-speaking fighter – this sent a shiver of panic through my body, and we quickly checked that every man in the company was accounted for, and that no one had been grabbed by the enemy. It was a fate we all dreaded far worse than death, and one that we were prepared to deny the enemy by the use of a final round, or grenade. Some days before, we had been advised from Battlegroup HQ that a pilot had had to ditch his aircraft over Helmand. Praying that he had not fallen into enemy hands, we sent the radio intercept to Battlegroup HQ. Nothing further was heard on the subject, which we took to be good news.

The enemy made their final push of the day at 2147. Their fire was thickest in the east, and following a day of attacks, we were in no mood to pussyfoot. Through Ray, I ordered the dropping of a 2,000 lb bomb. When it hit the enemy's firing point, smoke and debris climbed towards the heavens like a volcanic eruption. It was the final exclamation point on a day of rattling gunfire, exploding mortar rounds, and roaring gun runs. It was also the day where we learned a new term in the enemy's lexicon – 'throw stones'.

It meant to drop mortars, and in the days to come we would learn to fear that casual phrase.

The 2,000 lb bomb strike of the previous night did little to deter the enemy the next morning. As our friends and family in the UK went through the daily ritual of the school run, we went through our own morning routine – receiving RPG and small-arms fire from the enemy, and then beating back their attack by any means, and at distances that brought us close enough to see the detail of their faces as we killed them.

In the middle of the morning, three 107mm rockets screeched in from the north but mercifully landed short of the compound, their explosions shaking the ground as we pressed ourselves into the dirt. Our sniper pair got their eyes on a potential enemy fire controller at four hundred metres distance, and his own strike was answered with a rolling barrage from the guns of I-battery, our 7 Para friends in the desert.

Later that day there was some excitement when we were given intelligence that a high-value target was believed to be in a building less than three hundred metres from our compound. He was the type of enemy leader whose face made it onto decks of cards, and so, as the next contact was joined, we wasted no time in placing an F-18's thousand-pounder onto his position. Senior Taliban leaders came and went in the area, and in relentless pursuit of these high-value targets were TF-42, the British Special Forces operators who worked tirelessly to behead the enemy's snakes. The details of their operations were under wraps to us, but just to know that these bearded supermen were acting in our support was a huge boost to the men of Easy Company, who looked upon the warriors of the SAS and SBS as demigods.

The afternoon of the 29th passed in a sweltering silence. The phrase; 'It's quiet, too quiet', passed many a soldier's lips, and we wondered at this let up in the enemy's onslaught – had we beaten them into submission, or were they simply holding themselves back for a big push once the sun began to drop? It was with itchy trigger fingers that we awaited this expected attack, but it did not come. Then, as day gave way to night, an intercepted ICOM message revealed to us that the enemy's commander was worried that 'we let the foreigners rest today'. This caused great hilarity amongst Easy Company's men, and I heard one young soldier quip to his friend; 'Aye, I feel like I just had a fucking spa weekend.'

Late that evening, Terry tried to make up for his let up by firing a burst from a heavy automatic grenade launcher from the southern end of the bazaar. The attack caused a break from backgammon and shithead as we rushed to stand to, but it turned into nothing more than an exchange of shouted insults between the men in the Outpost, and the Taliban who occupied the nearby buildings.

'Thanks for the rest, Terry! See you tomorrow!'

*

At dawn, the Outpost drew the thickest part of the contact. According to intercepted ICOM, this was due to the fact that its machine guns were giving the enemy their biggest problem, and not because of the Irish-accented jeers that trailed every beaten Taliban assault. One of our two .50 HMGs had been destroyed in place by PKM fire.

After the first was broken by A-10s, a second attack began at 0806. The enemy got close enough to the south-east corner of the compound to lob grenades at the sangars. With the reserve section, I headed there to throw our own in return. The attack was broken with more air.

At 0922 three mortar rounds crumped into the area of sangar five, and the med centre, in the south-west corner of the DC. ICOM that morning spoke of capturing a spy, who was likely a poor local who was then tortured and killed. ICOM also made references to guests from Bagram, and a certain Mullah Koran. Though we were killing them by the dozen, there was no let up in the replacement of fighters and enemy leadership.

Sometime that day, the Household Cavalry's Mobile Operations Group was struck by an IED, and a huge contact ensued. We heard it over the battlegroup net, the enemy's ICOM, and in the rolling reports of gunfire and explosions that echoed through the town's empty streets. The MOG had been operating to support us by disrupting the influx of Taliban men and supplies, and now they were paying a price for that deed. There was nothing we could do but pace the ops room in frustration, passing on any ICOM intercepts that could help steer the air that would be needed to break the contact occurring no more than a dozen kilometres away. During that drawn-out firefight in the distance, every man in Easy became aware that he would rather be the man on the receiving end of attack than on the sidelines. There is no way to describe how useless and hand-cuffed you feel as a soldier when your fellow countrymen are being battered within earshot, and you can do nothing but pray the enemy break that attack and come at you instead. That didn't happen, and it took air power and exceptional heroism on the part of the HCR to break the contact, and slip the enemy's trap.

In the middle of the afternoon, Terry's attention turned back to us – four mortars whistled into the company, sending men diving for cover. There was nothing dignified about sheltering from these 82mm shells, and heeding a call of nature became a dangerous affair that needed to be finished as quickly as possible. Reading on the toilet was not a luxury we could be afforded, and men railed at this assault on dignity and decency.

'They can shoot at me all fucking day, boss, I don't have no problem with that, but trying to blow me up when I'm taking a shit? Come on, now. That's just no' fair.'

Though there had been no reference over the ICOM to the enemy switching tactics, one look at the ops room log made something very clear – the number of small-arms contacts was falling. The number of indirect fire attacks – rockets and mortars – was on the rise. Badly positioned and exposed as we were to direct fire attack, we were in even worse shape to stand up to a prolonged assault from the air. The sangars were without overhead cover, and though the buildings could withstand mortar strikes, we could not expect to sit in them without the enemy clambering over our walls, as they already threatened to do even with us fully manning the fire positions. As we had no choice but to stand and fight the enemy's direct attacks, there was no other option but to endure their rockets and mortars. It made me sick to think of what a direct strike from such a weapon would do to our unprotected sangars.

The next day, the deadly consequence of our exposed positions was made clear.

17

'A-10s are on station,' Ray whispered to me in the near darkness.

The A-10s were our favourite sight in the sky, the snarling faces painted onto their noses as beautiful as any girlfriend or wife back home. The A-10s and their gun runs had been the difference in breaking attacks again and again. I had no doubt that, without them, our casualties would have been far higher. Indeed, I doubted even that we'd be able to hold our position. They were the ace that I played again and again. The battlefield wasn't about fair play, but survival, and I wanted as many ways to kill the Taliban as possible. From gimpys to B-1 bombers, nothing else in the arsenal was proving as deadly as the 'Hogs'.

As the sky lightened, the silhouettes of the men on the rooftop began to take form. They were a lot leaner than the soldiers who had boarded that Chinook a week ago. The soldiers of Somme, here for weeks longer, were more skeletal still. There were ample ration packs to be had, but eating in the blistering heat is hard going. With the amount of calories we were expending through contacts and work parties, there was no way to keep meat on the bones. Cigarettes, brews, and stubborn pride was the fuel that kept our engines running. Bearded and red-eyed, we were not the well-groomed, well-fed soldiers our families had seen off from Colchester and Fort George.

DUMF – WHOOSH – BOOM!

'RPG!'

'Contact!'

'Contact!'

'Contact!'

Dozens of voices called out the redundant warning of

attack. Dozens of others began to lay down the curtain of fire that would keep the enemy pinned inside their positions, or drop them if they found the courage to try to move forward. It was a heavy contact – 'First light smash, as per SOPs' was how the blokes referred to it. The enemy tried to close the short distance, we killed them, and then the Texan pilots swooped in to pound the rest with cannon shells. The rising sun was blotted from the sky by a thick cloud of dust, chunks of rubble dropping down onto our own positions. When it cleared, the only visible enemy were the ones who lay still and lifeless in the streets.

I stood the company down as soon as possible once the contact was broken. Besides a few moments to argue over who had dropped the most enemy dead, men quickly began to shuffle down from the fighting positions. It was still cool enough in the day that it wasn't a hardship – and was, indeed, almost a pleasure – to enjoy a few moments in the sun to wash armpits and brush teeth. All of this needed to be done in the few areas that weren't overlooked by the enemy, and there was always the chance that the Taliban would send a surprise their way.

It was during one such lull that I decided it would be a good opportunity to clean my weapon, whilst Freddie announced that he was going outside to shave. Just a few minutes later the enemy launched an attack, and as I ran from the ops room with my stripped-down rifle in pieces in my hands, I felt like a recruit who had been surprised by his training staff. It was only as I ran outdoors that I realized my situation could have been worse – I came face to face with Freddie, his face obscured by dirty shaving foam stained by the debris of an explosion. We took one look at each other, and burst into laughter.

As armpits and weapons were cleaned throughout the company, men would fall into the rotation of duties throughout the sangars and fighting positions. We were a small company with a large perimeter, and so a soldier would be lucky if he found himself with thirty minutes here and there in the day to close his eyes, rolled-up body armour used as a pillow. The chances of seeing through such a rest were small, as the enemy were active. Small-arms attacks would require the company to stand to. Indirect fire would cause men to scuttle for cover, looking for a welcome depression in the earth in which to press their bodies.

Such an attack came at 0936.

Dumf – dumf – dumf.

The unmistakable sound of mortar rounds being launched from their tubes.

'Incoming!'

There is nothing dignified about taking cover from mortars. No one wants to be the first to dive, but no one wants to be the first to get loaded onto a casevac, either, and so begins a pride-driven game of chicken. Our own mortar men were most experienced in estimating the time of flight from a bomb's launch to impact, based on how far away the sound from the tubes seemed, and so they became the men to watch. If a mortarman is eating dirt, then it's time to get on your belt buckle!

The three rounds whined in.

CRUMP-CRASH! – CRUMP-CRASH!

The third was a dull thud. It was a blind, the round failing to detonate on impact.

My radio came alive. It was my sniper pair, Lance Corporal Hugh Keir and Private Jared Cleary – they'd identified a potential spotter.

With Ray and Abe, we made best speed to their position on the Alamo's rooftop.

'One hundred metres to the left of the white-walled compound,' the Welshman Keir directed me. 'Look through the binos, boss. You'll see him. He keeps popping up and down in the same spot, in that gap in the low wall.'

'I see him,' I acknowledged. 'Looks like he has a radio in his hand.'

'He has, boss,' Keir confirmed.

Given that the town was empty of civilians, and we had just been attacked, that was more than enough to convince me.

'Smash him,' I told my JTAC.

In no time I heard the report from the desert as 7 Para's guns opened. Soon, their shells were crashing around the spotter. I hoped that the mortars themselves were in his vicinity, but at the very least we had to try to neutralize the enemy's eyes – mortars are only as good as their spotter. Unfortunately, with the spire right outside our gates, and the radio tower not far away, even a novice fire controller could bring down rounds onto our compound with ease. They simply had to align with those landmarks that rose above all else in the town, and to figure out the distance from a map. Our district centre was the mortar equivalent of shooting fish in a barrel.

'Good job, lads,' I thanked my snipers and JTAC. Keeping low to avoid drawing the ever-present threat of fire, I made my way back to the ops room – Staff Wornham had more ICOM intercepts.

'They said they're disappointed with the results of their mortar attack,' he told me.

'Anything on the result of our own rounds?'

He shook his head. That could be good news or bad. Either our counter battery fire had been so well placed that it had killed the enemy, or it was far enough away not to raise concern over the radio.

I made my way over to the empty ammunition containers that had been converted into our stoves. Filled with sand then soaked with diesel, they were perfect for heating other containers, which we filled with water. As I waited for the water to boil, I wondered about the drop in the enemy's small-arms attacks. Now gone mid-morning, we had taken no direct fire since the heavy dawn attack. Like the previous day, I had the uneasy sense that things were too quiet. It seems ludicrous to think that I wanted the enemy to be trying to overrun us, but there is something to be said about having their intentions laid bare before you. Now, I could not help but turn over the possibility that they were massing for one huge attack. The idea that they had slipped from the town did not seem credible, especially when Ian Wornham reported an ICOM intercept from a Taliban commander, newly arrived with eighteen men.

'What do you think they're up to, Freddie?' I asked my intelligence officer, passing him a brew.

'They're still bringing more fighters in,' he confirmed. 'But the chatter has definitely been swinging from coordinating attacks to talking on mortars.'

I didn't say what was on my mind – if the enemy could bring a steady rain of mortars onto the compound and our exposed fighting positions, then our casualty rate could expect to climb rapidly. Freddie knew the same, and I could see that our inability to change that situation, lacking in supplies as we were, chaffed at the trained assault engineer, an expert in all things defensive.

'Feels strange, not having an attack every other hour, doesn't it, boss?' he confided in me.

I smiled. Freddie had been enjoying the contacts more than most. He was often to be spotted using one of the Afghans' AKs on the west wall. He had even launched an RPG from the Outpost. From gimpy gunner to grenade thrower, Freddie was relentless in his pursuit of the combat experience.

'It does feel strange,' I agreed. Then, confident that all had been done to recover from the morning's attack, we settled down to do what all infantry soldiers do in times of war.

We waited.

DUMF – DUMF – DUMF – DUMF!

'Incoming!'

'Hello, Zero, this is Cobalt Six, contact IDF at 1546; stand by for full contact report; out.'

Whoosh – BANG! Whoosh – BANG! Whoosh – BANG! Whoosh – BANG!

The four mortar rounds ploughed into the compound, dust shaken clear of the ops room's ceiling by the concussion of their explosion. Taking hold of my rifle, I ran out into the sunlight. As I crossed the threshold, my stomach balled into a knot.

The Alamo had been hit.

From the smoke and debris lingering over that position, there was no doubt. At least two of the rounds had smacked into that exposed rooftop. A rooftop where my men had been on sentry duty.

I fought down the urge to run to them. NCOs and medics were already moving to the site of the strikes. My job as company commander was to see that any casualties could be taken to surgical care as quickly as possible. Until then, we had to suppress the enemy.

'Ray! Abe!' I called for the JTAC as I crouched my way onto the ops room rooftop. They joined me within moments, a bustle of antennas.

'Let's smash the earlier firing point,' I told them. 'I want the Taliban kept busy whilst we get any casualties off that roof.'

The men nodded, then began talking into their handsets. In the desert, 7 RHA's artillerymen would be adjusting their guns back onto the morning's fire mission. As I spoke into my own radio, requesting a sitrep on the strikes, the 105 guns in the desert began to fire.

It was the snipers who had gotten to the site of the strike first. As they made their report over the radio, my guts froze.

'One T1. One dead.'

There was no time to mourn for the unknown soldier now. My sole focus had to be on the evacuation of his critically injured comrade. I got on the net to Battlegroup HQ.

'Zero, Zero Alpha. One KIA and one T1. Stand by for nine liner. Out.'

I turned to my JTAC. 'Ray, we're going to need some air on station. If they try and start a contact as we're getting the guys off the roof I want them smashed instantly.'

I looked towards the Alamo. The dust was still in the air, but already my men were extracting the casualties. Corporal French was there on the quad, and soon the two stretchered soldiers were racing on their way to the med centre, where Mike Stacey would be waiting for them. I knew that we couldn't hope for a better surgeon this close to the point of injury. With such faith in his skill, I turned my attention fully to the coming extraction. In the distance, 105 shells continued to pound the likely enemy firing point – I was in no mood to let up, and let them regather.

'Get the air on station, Ray,' I told my JTAC. 'I'm going to the ops room to call in on the satphone.'

By the time that my call to 3 Para's ops room had gone through, I'd received the confirmation from the doctor that we had a T1 casualty and a fallen soldier on our hands.

'They're going to know those hits caused casualties,' I told the ops officer.

'We can't lose a Chinook,' he said, knowing the dangers of flying a casevac mission to our exposed position. 'Is he stable?'

'For now,' I answered, relaying the doctor's words. 'He needs surgery, but he's as stable as he can be here.'

'If we can delay the casevac, then let's delay,' the ops staff said. 'The more time we get to cue up air and plan the fire missions, the better.'

'Agreed,' I finished, hearing the sound of small arms erupting from outside. 'I've got to go. It's just kicked off again.'

Hanging up, I ran to the rooftop. Tracer cut across the sky. The smoke of RPG launches drifted across the town.

'Air?' I asked Ray.

'Pair of F-14s. Five hundred and thousand pounders,' he replied.

'Right, let's use them.'

True to form, the enemy were attacking from their favourite positions. In no time, Ray had a 1,000lb strike lined up against a compound that was a persistent source of enemy fire.

'Cleared hot,' I told him, signing off on the strike.

The bomb shrieked in from the heavens. With hands over my ears and my mouth open, I watched as the blast wave ran out across the town, a pillar of smoke churning upwards, debris raining over enemy and friendly heads, the dirt bouncing from our helmets, dust creeping into our lungs.

It took another pounding to deter the enemy's attack. As the clouds of destruction smudged against the clear blue sky, I ran to the med centre.

Lance Corporal Paul Muirhead lay on a gurney in front on Mike Stacey. Heavily bandaged, he looked in a bad way.

'He's stable,' the doctor told me.

'How long can he stay that way?'

'He needs surgery, but right now, I'd say we're good for a few hours.'

Mike understood the situation. Though he would not put any of his charges in danger, he too knew the risk that came with casevac. Both of our priorities were to see that the men of Easy Company were treated by a full surgical team as soon as possible, but that could not happen if the Chinook was a burning wreck beside the HLS.

'Ranger Draiva?' I asked of the smiling Fijian who had been named to me as the second casualty.

Mike shook his head. Draiva's body lay on the far side of the medical centre, delicately covered with a sheet.

'It would have been quick,' he offered as consolation.

There was no time for me to mourn. I returned to the ops room, and called Zero. Battlegroup HQ had been busy planning their end of the casevac. The fact that we had just been forced to break a contact with fast air made them nervous about deploying the asset in daylight.

'Can he make it until darkness?'

'Too early to tell. The doctor's calling it hour by hour.'

'We can't bring it into a hot LZ.'

'I know.'

I returned to my maps with the JTAC. Along with Freddie, we began plotting all of the likely firing points that would need to be smashed should the enemy contest the casevac, as they were sure to do.

The planning session was cut short as RPGs and small-arms fire screamed out across the compound.

We rushed back to the rooftops, the whole company stood to, their fire and posture angry as they fought back against the enemy who had killed and injured their comrades. Word of the casualties had spread, and now every man was determined to beat back the enemy so that Paul Muirhead could be taken to Bastion's surgery.

As Easy Company pinned down the enemy with a savage weight of fire, I called up more 105 shells and air strikes. I wanted the enemy cowed, and the JTAC were tireless as they called strike after strike onto the Taliban's heads. Eventually, the contact was broken. Darkness was an hour away when Mike Stacey sent the word.

'He can't wait any longer. He has to go now.'

Lance Corporal Muirhead lay on a stretcher in the med centre. He was critical, and Mike Stacey had done all that he could – without surgery, Paul Muirhead would be dead before the end of the day.

I called Battlegroup HQ. 'He has to go now. The Doc can't guarantee him any longer.'

'Is he sure?'

'He's sure.'

There was a pause at the end of the line; 'Adam, you've been in contacts all afternoon. We can't risk a Chinook flying into that.'

'We can't leave him to die on a stretcher.'

There was further silence. Battlegroup HQ would have been weighing up the options all afternoon, as I had myself. It came down to a simple choice – leave Muirhead to die here, and protect the Chinook, or risk losing that helicopter and its crew to retrieve the man. Anything less than a successful retrieval would be a disaster, not only to the men involved, but also on a strategic level – there were simply not enough Chinooks in theatre to lose one, and such a loss would raise questions at home as to what kind of operation we were actually involved in – hadn't the government said it was a peacekeeping mission? Then, of course, there was the damage to morale that would be caused by leaving a man to die because he could not safely be extracted. Such a death would break the covenant between soldier, command, and government. How could the men of the battlegroup be expected to risk their lives for the people of Helmand when their own commanders would not sanction a dangerous casevac to retrieve them? There was no magical answer to the problem, only control measures. Retrieving Paul Muirhead – or not – could become the moment for which the campaign was remembered. Downed helicopters and rescue efforts live long in the public consciousness, and Task Force Helmand's commanders had no desire to star in the British *Black Hawk Down*. Neither did the men of Easy Company – we simply wanted our friend and comrade out, and in care.

'We'll launch the casevac,' they told me.

There was no relief for me at the news. I knew that it was just the beginning.

'Get me preliminary fires,' I demanded, referring to a fire mission that is launched before contact, in order to suppress the enemy before they get the chance to strike.

'We'll try, but it's unlikely,' they told me reluctantly.

'Lawyers won't sign off on it. We can't use any artillery or fast air unless you or the Chinook are under contact. Can't risk the collateral damage.'

I was disgusted by the answer, but not surprised. The lawyers had their job. I had my own.

'I'll get the company stood to.'

Easy Company wasted no time in preparing for the extraction. They knew what was at stake, and men rushed quickly to the rooftops as others prepared to act as stretcher bearers, or to push out beyond the HLS to come between the Chinook and the enemy.

I had the JTAC join me close to the HLS. They were tuned into the air net, and would keep me updated on the helicopter's progress. High in the skies above us, multiple aircraft had been put into holding patterns to support us should the enemy attack. Familiar with the enemy's favoured firing points, Ray knew ahead of time which buildings and compounds we would likely want smashing soonest. We couldn't get the lawyers to sign off on preliminary fires, but we could bring them on as quickly as possible once we were under contact.

No one in Easy Company lived under the false hope that the enemy would not put up a fight. The Taliban had seen the strikes, and they had seen the bustle the explosions had caused as the casualties were cleared away. It was impossible to believe that they were not watching, and waiting. I thought back to the pictures scrawled on the wall of the Alamo's jail cells – the crude sketches that Taliban prisoners had drawn of helicopters falling from the sky. Seeing the faces of the men about me, I knew that not one of us would allow that murderous fantasy to play out.

The two stricken Rangers were brought forth on their stretchers. Anare Draiva was enclosed in a body bag, the mates about him grim-faced and angry. Paul Muirhead was still attended by Doc Stacey. It made me uneasy to have the doctor exposed to the Taliban fire, but he had insisted that he conduct a proper handover to the surgeon on board the Chinook – full knowledge of the patient's injuries and treatment could prove vital on the flight to Bastion.

'How is he?' I asked Mike quietly.

'He has to go out on this one.'

There was not an ounce of doubt in his voice. Either Lance Corporal Muirhead got out on this Chinook, or he died.

'They're two minutes out,' Ray told me.

No sooner had I relayed the words onto the company net than I heard the deep rhythmic sound of the blades in the distance, heavy as they beat the air, the unmistakable herald of a Chinook's approach.

The Taliban knew it as well as we did.

They opened fire.

As if the town's mayor had thrown the switch for Christmas lights, muzzle flash blinked and spat from the buildings all around us. Tracer shot across the darkening sky, ricocheting and bouncing as it ploughed into our fighting positions.

'Rapid fire! Rapid fire!'

Easy Company returned fire with everything we had.

'There's no time to get fast air in,' Ray told me, shaking his head. 'The bombs would be dropping as they go wheels down.'

The enemy had kept their discipline long enough to deny us our ace card. Now that the IRT was a minute away, even our mortars had to be pulled from the fight – we couldn't afford a bomb hitting the Chinook in mid-air. Now, it was nothing but a small-arms slog between British infantrymen and Taliban fighters.

NCOs ran and jockeyed between their men, giving fire-control orders and managing the weight of fire. Machine gunners rattled off long bursts of red tracer. Mortar men, their fire missions on hold until the Chinook could get clear, rushed with their rifles to the fighting steps.

'Thirty seconds!' Ray called, and I broke from my firing to relay the message. As I did, I looked into the direction of the

Chinook's approach. The ungainly beast was drawing fire from all over the town, tracer arcing up to it with deadly beauty. The Chinook's own door gunners were firing back, constant streams of tracer whipping the ground below them like red lasers. To either side of her flew an Apache, the attack helicopters blasting an air corridor, smashing everything in their path with cannon, rocket, and Hellfire missiles. It was an awesome sight to behold, and as these murderous payloads began to batter the enemy positions north of the HLS, the enemy fire slackened as they sought cover. There were still bullets in the air, but this was Muirhead's one and only chance – I would not call it a hot LZ, and abort the mission. The pilots could see the battle ahead of them, and it would be their brave decision to fly into it regardless.

They did.

'Stretcher parties! Prepare to move!' I called, and like sprinters, the crouched men readied themselves to rush their stricken comrades onto the HLS.

I looked back to the sky, feeling the wave of dust and dirt smash me as the Chinook flared its huge body, the twin rotors churning the air around it into a brown haze of grit.

'Go! Go!' I shouted to the stretcher teams, and they were away, no thought for their own safety as enemy bullets still stung the air. As the Chinook's big wheels sat down and bounced on the dirt, the stretchers had already reached the tail ramp and were on their way aboard. The portside door gunner continued to stream tracer at the enemy to our north, but others aboard began to bundle out the ammunition and sandbags that we so desperately needed.

The stretcher parties grabbed at these supplies as they sprinted back towards the gap in the wall that allowed their entry to the compound. Within thirty seconds of touching down – and as the Apaches prowled overhead like angry angels, spitting cannon fire and missiles – the Chinook was lurching into the air, and away.

'Once they're clear, we smash those fire positions,' I told Ray.

'Got A-10s ready to go,' he replied with a thumbs-up.

'Collapse the HLS,' I ordered into my radio, and Johnno began the process of fire-and-manoeuvring his men back inside the walls, grabbing the stores as they went. The contact was not broken, but as the Chinook and her escorts escaped over the rooftops, there was a noticeable slack in the enemy fire – they knew that they'd missed their chance, and we knew that we'd taken ours. It had gone as well as we could have expected, I thought to myself.

And then Ray grabbed my arm. 'Boss, the Doc's on the Chinook.'

'What?'

'He was doing the handover and they took off with him. The pilot just told me now.'

I cursed, knowing that there was no way we could risk a second run in to return him. Alongside the JTAC, the doctor was the most valuable asset of Easy Company. Without him, Muirhead would not have survived to have made it onto that helicopter. As our casualties had begun to climb, so too had the men's faith that there was such a surgeon to attend to their injuries. As word of the mishap began to spread, looks of concern shot over the men's faces. Many uttered 'fuck', just before their shoulders slumped a little.

'We'll get him back,' I promised. 'But not back into this.'

It was time to break the contact.

'Bring in the A-10s.'

18

'Chinook is wheels down at Bastion, boss', Signaller Jones told me in the ops room. 'They're going to update us on him when they get out of surgery.'

I stepped away from him and lit a cigarette.

'We got away with one there, boss', the sergeant major said as he took it from me and puffed. 'Luck won't hold forever.'

'Let's take another look at the maps', I said. 'See if we can find a more suitable HLS.'

'I'm sure we can find plenty, sir, but it's whether or not we'll make it to them.'

By 'making it to them' he was referring to our inability to secure another HLS; we were too few and too besieged.

Now that more of the company had died in the game that the men were referring to as 'capture the flag', it would be my task to ensure that morale did not fall with their friends. It was one thing for a soldier to question his orders – something that can be beneficial to his commanders, to seek out weakness in plans and ideas – but he cannot be left without answers. Simply saying 'you're doing this because I told you to' is not enough for a soldier who may be asked to lay down his life at any moment. And so, I brought together my platoon commanders and senior NCOs, reiterating to them again the 'why' of the mission – that we were here to fight and beat the Taliban so that the population could enjoy such basic rights as education and equality, and explaining to them that, despite how it might look on the surface, we were not alone out here. From the aircraft overhead to the guns in the desert and the Special Forces who knows where, there were a lot of assets being directed in our support.

'It's hard all over the battlegroup,' I told my leaders. 'Nobody's getting an easy time in Helmand.'

They took it with stoic acceptance. Deep down, I was certain that this was how my men would want it. If anyone was to have their backs against the wall, better it be them than their friends, and not only because they wanted to take on the risk – they could not stomach the thought of their friends lording it over them post-tour, bantering for the rights of who had had it easy and who had seen the most action.

'The Doc's coming in at 0430,' I then reassured my men. 'We'll have him back before first light.'

'Blokes will be relieved to hear that, boss,' Somme's sergeant spoke up, smiling. 'Some of the guys haven't taken their helmets and body armour off since they heard he left.'

It was a light-hearted comment, but we all knew the truth behind it – every man in the camp would fight harder, and breathe easier, knowing that there was a skilled surgeon like Mike within the same walls.

'We had a shit day today,' I concluded, not wanting to sugarcoat or forget the fact that we had lost two good men, and one of them for eternity. 'But I couldn't be more proud of how everybody cracked on. We're still up against it here, but we're hurting the fuckers every time they try it on. Sooner or later, something's going to break.

'Stand to at 0400 ready for the Chinook. Sangars and fighting positions only, no pushing out into the HLS. We can't project out far enough to buy it real security, so let's keep the guys behind hard cover. See you in the morning.'

It seemed I had barely closed my eyes before it was time to stumble half asleep into the ops room, and to prepare for the Chinook and its precious cargo.

I found Ray smoking a cigarette in one of the plastic chairs, tuned into the air net.

'They're going wheels-up in ten,' he told me. 'Then a thirty-minute flight time.'

'Well let's get the brews on, then,' I suggested, and as we drank the hot mixture of caffeine and sugar we looked over the maps at the route the Chinook would be taking in to us. Due to the layout of the buildings surrounding the HLS, there was little option but to bring her in from the north-west. As per SOPs, the Chinook would be accompanied by a pair of Apaches, but their guns would remain silent unless contacted. Stealth was our ally here, and we hoped that, by bringing in the Chinook before first light, the Taliban would be taken un-awares. They had seen us casevac our wounded the previous evening, and had little reason to suspect that another Chinook would be inbound. I had pressed HQ to take advantage of this, and to send us a section or two of reinforcements if possible, but the battlegroup's barrel had been scraped dry – there wasn't a single sub unit in Helmand that wasn't crying out for more men.

'Why don't they send more battalions over?' Ray asked me between drags. 'How many infantry battalions in the army?'

'About forty,' I told him.

'And we've got one here, plus call it a half for the other couple of companies. How many in Iraq?'

'Now? I think five or six.'

'So somewhere, there are thirty-four or five infantry battalions that aren't doing anything. If they sent us five here, we could dominate this place. Think about it, boss. Imagine we had a battalion here. You use one company to guard the DC, like we're doing, and then you have all these other companies to get out there and smash the fuckers.'

'I'm not disagreeing with you, Ray.'

I had thought about the question long and hard myself. In Sangin, as part of a deliberate battlegroup operation, I had seen the impact that we could have when a few companies' worth of soldiers were deployed into one area. Outmatched, the Taliban would not face us. Once that force had been dispersed, and all that remained was a solitary company stretched between a district centre and platoon houses, then the enemy would pick up their RPGs and attack those weaknesses. Strung out as we were, we were holding the enemy off, but that was as much as we could do. I had no doubt that, with two or three full brigades in theatre, we could have beaten down the Taliban in a matter of weeks, securing the way to build and improve the lives of the locals, as we had promised. With the local populace on your side, the insurgents' campaign cannot survive.

I looked at my watch. '0415. Let's get up on the walls.'

We shuffled to our positions in darkness. A few hounds barked in the distance, but all else was still.

'Five minutes out,' Ray whispered beside me.

And then, there it was, the unmistakable whump-whump-whump of a Chinook's rotors.

I looked out at the town through the NVGs, seeing compounds bathed in eerie green light, cavernous holes in the mud walls yawning at me like toothless mouths.

'Two minutes.'

Whump-whump-whump. It was getting louder now. In my mind I pictured Taliban commanders being shaken from their sleep, fighters rushing to rooftops as they attempted to pick out the beast in the black sky.

'One minute.'

'Anything on the ICOM?' I asked over the radio to Staff Wornham.

'Nothing, boss.'

'Thirty seconds.'

There was no hiding the approach now, the Chinook's blades causing a tempest as she flared above the ruin of the town and made her descent. Now began the sixty seconds of greatest vulnerability where all speed was lost, and the lumbering airframe became a static target. A dream target. A target that would make the RPG gunner who hit her a legend in Taliban lore.

Dust and grit was thrown out in a dark storm. I saw her on the HLS, a figure running from her ramp, stores piled out even as the pilot took her up. From wheels down to up had been no more than ten seconds, and now she was gone, leaving nothing in her wake but bundles of supplies, grit in the air, and relief in the hearts and throats of every man of Easy Company.

We had our doctor back.

Leaving the men stood to in preparation for the inevitable dawn contact, I hurried down to the ops room. Mike had beaten me there, and I had never seen a man look more sheepish.

'Don't,' he said, smiling.

I said nothing. Instead, with every other man in the ops room, I began to sniff at him. 'Is this what soap smells like?'

Dressed in a fresh set of combats, looking parade-ground smart, he took it all in good humour.

'Leave me alone and let me get into my kit.'

He shooed us away, plunging his hands into a patrolsack, cheers following the emergence of all manner of contraband he had liberated from Bastion.

'The loadmasters threw the mail off the Chinook,' he told me, and sure enough, the reserve section began to appear with the angular bags of parcels and letters. As those were stacked into the corner of the ops room, Mike went about emptying every pocket of his kit and person. When the last sachets of salt and pepper had been thrown down onto the ops room table, Mike finally threw his hands up in surrender. 'That's the lot.'

'No beers, sir?' Signaller Jones asked.

'No beers.'

I looked to the mailbags in the corner, knowing that what was in them was as vital to Easy Company as water and ammunition. To hear from loved ones was the greatest morale booster for the soldier in the field, but, like ammunition, there was the danger that it could go off in the wrong way. News of a child speaking her first words was wonderful. News of a cheating girlfriend could be devastating. As pushed as we were, even welcome distractions would need to be handled with care.

'We'll get this sorted later in the morning,' I told the reserve section, who were eyeing the mailbags like toddlers on Christmas morning. 'You lads get to your place. Everyone else up onto the fighting positions. Mike, do you think you can find your way back to the med centre, or are you back off to Bastion?'

He took the jab well.

'Fuck off,' he said.

I left the ops room and scrambled up onto the roof. I expected that the Taliban would be angry that a Chinook had slipped in and out without them getting off a single shot at it, and reckoned there was a good chance they'd vent their spleen once dawn stalked over the horizon, but as the grey light ghosted across the bitten compounds and gnarled streets, there was no sign of our enemy.

The absence of violence set me on edge more than any crashing explosions or zipping rounds would have done. Looking through the green haze of my night goggles, I wondered if this was some new tactic of the enemy's, and that they were attempting to creep towards us in the morning's shadows, but the only movement came from Afghan hounds that loped amongst the rubblized streets. All about me, I felt and heard the discomfort of my men as they fidgeted in their positions. The wait is always the worst, those moments when a soldier has nothing to do but ponder the choices that brought him to this place, and the consequence of those actions. He has time to think about what his girlfriend is doing at this very moment – sleeping alone, he hopes. What his mother's reaction would be if a sombre, uniformed man appeared on her doorstep – collapsing from grief, of course. And what his friends would say at his funeral – best soldier they ever knew, and never slow to pass out his fags. Never again in his life would the soldier know such clarity of thought and vision as he did now, crouching in the dawn, the grit of the rooftop digging into his knees and elbows, his mouth already dry from a heat rising with intent. In these moments the mistakes of his life were laid bare, his true friends known, and his future planned. After this, they would all become a jumbled blur once more. Perhaps, as an old man on his deathbed, they would crystallize again. Until then, this moment as an eighteen-year-old tucked in behind a machine gun, was as clear a perspective on life as the soldier could ever hope to get.

'Where the fuck are they?' one man, growing anxious, hissed to his fire team.

'Shut the fuck up and watch your arcs,' his NCO told him, the harsh reply betraying his own stress at the inactivity.

I turned to Ray on my shoulder. 'If it stays quiet like this, we'll bring the A-10s in to take a look over the town. See if they can spot anything.'

'Now?'

'Give it another five minutes.'

I could not shake the feeling that the enemy would attack. They had done so every morning without fail, and it was a tactic they pursued throughout Afghanistan. They had hurt us the day before, and so it seemed unlikely in the extreme that this was the moment they would take their foot off the pedal and allow us to catch our collective breath.

'Maybe they forgot to set their alarm,' Ray joked. I have no doubt that the same words were being repeated in every sangar, and on every rooftop.

'Runner,' I whispered to a soldier close by. 'Go and ask the terps if today is any kind of religious holiday.'

It wasn't.

'What the fuck's going on?' the gimpy gunner growled, angry at the break in routine. Angry at the uncertainty.

I had no answer for him. I only knew that I had no intention of standing the company down. I could see no sign of our enemy, but my gut told me to be watchful, and to be ready. Dawn was becoming day. That meant combat, and death, but the only blood to be found this morning gushed forth from the rising sun, a violent crimson that leaked across the silent horizon.

Birds called. Dogs barked. Soldiers swore, complained, and muttered beneath their breath that, 'Terry's a fucking pussy.'

The agonized calm could not last forever.

And it didn't.

CRUMP – CRUMP!

CRUMP – CRUMP!

CRUMP – CRUMP!

'Incoming!'

Mortars. Two barrels. Six shells.

'Get your fucking heads down!'

Whoosh-bang! Whoosh-bang! Where there had been quiet and uncertainty, now there was the roar of chaos, and the muted whispers of soldiers who wanted nothing more than the uneasy calm to return. A stand-up fight with Terry was one thing, but these mortars were unseen death from above. They were dispassionate weapons of war whose sprayed shrapnel cared not for the skill of a soldier. It didn't matter how fast you were, how good a marksman, or how keen-eyed a sentry. The shrapnel was looking for the good soldier and bad alike. For the fast and the slow. For the well protected, and the exposed. Run. Hide. It didn't matter. They could fall in your lap, and that well-protected sanctuary you had thought would see you through this was now nothing but a convenient container for the scattered parts of your body.

I hated those fucking mortars. I hated them for their randomness. I hated them for their detachment. I hated them

– and I know how English this sounds, and I don't care – because they weren't sporting! They were a window into what it must be like to be our enemy. To suffer artillery and air strikes on a rolling basis. As the mortars now screamed into our compound, hissing shrapnel searching for exposed flesh, I had some insight into what our enemy had been withstanding. In that moment, I felt some connection to them as warrior to warrior, but the camaraderie ended there – I was here to kill them.

'Abe! Ray!' I shouted for my JTAC. 'Get I-battery on the net. Smash every fucking known firing point.

'Any casualties?' I then asked over radio and by voice.

There were none, and I spoke a quick prayer of thanks.

'Firing now,' Abe told me, and seconds later, I heard the sound of our 105s firing from the desert.

We raised our head above the parapet and watched the shells crash into the town, a rolling barrage of high explosive, each concussion a gentle slap in our faces. Having experienced the enemy's 82mm mortars, I could only imagine what hell it would be to be caught beneath the bigger shells.

But the enemy's welfare was not my concern, nor that of my men.

'Enjoy your breakfast, Terry,' one of my Irishmen called out. When we were done laughing, I stood the company down.

It had been our first dawn without a direct attack from the enemy, but those optimists who thought that our adversaries had quit the town were soon proven wrong when a second mortar attack followed the first. Four rounds hit inside the compound, and I counted my blessings once more that we had come through the attack unscathed.

'Got some good gen on Moslem,' Staff Wornham informed me, referring by name to a man our interpreters had identified as the enemy's mortar fire controller, and, as such, a man we were very keen to kill.

'Sounds like he was making adjustments on those last strikes,' the signaller went on.

'You think you can work out where he is?' I asked Freddie.

'Give it our best shot, boss,' he replied, keen for any puzzle. 'Best guess so far is to the north.'

'All right. I'll send the snipers up to the Outpost.'

The sun was now high in the sky. If the threat of enemy fire wasn't enough to keep us in the shadows, then the scorching heat would see us seeking shade like the hardy Afghan weeds that sprouted from cracks beneath the compound walls. Such spots were also favoured by the insects that lived amongst us, and every potential resting place needed to be carefully checked for scorpions, or the horrifying camel spiders – many a hero in combat had been reduced to childlike screams at the appearance of such a monster. Bored soldiers were fond of ranking things that they liked and things that they hated, and to be bitten by a camel spider was considered worse than a gunshot wound. At least a gunshot was a heroic story for the ladies. No one wanted to be the guy who got casevaced for an infected spider bite, and had to suffer merciless piss-taking for the rest of his army career.

I was looking for my own spot in the shade to read a letter – brought in with the doctor that morning, and which turned out to be an overdue water bill – when the sound of automatic weapons fire crashed out over the compound. It was three hours after dawn, but finally, the small-arms battle had begun.

'Contact!'

I ran to the rooftop and began to suppress to the east. In mere moments, the men of Easy were at their fighting positions, and rifle and machine-gun fire belted out towards the enemy firing points. They seemed to be making no attempt to manoeuvre forward, and after twenty minutes a Harrier rocket attack was enough to convince them to break off. Given the scale of the fighting we had seen so far, this seemed little more than a harassing attack. An attempt to remind us that we were both unwelcome and surrounded.

That was not news to us, and after the quiet of dawn, and now the quick breaking of this contact, it was with an effort that I batted away the idea that we were gaining the upper hand in the town. I could have had no idea that, in an hour's time, I would lose an entire section of my men.

At 1048 heavy contact erupted from the east. In those first few moments of rapid fire, and as the air was torn by the scream and explosion of RPGs, all thoughts that the enemy had backed off were quickly dashed.

'Stand to! Stand to!' NCOs called the order, but men were already falling over each other as they raced to the firing positions. Salted veterans now to a man, they knew by the weight of fire that this was no ordinary harassing action – this was a push. Terry was trying to suppress us so that he could breach our walls and slit our throats. With urgency, we sped to our assigned positions to kill him.

I threw myself flat onto the ops room rooftop, a burst of machine-gun fire coming so close to my head that I could feel the rounds breaking the air.

'What have we got?' I asked my JTAC. Ray and Abe were in constant communication with our assets throughout the day, aircraft replacing aircraft as they were forced to leave our patterned protection to refuel.

'The French,' Abe told me, pulling a face.

'For fuck's sake,' I groaned as more machine-gun fire bit at the wall's lip. Any air cover was better than nothing, but the French pilots were loath to fire more than a single cannon round on their strafing runs. The chances of that round finding a Taliban fighter were minuscule. Those in air-conditioned offices reasoned that the mere threat and sound of the aircraft would be enough to deter an attack – a so-called 'show of force' – but to soldiers who had seen the Taliban press on through devastating barrages of artillery, bombs, and cannon fire, that idea was laughable.

'See if you can get us A-10s or Harriers,' I asked my JTAC, turning my attention to the enemy firing points in the east, where dark shapes moved and fell. I saw an RPG gunner step into an alleyway to fire, but before he could loose his charge he was cut down by a burst of machine-gun fire, the red tracer skipping about his body and off the walls.

'Incoming!' a soldier called, and I heard the screech a split second later as the mortar rounds came to earth, detonations rolling in their wake. As I raised my head, tiny chunks of debris pattering against my helmet, my stomach froze into a knot. Once again smoke and dust rose over the Alamo. A direct hit on a position full of men.

My men.

I ran for the steps.

Hitting the ground, I saw a figure emerge from the ops room.

'I've got this one, sir!' Sergeant Major Scrivener shouted as he charged heedless of the enemy fire in the direction of the mortar strike. There was nothing else on the man's mind but the safety of his troops, and as the tracer cut the air above him, and I felt the lull in the fire of our guns on the Alamo, I knew with sickening certainty that we had taken casualties.

'Prep nine liner!' I called into the ops room as I clambered back onto the rooftop. Skirting the men as they fired and changed positions, I took hold of the landline field telephone and tried the Alamo. It was dead. The strikes had cut the line.

I took to the company net instead. I cursed as I heard the sergeant major's reply to my requested casualty report.

'Nine casualties.'

Nine casualties, from a company strength of sixty-six. We had just lost 15 per cent of our manpower; 15 per cent of our *fire*power. The gimpys on the Alamo had begun to fire again, but with nine men down, and others needed to treat them, we had taken a serious hit in our ability to beat back this determined assault. For their part, the Taliban had taken advantage of the slackening fire and were steadily creeping closer. I had to make a decision quickly – did I leave the wounded to look after themselves, and throw the reserve section up to beat back the attack, or did I send them to clear the casualties from the Alamo's embattled rooftop?

'Reserve section! Get to the Alamo! Move the casualties to the med centre and get back here! Go!'

They went. I turned to Ray. 'Please tell me we've got something else.'

'A-10s.'

Thank God.

'Cue them up for gun runs north to south on the eastern side, buildings 186 to 188. I want those now.'

'You've got it, boss.'

I spoke into my radio. 'This is Zero Alpha. Unless casualties are T1, triage and hold them in the Alamo. We've got gun runs coming in. We'll move the guys once we've suppressed the east. Read back, over.'

Panted confirmation of my orders came back to me from officers and NCOs, but one voice was conspicuous by its absence – Paul Martin, Somme platoon's commander. I knew at that moment that he must be one of the casualties.

'Air's stood to, boss,' Ray told me.

'Clear hot. Go.'

They came from nowhere, the A-10s' pilots skilfully gutting the compounds on our eastern flank.

'Move now,' I ordered. Forced to keep my head low from enemy fire on our other flanks, I watched as my men bravely hurried their wounded comrades in the direction of the med centre.

'One T1, two T2, five T3,' came the report over the radio; so it was eight men, not nine. One critical, two stretcher cases, and five walking wounded.

'Status on One Zero Alpha?' I asked, giving the call sign used by Paul Martin on the net.

'T1.'

I swallowed. There was nothing I could do for him or the others now but break this contact and clear the way for their evacuation.

'Let's smash the east again,' I told Ray, the rattle of PKMs still cutting across our compound.

'A-10s are guns empty,' he told me. 'Waiting on our hand-over now.'

'OK. Let's smash them with arty until we get it.'

Calling in fire to our east was a risky business. Not only was it danger close, but the rounds would have to travel over our heads as they came from the guns to our west in the desert. If one was to fall short, it could cause more carnage than the enemy's own indirect fire had done, but the fact remained that we were a section down, and at least one of those men was critical. If there was a time for such a risk, it was now.

I gave the order.

The rounds roared through the air, forcing every soldier to press himself into the dirt and rooftops, hurried prayers whispered that we would not die at the hands of our comrades in the artillery.

WHOOSH – BOOM! WHOOSH – BOOM! Again and again. With my JTAC, I watched as the skilled men of 7 Para put round after round onto the nose of our enemy. It was a brutal pummelling. An angry reply to the blow we had ourselves been dealt.

'We've got F-18s,' Abe spoke up. 'They've got thousand pounders.'

We put those huge bombs to good use. The air was momentarily sucked from our lungs as they exploded, the concussion rocking our innards a split second later. Huge pillars of smoke rose from the ground like awoken titans and, as if awed by their presence, only the most desultory rate of enemy fire remained. The contact had been broken.

I ran for the med centre steeling myself for the worst. I prepared myself to see a young platoon commander on the precipice of death; to see the broken bodies of my men.

'All right, boss?' one of those young soldiers greeted me cheerfully. Bandages around his head and arms, he couldn't have been more casual had I just ran into him in the pub.

'Hey, boss,' an Irish lance corporal piped up, his desert fatigues stained dark with blood. 'I'm all right to go back up now. Can you tell the Doc, please? He's not letting me go.'

I didn't know what to say. Here were soldiers. Here were *men*. Not one amongst them was older than twenty-five, and yet they sat quiet and uncomplaining as their shrapnel wounds were dressed and treated. Others joined in the petitions of the lance corporal, asking to be allowed to return to the fighting positions. Their wounds were 'no bother'. 'Not worth making a fuss about.' Never had I been more proud to be a commander, a soldier, and a comrade to these fighting warriors of the Royal Irish Regiment.

'Stay where you are,' I told them, though I could not hide the trace of a smile. It grew as Paul Martin caught sight of me, and gave a thumbs-up as Doc Stacey worked over him.

I looked over his injuries. Tubes had been inserted into his chest to drain the fluid from his wounds. Without doubt he would need casevacing as soon as possible, but a simple look from the glacier-cool Stacey was enough to tell me that it did not need to be imminent.

'He walked here himself,' the doctor told me, shaking his head in admiration for the young commander.

His words took me aback. To say that was some feat was an understatement. To reach the med centre, Paul had been forced to navigate the trapdoors and ladders of the Alamo, then cross the open ground to the doctor, all whilst under fire, and with a chest torn open from shrapnel. It was staggering.

Down time. Cards and backgammon, favoured by soldiers for millennia. Left to right: Cpl Hugh Keir, Bdr 'Pritch' Pritchard, Cpl Abe Williams, Sgt Freddie Kruyer, me, and Pte Jared Cleary, hoping to win a game of shithead!

Watch and shoot: Cpl Cliff Tweed engages the enemy from his fighting position on the eastern wall.

Inside the ops building immediately after a firefight. Left to right: LBdr Wright, me, Sgt 'PJ' Brangan, and Cpl Lee Simmons 'Wire Under Fire'.

Exemplary air support from the A-10s. 384th Expeditionary Fighter Squadron, based out of Bagram, repeatedly put bombs and strafing runs as close as twenty metres from our positions.

Strafing run across our perimeter (foreground) towards 186 complex.

Organic fire support from our mortar section. Our own 81mm high explosive bomb detonates to the east of the compound.

LCpl Paul Muirhead and Rgr Anare Draiva en route to the Alamo, 1 September 2006. *Faugh a Ballagh.*

Lt Paul Martin receives medical care at point of injury. Wounded on the Alamo, he made his own way to our clinic.

The reserve section waiting in hard cover. They were thrown at the pinch point every time we were losing the battle.

Bending, not breaking: Rangers enduring the bombardment. Left to right: Rangers Norman Russell and Joe Ward, and Cpl Cliff Tweed.

The operations room. Left to right: Signaller 'Tash', LCpl Rab McLurg, Cpl Lee Simmons, Sgt 'Gillie' Gillespie, me, and Cpl Mick French.

Unexpected development: a 'cessation of hostilities'. The elders and the Taliban gather for the initial meeting with Naz and me.

With a negotiated resupply through enemy lines we received medical supplies and generators. Left to right: Rgr Danny Ross, CSM Jon Scrivener, Faz, and me.

Capt Dean Whiten, Barossa's replacement platoon commander, and Sgt Freddie Kruyer. The northern side of the Alamo and Freddie's shower are in the background.

A time to build. Impossible during the fighting, Rgr Elia 'Leo' Manoa and Cpl Cliff Tweed rebuild the fighting positions with locally purchased mealie bags.

Irregular extraction: Rangers aboard a jingly truck on the way out of Musa Qala.

Right hand man: with Naz, fiercely loyal and strong to the end, saying farewell to the elders.

Head shed: Captains Mark Johnson and Mike Stacey celebrate at the Commando RV.

At the Cdo RV with Lt Col Matt Holmes, 42 Commando's exemplary CO. Estonian LAVs are in the background.

On the Chinooks to Bastion. Above, left: Cpl Hugh Keir and Pte Jared Cleary.
Above, right: SSgt Ian Wornham, Sgt Stef Crouchman, and Sgt 'Gillie' Gillespie.

A time to mourn: after our
remembrance service.
This was to be our final act
in Helmand.

HOME.

'You bloody madman.' I smiled.

With a chest drain in place, Paul could only answer me with his eyes. I'm almost certain that they told me to 'bugger off'.

Beating away more pleas to be allowed to return to the fight, I left my wounded and doubled to the ops room.

'Great job, Sergeant Major,' I told the man, his combats stained with blood.

'We're going to need more blokes, sir,' he told me matter-of-factly.

'They've already scraped the barrel to come up with us,' I reminded him. 'Let's see who else they can pull out.'

I got my answer on the satellite phone – B Company were in Bastion, and a section of riflemen would come in on the casevac to replace our wounded.

'They're also sending us a platoon commander, and a company second in command,' I told my ops room staff.

'You mean your replacement, boss,' Ray joked darkly.

'Very funny, you bastard. Anyway, Doc says that Paul is critical, but stable. The rest of the guys are T3, and so we don't need to rush into a casevac. Zero and I are both in agreement that we plan this one out as much as possible as far as coordinating air and arty goes. It will also give them time to get the replacements on board, as well as loading them up with gimpy link and eighty-one rounds, of which we're practically out.'

'Got enough for one good fire mission,' Scrivs put in, to raised eyebrows.

'Exactly,' I told my men. 'So let's not rush this if we don't have to. All things considered, we've gotten away lightly from that strike. I don't want us to fuck things up now, and stick a downed Chinook on the HLS.'

'Wouldn't do much for your career that, boss,' said Ray, smiling.

'What career? You told me my replacement's on the way,'

I laughed back. 'OK. Back to routine. JTAC with me to get plotting this air. We've got eight of our blokes hurt in the med centre. Let's get them home.'

19

The Taliban kept up the pressure that afternoon. Almost certainly they would have known that their mortars had struck one of our most heavily manned positions, and seen the brave efforts of Easy Company's men to recover the wounded. At 1352, one of our sangars spotted the enemy moving into position, and opened up on them with a GPMG. It kicked off a big contact that was fought in every direction, broken only by the use of 7 Para's guns in the desert, and our constant guardian angels in the sky. A section of men down, we were more pressed than ever, and I had to avoid the temptation to throw the reserve section in from the outset. Holding those eight men back played havoc with my nerves, a constant second-guessing of how, when, and where they should be deployed, but once a commander commits his forces they are not so easily pulled back. With the ever-present threat of multiple casualties, and the enemy pressing in from all sides, I had to discipline myself to commit them only when a tipping point had presented itself. Then, it was a case of overwhelming that point with maximum firepower in the shortest space of time, before pulling them back, and awaiting the next moment. Every section spent time as the reserve, and each of them became skilled themselves at judging the ebb and flow of battle, and would prompt me to pull them back once their own battle within a battle had been won. So it was this day, and with the assistance of my veteran NCOs, the reserve were pushed and pulled from one wall to the other until finally the enemy ceased in their attempts to push forward, and a final air strike convinced them to break off the attack.

'We can't bring a casevac into this.' I spoke the obvious

words to my ops room team. 'Doc Stacey says Paul is still T1 but stable, and so we'll keep holding off as long as possible.'

'Moslem's been busy on the ICOM,' Freddie told me, referring to the man who seemed to be the enemy's principal mortar-fire controller. 'Looks like they're trying to find the MOG and our guns out in the desert. We've had six intercepts from them on that.'

'That's probably a good thing,' I suggested. 'Means our arty fire must be hurting them.'

Freddie nodded in agreement. 'What isn't so good is that they're certain they caused casualties earlier.'

The statement only confirmed what we could feel in the air. With an eye to the coming casevac, I left the ops room and visited our mortar section.

'We've got enough HE for one good fire mission, boss,' Danny Groves, the Royal Irish Ranger from Birmingham, told me. 'Would be great if we could get some in on the casevac.'

'That's the plan,' I agreed. Of course, like all plans, that was subject to surviving contact with the enemy.

'We can use the fifty-ones more for now,' the experienced mortarman suggested, going on to explain that, unlike the 81mm mortars that needed digging into the ground with their heavy tripods, the smaller mortars would be better deployed on positions like the Outpost and Alamo. The very lack of cover that made them susceptible to enemy mortar fire also made them great places from which to launch our own.

I looked at the shipping container that was used to store the mortar rounds, and to shield them from a direct hit that could cause catastrophic secondary explosions. The container had been full when we arrived. Now it was scarred from shrapnel, and almost empty. At least it provided good hard cover for the men of the mortar section, and I laughed as Danny showed me what one of the Rangers had daubed on the container's wall – THIS IS WHERE WE COWERED LIKE LITTLE GIRLS.

After calling in to check on the casualties – finding Paul

still stable, the walking wounded restless and still asking to leave the med centre – I returned to the ops room and called in to HQ. Following the big contact of the afternoon, they were more on edge than ever about sending a Chinook and its crew into our exposed HLS, and were greatly relieved to hear the news that Paul was stable. I imagine there had been some very uncomfortable conversations both in the battalion ops room and in Brigade that day, the tier of command that sat above 3 Para's battlegroup. I knew that there was not one officer in the army who would *want* a casualty to die when he could have been saved, but the ugly truth was that flying a Chinook into a heavy weight of fire was as likely to doom ten men as one, and that earlier casualty would still die waiting for help. I hated that we had been forced into this position by taking over a compound that was not fit for purpose, but we were here, and there was nothing else I could do for Paul and the other wounded than ensure that Easy Company were as prepared as possible for when the time came.

In the early evening, two more mortar rounds slammed down into the compound, the impacts sending tremors through our bodies and our deepest fears racing through our minds. Thankfully, there were no casualties, and Easy Company shook off the attack with laughter and banter.

After a call to Bastion, I gathered my leaders in the ops room. Their bearded faces were haggard, but morale was high. Even a section down, we had once again beaten off the enemy's attacks. Now we would see our wounded comrades away to safety. Easy Company had been bonded tightly through days on combat, and our own comfort and rest was far from our minds as I briefed my men on the casevac.

The army has a formal orders process that is drilled into its leaders, refined from centuries of warfare and the hard lessons learned by our forebears. It covers everything from timings to the situation of enemy forces – something that we were all intimately aware of by now – but often the most important section is that of the 'actions on', which is essentially where a commander will deliver his intent on what actions should be taken following any given scenario. That evening, the commanders of Easy Company listened intently as we outlined such sickening thoughts as 'actions on downed helicopter' – if that happened, seconds would make the difference between a tragic night and an unmitigated military disaster.

I wrapped up the orders and the NCOs filed away quickly, needing to disseminate the orders to the men, and to try and find a moment for a quick cigarette and brew. The casevac would take place at the cusp of darkness. As we did at dusk every evening, the company would stand to. Under the rules of engagement, we could only fire if we spotted armed fighters moving to attack. I told my men that, for tonight, we would hold off on being the first to engage – I did not want a chance shot at a solitary enemy fighter to kick off the contact that would see the air thick with lead, and the Chinook unable to land. I urged restraint, and I had no doubt that, with their wounded comrades at risk, my men would have no trouble displaying it.

The day's fierce heat was dying, the sun dipping behind a distant mountain range, an orange disc against deep red. Afghanistan delivered nightly on sunsets that were unrivalled in beauty, but here in Musa Qala there was no chance to sit on a rooftop and marvel at nature. Instead we crouched, eyes peeking nervously over pockmarked walls, ears straining for the telltale whump that would announce the Chinook's approach.

Below, the injured men began to shuffle towards the HLS. They would remain behind a wall until the last moment, there to be rushed on as their replacements came off. How would that feel for the new arrivals of B Company, stepping off to see a man on a stretcher, tubes in his chest? If they had any doubt about the danger that they were landing into, then it would be gone before they had left the Chinook's ramp.

Doc Stacey waited alongside Paul Martin's stretcher. I had made a final visit to see off my young platoon commander. Of course, the trip had also been necessary for some merciless piss-taking.

'I've been on the net to the loadmaster, and told him to throw you off the Chinook if you try and go on another holiday.'

'Why would I leave?' the doctor asked me, deadpan. 'I've heard Musa Qala is great this time of year.'

The rest of the casualties made their way to the HLS under their own steam. Undermanned as we were, we needed every rifle and gun on the walls, and so the walking wounded hobbled their way on makeshift crutches, the men with lower body shrapnel injuries supported by those with upper. There was nothing cheerful about their manner, or the fact that they were leaving the fight. Quite the opposite. Some of them accepted it with weary resignation, others protested. None wanted to be jack and to leave their comrades behind. Not when there was still such danger. As the young soldiers handed over cigarettes, ammo, and creature comforts to the men that they left behind, they knew that there was a chance they would never see each other again. Such unwanted or unrelenting thoughts lead to discomfort for a man to whom masculinity is all, and so he will hide this uncomfortable intimacy between an insult, a joke about his comrade's mother, and a final, firm handshake.

Ray and Abe joined me on the rooftop.

'Beautiful night,' Abe observed.

'Bloody gorgeous, isn't it?' I replied. 'How we doing on the air?'

'In comms with the A-10s, but they know to keep well away unless things go noisy and we call for them. We've set up boundaries for them, so there's no way they come over the town and risk setting things off unless we call for it.'

'Perfect.'

A week ago, I would have considered flying the menacing aircraft low and fast over the town in an attempt to persuade the Taliban that any attack was a bad idea, but after seeing our enemy soak up air strike after air strike, and still come at us, I knew that such an outcome was wishful thinking.

'Boss. Boss.' I heard the words gently called up from beneath me. I moved to the stairs, and found Staff Wornham.

'Got some good news off the ICOM,' he told me. 'Some of the enemy groups are moving out of Musa Qala.'

There would be time later to wonder how and why that was. For now, I simply hoped that such a changeover in enemy forces would mean that they were pulled back from our compound tonight, and would be in no place to threaten the Chinook.

'They've just gone wheels-up in Bastion,' Ray informed me.

It would take thirty minutes for the Chinook and its Apache escort to reach us. Half an hour of nervous fidgeting, wide eyeballs, and muttered prayers. The vivid colours in the sky were gone, overwhelmed by deep blue darkness. Night was drawing close, and across its canvas we were used to seeing the red and green dance of tracers as the enemy pressed the final attack of that day. Tonight there was nothing. Not a single shot. Not a single mortar. As Ray counted down the minutes, I began to hope.

Whump – whump – whump – whump.

I looked east on instinct, knowing that the casevac was coming from that direction. I could see nothing but murky sky, and so I pulled down my night-vision goggles – one of the six pairs in the company – and tried again. There was nothing to see, their range limited to closer quarters. I scanned the buildings about us, seeking out enemy movement, but the town seemed lifeless. A bled-out corpse abandoned to darkness.

I looked down to the edge of the HLS. Walking wounded and stretcher cases became bathed in green and yellow hues.

It would be my final sight of them in this place, an eerie collection of shuffling shapes, brave men made ghoulish by
technology. I fought back the urge to make my way down to
the LZ to see them one more time. I wanted to tell them how
proud I was of every single one of them, but my job now was
to see them home. For that, I needed to be their commander,
and not a fellow soldier who had nothing but admiration and
love for the courageous and selfless actions of these bravest of
men.

Whump – whump – whump – whump.

'Two minutes,' Ray whispered.

I passed the message along, then turned to look up once
more. This time I found the Chinook, a darker smudge against
the sky. Tracking her through the night vision was like trying
to catch a fly in a dark room. As she came and went from my
sight, the sound of her grew louder. Now, against the beat of
the Chinook's heavy rotors, I could hear the higher pitched
whine of the Apaches – they were known to the Taliban as
mosquitoes for a reason – and I saw them in the sky, angular
brutes dripping with payloads of promised death.

I swallowed the lump in my throat. No fire. No movement.
Could it hold? The Chinook was a minute away now, and I had
what we all wanted – a cold LZ – but a voice in my head told
me that this was all too good to be true. That surely the enemy
– who knew we had taken casualties – would not simply let the
Chinook pass in and out of their midst unmolested for a
second time. And yet, as it lost its final metres of altitude, the
heavy pressure of calm held. It was all so perfect that my gut
screamed it was a trap, but I told myself to be steady. To
concentrate on what was in front of me, and not what was in
my head.

'Tell her it's ice,' I told Ray, and he passed on the order, the
HLS was not hot.

There was no missing the shape in the sky now, a fat
bumble-bee that flared its nose to the sky and sat its thick body

down towards us with beating wings that churned dust, driving it into our exposed ears and nostrils. Goggles saved my eyes, but visibility plunged in the near-black. I knew that the first sign of disaster now would come through sound, not sight – the dumf-dumf-dumf of mortars leaving tubes; the whoosh of 107 rockets launching from rails; the bumf-whoosh-boom of RPGs; the peck-peck-peck boom-boom-boom of an automatic grenade launcher; the rattle of automatic weapons fire; the frenzied cries of men intent on killing or dying.

I heard none of it. There was only the beat of the rotors. Already the stretcher party was running. Already the walking wounded were shuffling. On the Chinook's ramp, I saw the figures of our replacements emerge, dragging and throwing stores clear. Every second the Chinook sat on the open HLS I expected the Taliban to wake from their slumber and attack, but there was nothing – no sight, no sound. Within moments the replacements were clear and the casualties were on board. The pilot – doubtless praying hard and swearing harder – wasted no time in clearing from the kill zone, and the bird lurched and beat its way from the open ground, leaving behind it a pile of stores that the new arrivals hastily dragged into the compound.

'Chinook's at altitude,' Ray told me, relief in his voice, and no wonder – the Chinook had now climbed to a point where she was safe from the enemy's small-arms and RPG fire.

'I don't fucking believe it,' Abe uttered, and I could sense the silhouette of the JTAC men sag against the wall.

I pushed my NVGs upwards and ran a hand across my face. I was in disbelief, and relieved beyond measure. Not a shot had been fired, and my men were away safely and on their way to a fully equipped hospital attended by the best surgeons in the world. For a British soldier, there was only one way to celebrate such a victory.

'Let's get a brew on.'

20

I stayed awake long enough to hear that Paul Martin's surgery had gone without complication, and then I slipped into a comatose state for an hour before rough hands shook me awake for my turn on radio stag. During those early morning hours, I thought over how lucky we had been the previous day. Firstly, because we had suffered only wounded and not killed, and secondly, because the casevac had gone off more quietly than I could ever have hoped for.

As I sat alone in the ops room, smoking cigarettes and sipping coffee, I wondered why that had been. The Taliban had announced on the ICOM that they knew they had inflicted casualties, and so to let the Chinook slip so easily through their net was doubly puzzling. In the end, I decided that the intercepted radio message in the evening was the most likely explanation – that with some enemy fighters leaving the town, there had likely been a decision taken to pull back those closest to our positions to ease the handover between Taliban groups. There was also the possibility that we had simply worn our enemy out in the previous days, and that they had been forced to pull back due to casualties and fatigue. Such a thought gave me immense pride in my own men, who, though hollow-eyed and gaunt-cheeked, still functioned as skilled infantrymen despite subsisting on an hour or two's sleep a day.

The new arrivals in Easy Company were conspicuous by their fuller flesh and brighter eyes. The eight-man section from B Company, led by Corporal Bri Price, were no strangers to the Taliban, having been in Sangin, and Price was keen that his fresher blokes take on extra duties immediately to try and buy a few more hours' snatched sleep for the men of Somme and Barossa. My two newly arrived captains, Dean Whiten and

Austen Salusbury, were equally insistent that I get a full night's sleep, but I wanted the time to plan for the inevitable contact in the morning, and so I had refused their offers to cover my duties, though I was greatly lifted in my spirits to have two more 'headshed' in the company. Dean, who was replacing Paul Martin, was a young Para who had been halfway to becoming a Chinook pilot before he had decided he would rather be running off the back of helicopters than flying them, whilst Austen, my new second in command, was your proto-typical Guards officer, strikingly tall and with that privately educated accent that is so common in the Household Division – in his case the Welsh Guards. Since I had once been a Guard myself, we had many mutual acquaintances, and I was certain that the company would be in good hands should I be the one who was next to be loaded onto the back of the Chinook.

Sitting in the ops room, I drew up as many notes for Austen as I could think of. There would be time the next day to discuss everything, but having my head in the wrong place in the morning's contacts could see that conversation never taking place. There was nothing macabre in writing my intent for my subordinate should I die. It was simply a necessity, and nothing more. If you overthought your own mortality, you'd never put your head above cover. Better to simply accept it and crack on. We were all in the same boat, and as captain of that vessel, it was down to me to set the example.

I set the scribbled orders for Austen aside and paced the room. There was a lot in there that I could not tell him, and that he would simply have to judge for himself. I knew that yesterday would not be the last time we needed to bring a Chinook into that hideous HLS. I knew that it would not be the last time we'd have to balance one man's life with the crew of others. I hated that we had been forced into this position, but every attempt I'd made to convince HQ to allow us to change position was beaten down in a heartbeat.

*

Easy Company's replacements were baptized by fire in the morning, the enemy showing up in force as the light snuck wickedly over the horizon, bringing with it a barrage of RPGs, and a weight of fire so thick that it seemed impossible that a man could raise himself into it and not be hit. Perhaps the enemy had been resting last night, because they came with fresh vigour. Or perhaps this intensity was born of anger, a savage backlash for missing the Chinook that had landed and left untouched.

The contact was beaten off with air strikes, and I stood the company down as quickly as possible. Yesterday had been a long day, and there was no reason to expect that this one would be any different. Men needed to clean weapons, re-distribute ammunition, eat, and rest, as quickly as possible. Good NCOs ensured that these tasks were achieved in that order, repeating the mantra learned in the early days of basic training: 'My rifle, my kit, myself.' A fully rested soldier was little use if his rifle was clogged with dirt and carbon.

At 0615 the Taliban returned, but in less force. Easy Company were in their fighting positions when five mortar rounds screamed in. I felt dread in my stomach at the sound of them, the concussions slapping me in the face and lifting my guts. I knew instantly that they had landed in the compound, and could only thank God when it became clear that they'd landed in the open space between the headquarters building and the Alamo. Hasty checks were made to all positions to ensure no casualties had been taken, whilst Sergeant Major Scrivener and the reserve checked all nooks and crannies to ensure that no man was bleeding out alone and isolated. Eventually the headcount came back confirmed, and I offered up another prayer in thanks.

We returned the enemy in kind, battering their likely firing positions with our own mortars, artillery, and A-10s. The enemy either died beneath the weight of fire or retreated under the thick cloud of debris that polluted the town's sky.

'That was rather tasty,' Austen said in greeting once the dust had settled, and the company had stood down. 'You've been doing this every day since the twenty-fourth?' he asked, a little incredulous.

I took off my helmet and wiped sweat from my eyes. 'Somme Platoon have been here three weeks longer than that.'

'Bloody hell.'

'What do they think's going on up in Bastion?' I asked him.

'Everyone knows you're – we're – up against it here, but it's hard to appreciate it until you actually see it first-hand. This compound's fucking awful. Absolute liability.'

'We're stuck with it though,' I told him. 'Governor won't stand for us moving.'

'So I've heard,' Austen replied. 'Someone up the chain needs to grow some balls.'

Staff Wornham joined us, his shirt patched with sweat from where he'd fought up on the rooftop. 'Got an intercept, boss. They're requesting more ammo for their grenade machine guns.'

'Well, that's something to look forward to.' I smiled at Austen.

'Can't wait.'

'Other good news,' Wornham continued, 'is that we killed one of their commander's sons. Looks like the artillery was bang on.'

'By son you mean a fighter, I take it?' Austen asked the signaller.

'There's no civvies in the town, sir,' Wornham confirmed. 'Fucking ghost town. Last bit of gen is that they're planning a casualty convoy to take their wounded to Gereshk.'

'It's like this most days,' I told Austen. 'We knock them out by the dozen, but there's always more groups coming in.'

And that was the crux of the problem. No matter how many of the enemy we were killing and wounding, they were still coming back at us each and every day. Committed to hold this compound by our commanders, there was nothing we could do but soak up both the attacks and the steady stream of casualties that was in danger of becoming a daily occurrence for Easy Company.

This day would be no different.

The four rounds struck the compound with sickening thumps. There had been no warning of their launch, only a split-second shriek, and then the chunks of dirt and plaster were flying, deadly shrapnel singing as it bit into walls and men.

From the doorway of the ops room I saw the first round strike the rooftop of the Alamo. I cursed as my guts twisted up towards my chest – I knew that there would be casualties. I waited impotently until the fire ceased and I could raise myself from off of the floor.

'Reserve section on me!' I called, grabbing at my gear.

Thudding across the open space, I expected the enemy to follow up their attack with small arms at any moment. There was no way to disguise the fact that they'd scored a direct hit, and I could only be thankful for every second that they didn't fire on our positions, and double our problems.

The round had struck the east side of the Alamo, which was a maze of archways. There we found four of the ANP, the men having taken cover beneath an arch as they heard the round whistle in. It had not been enough. They had been punctured from head to toe by shrapnel. Without helmet and body-armour to protect heart and head, one Afghan was already dead. Bleeding beside him were his three comrades. These we triaged, and as Corporal French arrived with the quad, we bundled the men as quickly as possible towards the skilled care of Doc Stacey.

The Afghan Police commander arrived on the scene and looked at his dead man. His face was as emotionless as that of his fallen comrade. The officer had fought the Russians as a young mujahideen, and had been in battle ever since. Death and wounds were woven into his life, and he had the righteous shroud of religion to protect him from their touch.

'Inshallah,' he said, 'he is with God, now.'

They were the same words we heard our Taliban enemies speak when they talked of their own fallen. Both sides claimed to be on the right side of a religion I knew little about, other than that it could give men great strength and comfort.

I went to the ops room to begin the process of casevacing the Afghan wounded. They would receive exactly the same priority and treatment as British wounded, and as such, we were once again cast into the deadly game of weighing up wounded men's lives with that of the helicopter crew. As such, it was a great relief when Doc Stacey called to tell me that all three men were stable and in no immediate need of casevac.

After apprising the Battlegroup HQ, I stepped outside and lit a cigarette. Looking across at the Alamo, I wished that there was a better way to protect the soldiers that had to man it. We still had no equipment to build overhead cover. The sandbags that we did have were shot up and deployed on the sangars at key points around the compound. Leaving the Alamo un-manned was simply not an option, as it afforded some of the best all-round arcs. Without the machine guns there, we would have struggled to beat back many of the advances. There was nothing we could do but suck up the enemy's fire. The only thing that I could do personally was to spend more time on the Alamo rooftop with my men, to show them that I was willing to take the same risk that I was asking of them.

Thinking of my soldiers, I grabbed my fighting gear and rifle, and made a tour of the positions. The Irish soldiers in the Outpost had been joined by a terp, and he was busy teaching them Pashtun insults that they could call to the Taliban who sheltered in a building not thirty yards away. Other men used the more traditional greetings of home.

'Yer bollix, yer!'

'Yer shooting's shite!'

'Yer mam's a slag!'

The Taliban responded in their best English. Following the mortar strike, both sides seemed content to trade badly accented abuse rather than small-arms fire and grenades.

The late afternoon passed quietly, a steady traffic of radio intercepts giving us the likely reason – the enemy were co-ordinating several resupplies of ammunition. Like us, they had fought themselves almost dry.

That evening, on the cusp of darkness, we stood to and waited once more for the crew of a Chinook and its medical team to pick up our Afghan casualties. I had nothing but ad-miration for the bravery of these born warriors. For their part, they hero-worshipped the British medical team, who treated them as if they were their closest kin. There were tight bonds between Afghan and Brit throughout Easy, and the men of both nations could often be found sharing cigarettes and brews, the terps in high demand to help answer questions about distant homeland and families. Born half a world apart into different cultures, Afghan policemen and British soldiers found that they had much in common – a love of family, a desire for a better life, and a joy in killing Taliban fighters.

The sun dipped below the horizon. The Chinook snuck towards home like the visiting boyfriend of a teenage daughter. The Taliban were either uninterested or in no position to con-test the casevac. After a few minutes during which my heart was in my throat, the beast was gone, and with it the body of an Afghan warrior, and three of his wounded comrades.

As the heavy rotors beat against the hot air and vanished into the distance, I thought back over the events of the past three days, and the consecutive mortar strikes and casualties. How long could we keep taking such losses? How would my men cope, knowing that next time it could be any one of them?

How would *I* cope?

I did not have the answer. I could only wait for dawn, the Taliban, and their next attack.

21

If there had been issues with the Taliban's supply chain, they had been resolved and then some – first light saw tracer zip over our heads in long green coils. RPGs blasted holes in our defences, leaving our ears ringing and skulls concussed. We picked off black shapes that ghosted from cover to cover, yelling to claim the prize of the kill. Taliban gun teams appeared on the rooftops and died before they could bring their weapons to bear, our own gunners and snipers cutting them down like rabbits, but the enemy were not afraid to die – in fact, it was the highest reward for them – and they were not deterred by these casualties. They pressed on into our fire and, with resignation, I knew that we would once again be required to destroy parts of the town we had been sent to protect – it was the only way to save our own lives, and to keep the enemy from the literal gates.

We called on our friends in the sky. So regular was their company now that our JTAC could distinguish each of the Texan pilots by voice. These Air National Guardsmen were part-time in the way that the Reserve Army operates in the UK, but their skill was of highly drilled professionals – time and again they came, strafing sometimes fifty metres from our own positions. To call attacks so close, our faith in the American airmen had to be absolute – and it was. Many members of Easy Company owe their lives to the men who flew these shark-faced tank-busters. They were our deadly ace in the hole, and again that morning, they churned buildings and Taliban fighters into pulp, and allowed us to see in another day.

The fourth of September was quiet. A reprieve. After the savage attack in the morning, the Taliban made no more attempts to assault. Even their mortars were quiet and this lull in the battle gave Easy Company some much-needed rest. That is not to say that the day was slept away – the necessity of manning fighting positions meant that a soldier could expect two hours' uninterrupted sleep at best – but it did give a man the chance to take his daily total of gonk from two hours to four. Such a rest may seem inconsequential to someone who has never suffered true sleep deprivation, but for Easy Company, it was as if we'd been given a week's leave, and smiling soldiers showed their appreciation of such things through increasingly savage insults to their friends. Not wanting to neglect our neighbours, the terps were called frequently to the Outpost – Terry needed his fair share of verbal abuse, too. 'Your mum loves a bacon butty you smelly bastards!'

I doubt the Taliban paid much attention to the shouting infidels. The ICOM was busy with the chatter of their commanders, and the topics of the day were resupply and casualties. They made reference to understanding the meaning of sacrifice, particularly to the foreign fighters in their midst. It was strange to hear them pressing such an issue. Their attacks had seemed almost suicidal, and I wondered what more was expected from their men. What *was* clear was that we were killing and wounding them in droves.

As dusk settled, and if all was quiet, we would allow them to come unmolested to collect the bodies of their fallen comrades from beneath our sights, but that was a simple matter of decency that needed no explanation to my troops – the enemy dead were of no threat to us. Let them be collected. Let them receive their burial. We had no wish to see bodies chewed upon by local hounds, no matter whose they were. We knew well enough that the Taliban would never show us mercy – worse, they would torture us slowly before sawing open our throats – but we had no desire to desecrate bodies, or to cause further suffering. We were professionals. An attacking enemy was a target to us, nothing more. When that target dropped, just as they had done on the ranges of Sennybridge and Otter-burn, we would move on to the next. There was no desire to mutilate. There was no desire to hang bodies from walls. If the Taliban were a cancer, we saw ourselves as the scalpel that would cut it out. Nothing more, and nothing less.

The day finished with death, though it was a distant one. Over the radio, we received the news that Steve Irwin, the Australian TV celebrity known as the Crocodile Hunter, had been killed by a stingray. Many of the men chose to see this as a prank by headquarters. For those who did believe it, it was a bizarre reminder that life carried on outside Musa Qala, and that death could be delivered in many ways.

The next day, a lone RPG at dawn was the solitary call of de-fiance from our enemy. A few hours later, one of our sangars spotted the enemy moving around the battered shops of the market area, and unleashed a GPMG on them, beginning a one-sided contact of our mortars and small arms. We poured on until we were satisfied that the sneaking fighters were dead or had escaped, and then the calm returned, a weary silence beneath the baking heat of the Afghan sun.

'Feels like they're waiting on something,' Scrivs confided to me in the ops room. 'All these resupplies and hardly any con-tacts. Bit dodgy, isn't it?'

More ICOM intercepts seemed to confirm the veteran's gut feeling. Taliban commanders – now recognizable to our terps by voice, and so pinned to a likely sector – made plans for an attack the next day. It would come from two directions, they said, and they would do what was necessary to see that the foreigners did not escape, and died to a man.

Later that evening another enemy commander requested English and Punjabi speakers to help translate to his men. It was further confirmation of what we already knew – this was not a bunch of disgruntled opium farmers that we were fighting, but jihadis from the world over. I sent this information up our chain of command, and was surprised by their answer.

'There are no foreign fighters in Helmand,' I was told. 'The Taliban are recruiting people angry that they can no longer grow opium. This is a local problem, and nothing more.'

I choose to believe the evidence of my own eyes and ears – we had even received messages about 'our friends in Lahore'. Why Battlegroup HQ were so keen to deny the truth laid out before them I could guess at – it did not fit the party line, and for a campaign that was already being carried out without the presence of the British press, it would not do to 'make a fuss'. Such politics annoyed me, but were not my real concern. Whether my enemy was from Kabul, Karachi, or London, we would fight him just the same, Taliban, Al Qaeda, Iranian or Pakistani farmer or not.

'Something weird's going on outside, boss,' one of my platoon sergeants told me, sticking his head inside the ops room. 'Think they're singing, or something.'

I followed the man out of the building and onto the rooftop. Sure enough, the sound of Afghan voices could be heard in the cooling evening air.

'What are they doing?' the sergeant asked me.

'I don't know.'

But I could guess. Though I had no grasp of the language, the tone was universal. It was mournful. A lament. Without doubt, this was a remembrance of fallen comrades.

Naz, one of our terps, confirmed it. 'They are singing prayers for the dead. All dead that have been fighting here.'

'Does that mean they're leaving?' I asked, thinking of that final scene in *Zulu*, and how the redcoats' tribal enemy had sung a chilling hymn on a mountainside before slipping away and leaving the garrison with the hope of life.

Naz shook his head. 'I don't think so.' Then, he went on to point out the parts of the songs that referred to the enemy by name. We knew some of them, commanders who frequented the radio waves we intercepted. We had noticed a steady turn-over in voices – or at least, our terps had – but here was our proof that these men had gone to meet their maker, and had not simply been rotated by their chain of command.

'Good.' The platoon sergeant smiled. He wasn't the only man grinning. This was our enemy, and the more they mourned their dead, the less we would mourn our own. This was war, and pity could wait until my men were returned safely home, if ever, for this was no ordinary enemy – this was the enemy who stoned women for committing adultery. This was the enemy who beheaded prisoners. This was the enemy who tortured and butchered in the name of their cult. I had to remind myself of that, as their singing sounded so recogniz-able. So human. But they were not like us. Not once you opened souls, and peered within. At no time in Musa Qala, or at any other point in my life since, did I question the righteous-ness of my use of deadly force.

After a while, men became bored of the singing and moved away. It didn't do to be exposed at any rate, and so they shuffled off to find quiet spots to smoke and play backgammon. Dusk would be coming soon, it would be better to go without the short rest than to suffer the agony of rousing weary brain and bones from the floor for the sake of twenty minutes' oblivion.

I took a final measure of the Taliban's sorrowful song, then left the rooftop and made my way to the ops room. Freddie was poring over ICOM intercepts. You could see the cogs turning under his bushy thicket of hair as he tried to glean some piece of information that we could use against the enemy. He was tireless in his pursuit of it, and already our greatest success had owed a lot to this Para. From fixing engines to fixing enemy positions, he was an absolute asset.

'What's new, Freddie?'

'ACM say they have a professional arriving tomorrow.'

'A professional?' I asked him, raising an eyebrow. 'What, like Léon?'

'What?'

'You know, the movie with the French guy.'

'Gérard Depardieu?'

'No! Jean Reno? I think that's him.'

'Ah. OK. Anyway, no more information than that. What did he do in the movie?'

'He was a cleaner.'

'A cleaner?'

'Hitman.'

'Ah. That would be interesting.' He thought for a moment. 'A proper sniper would be bad news.'

I nodded my head as I lit a cigarette. 'It would. There's no hiding in those sangars.'

Freddie had erected sniper screens in exposed areas, as well as hanging them behind sangars to diminish the silhouettes of the sentries, but with such an open compound, we were vulnerable to any sharpshooters.

My intelligence officer pointed to the log of intercepts. 'The rest of it's been pretty constant all day. Resupply, and lots of new troops coming in.'

'Brilliant. Hopefully they can have some songs sung about them soon.'

'Bit eerie that, isn't it?' Freddie shrugged, pulling a face.

As was the norm in the evening, my leaders came together for a quick recap of the day before we stood to. Everyone was talking about the singing. There was a real sense of pride that we had been grinding the enemy down, and a sense of hope that soon they would have to accept that we were going nowhere, and their best course of action was to 'fuck off back to their goats.'

During the informal briefing, I told my men that we were low on diesel for the sole generator that charged our batteries and so we would no longer be running our radio net with Battlegroup HQ unless we were in contact. Instead, we would tune in once a day at 1800 hours to deliver our daily sitrep, and to receive any news from HQ. This was certain to add to our feeling of isolation, but men fretted for another reason – until now, we had been able to listen in to the long list of engagements taking place in other parts of Helmand. Contacts that our mates were engaged in, and were increasingly being hurt fighting in. The battlegroup net was our way of cheering from the sidelines, and for willing on the casevacs that went in to rescue our wounded or fallen comrades. Helmand that summer was not an easy time for anyone.

The brief was concluded quickly. As we waited on the moment to stand to, we talked amongst ourselves. There was a sense amongst all of us that something had changed. The enemy were not pressing us throughout the day with small-arms attacks. No grenades were being exchanged. Something was in the air. We had no idea exactly what, but the talk of resupply and reinforcements could lead to an educated guess – the enemy were holding back for a big push.

They did not leave us alone that night. They came in the late evening, as the sky was a riot of angry orange. Our red tracers arced and ricocheted across this livid canvas like fireflies. The enemy jabbed with RPG, and we threw hooks with mortar and artillery fire. The uppercut came from our air, a B-1B that dropped a 2,000 lb bomb on the densest concentration of firing points, the air sucked from our lungs as the hungry explosion drew in all about it, then spat it upwards in a billowing cloud of broken buildings, and shattered bodies.

Such carnage was a thing of beauty to men who were not on the receiving end. Irish soldiers were now joined by Corporal Price's 3 Para section as they whooped and jeered at the Taliban. As the enemy fire petered to nothing, one light machine gunner called a final insult to a burst of laughter: 'You fight shitter than you sing!'

The ICOM was busy after that. Talk of dead and wounded fighters. Casualty convoys to Gereshk. Such talk of death was our own pleasant music as we opened up a deck of cards, and passed around a mug of tea.

Another day was done.

22

September the fifth. Dawn.

Dawn was eyes cracked open through dust and grime. Dawn was aching knees, scraped elbows, and dehydration so severe that it hurt to piss. Dawn was all of these things, but above all, the pale glowing light was the reminder that today it would all begin again, and that in a few minutes' time, you could be dead. Set against that fate, the creaking joints and tired eyes were experiences to be savoured.

Another dawn, another contact. It seems so flippant to talk of it that way now. At the time it was an intense blur of organized chaos, guns rattling and RPGs screaming over our heads. It was Taliban dead in the street, and moments of intense fear as their PK gunners drew a bead on you, their bullets ripping apart the wall behind which you were sheltering. It was shouted fire-control orders and target indications. It was the seconds of dread when a soldier would lose his footing, and you wondered with heart in mouth if it had been a trip or a bullet. Contact was all these things and more, and that morning it was brought to an end with the strafing runs of an American AV-8B Harrier, the jet pouring cannon and rocket fire into the Taliban firing points. The ordnance flew through the air like fireworks, sparks hissing. It was too much for our enemy, and they broke away.

Their exposed dead lay behind, leaking dark blood into the dirt. There was no breeze to stir their clothes. Their stillness was absolute, and eternal.

I patted my men on their shoulders, feeling the soak of sweat beneath their body armour. With the company stood down, I took to the ops room, there receiving the news via radio intercepts that we had killed another of the enemy's commanders, taking the tally to over half of their original number since our arrival. The intercepts also made reference to a number of Pakistani casualties – these I would flag up the chain of command later that day, and again I would be told that my ears were deceiving me. There were no foreign fighters in Helmand, they said. These are angry opium farmers.

Hours passed in the tedium of a company on the defensive. Sleep if you can. Take sentry when you must. In between, play backgammon and shithead.

The Taliban came at us twice that afternoon with RPG and small arms. A few months ago, these would have been the kind of contacts I dreamed of. Now, they were a minor irritation, shrugged off with the same indifference as a rugby tackle in school.

'This one's a bit different,' Freddie prodded me, pointing out the most recent ICOM intercept on the log.

I read it twice, as it seemed so unlikely. 'They're discussing a ceasefire? Where?'

Freddie shrugged his wide shoulders. Given that we had just plastered Taliban firing positions a few minutes ago, we knew that it was anywhere but here.

We mulled it over as we took to another game of shithead. Wherever it was, it would not be in Helmand. There was no chance of that taking place with British troops, as our government was firmly against talking to terrorists, and the Taliban fell into that camp. Our best bet was that it was between some kind of tribal factions, as the Afghans were as likely to be fighting each other as NATO forces.

'Fucking love a good scrap, these Afghans do,' Freddie concluded.

No one argued that point. I put the next card down. Two minutes later, three mortar rounds hit the compound.

Our time in Musa Qala would never be the same.

*

Two of the rounds hit the southern edge of the Outpost. There was an observation post there, and one look at it from the headquarters' building told me that it would be bad – it was trashed, sandbags spilled, smoke hanging mockingly in the air.

'Prep the nine liners!' I called inside to Austen – there was no way we'd get through such a strike without taking casualties.

Confirmation came a moment later via the radio – six of them; one T1, one T2, four T3. It was another mass-casualty event, but this time, the enemy would not leave us in peace to collect our wounded.

'Contact! Contact!'

In the first moments following the strikes there had been an eerie peace, the only sound in our ears the ringing of explosions and the pumping of blood as we considered our casualties. Seconds later, there was the clatter of machine-gun fire, the swoosh and bang of RPGs, and the crack of rifles. The enemy had initiated contact, and from the swarm of bullets above me, it sounded like they had done it from all sides.

'Stand to! Stand to!'

Men were already hurrying to the firing positions, some in nothing but a pair of shorts beneath their body armour. They ran crouched in the practised motions of the besieged, then crawled on hands and knees as bullets tore into the walls from which they now fought.

At the first impact of the mortars, Austen had turned on our radios to report that we were under contact. What he had stumbled onto was a net alive with chatter. We were not the only ones under fire. We were not the only ones with casualties.

'It's Sangin,' he told me. 'They've got a really bad T1. The IRT is on its way there now for casevac.'

If the IRT was on task, it would mean more time before it could get to us. There was no second Chinook available, but that mattered little at this moment. The air was so thick with Taliban rounds, there was no way that we could bring anyone onto the HLS without it ending in disaster.

'I'm going up onto the roof!' I told my team, and headed back outside in time to see an RPG leave a sooty trail against the brilliant blue sky. My duty now was to be a commander, and not to get sucked into the extraction of my men from the Outpost – I had to delegate, and trust my soldiers to do their own duty. I had no doubt that they would.

In the Outpost, men were clearing a path to the wounded on the rooftop. Given its proximity to the Taliban – who could be as close as the other side of a wall – moving into that position required the same stance as a fighting patrol, and a section at least would be needed to secure it, let alone extract the wounded. I got onto the company net, and ordered that the casualties be held in the Outpost until contact was broken – we simply could not afford to commit the men needed to pull them out without leaving ourselves critically weak in other sectors of the compound. It would be futile to get the men to the med centre, only for the Taliban to push through the ruined mosque and over our wall.

As the rounds zipped by within feet of our heads, I pointed out to my JTAC where I wanted the first strafing run.

'Get them in now, Ray,' I told him. 'We've got to break this fucking contact.'

'The A-10s are tied into Sangin,' Ray answered, disappointed. 'We've got F-18s. Five-hundred and thousand pounders,' he explained.

I took my map from my pocket, and pointed out which buildings I wanted hit. Like most of our strikes, they would be danger close, and almost down our throat – Ray and Abe called them in without blinking.

The word passed around. Men hammered rounds at the enemy until they heard the piercing shriek of the bombs as they hurtled to ground. Then there would be a split second to duck into cover as the ground was torn open, and rubble was spat outwards for hundreds of metres, chunks of Afghan soil and who knows what else spewed over our compound to bounce off of rooftops and helmets. Within a second of the detonations, men were back on their feet and firing – we all knew what was at stake, and no one wanted to let up on the enemy.

It was enough for the Taliban. As pillars of smoke rose towards the sky, scarring the horizon, the enemy ceased fire and melted away.

I ran to the base of the Outpost. Though I needed to maintain a sense of detachment so that I could oversee the overall casevac of my men, I had to hear the news face to face.

I found the platoon sergeant.

'Four ANP casualties, two Irish,' he told me, sweat pouring down his face. 'Matanisinga and Whitehead. Matanisinga's throat's torn open, boss, but Frenchie is with him now.'

'Can you get them down?' I asked, thinking of the perilous route to the roof of the Outpost, and how part of it led over an open mezzanine that had to be jumped from the opposite rooftop.

'We've laid ladders over the gaps. We'll carry them across there.'

And so they did, totally exposed to the Taliban-occupied buildings not thirty metres away. It was an act of comradeship and immense bravery, and I would later seek official recognition for the men who performed such a dangerous task.

I ran back to the ops room. I knew immediately from Austen's face that we had bad news.

'They had to call off the Chinook in Sangin,' the Guards officer told me. 'As it was coming in, all hell broke loose. The HLS was too hot. There was no way they could get in here, either, so they've gone back to Bastion to reset.'

I understood the decision – the Chinook could not stay in the air forever – but I was deeply troubled by the implications;

two locations, two sets of critical casualties, one Chinook, and two hot LZs. Our situation had never looked so precarious.

It was about to get worse.

'T1 casualties in Kajaki,' the signaller reported, grim.

I swore, then used the landline to call the med centre. It was now forty minutes since the mortars had struck, and the casualties were finally in front of a doctor.

'I've done what I can to stabilize Matanisinga,' Doc Stacey told me over the phone. 'The others are all stable. For now, they're nothing to worry about, but Matanisinga needs surgery ASAP.'

'How long can you keep him stable?' I asked.

'Six hours at the most, but that estimate is only going to go down, not up. I can't guarantee him, Adam. I can't stress enough how badly he's hurt.'

'Thank you, Mike.'

I hung up the field telephone, and felt once again a surge of admiration for our doctor – he was performing miracles under the greatest pressure. Then, armed with the knowledge that he had given me, I called Battlegroup HQ on the satellite phone, and we made our plan to get our wounded home alive.

Sangin was still in contact, and so it was decided that the IRT would make its first attempt at saving lives by flying to us in Musa Qala. The attempt would take place at 2015, almost three hours after red-hot shrapnel had struck down six of my men. Though we all wished that it could be sooner, we understood that later was better – twilight had been our ally so far, and we hoped that it would continue its coalition with us on this day.

The mood in the company was grim and born from simmering anger, but anger towards our enemy rather than towards our own situation. Some men questioned why their comrades – and their Royal Irish brothers in Sangin, too – had not been casevaced sooner, but all understood that to bring a Chinook into a hot HLS was more than simply counter-productive – it was suicide.

Staff Wornham, as sombre-faced as any man, gave me more bad news in private. From radio intercepts, we knew with certainty that the Taliban were aware that they'd caused casualties. I chose not to share this outside of my leaders. I felt that it would only dampen spirits, and I wanted my men's state of mind to be as it was now – burning with determination to see their comrades home.

I took a moment to be alone, finding a perch in shade where I could drag on a cigarette, and think. There was so much that could go wrong. Not only here, but also in Sangin. It didn't take Sun Tzu to see that we were overstretched and badly positioned, and yet brooding over such things would do me no good. What I *could* do was run over the countless 'what if' scenarios that could take place during my casevac, and to think over my response for each. I hoped that, through this exercise, I would not be caught short.

I looked at my watch. The face was dusty and scratched, and told me there was forty minutes until the Chinook would appear. In thirty minutes I would move the company up onto the walls, from where I prayed that they would not have to fire a single round. At the same time the casualties would be brought from the med centre and placed in the ops room. They'd remain there in hard cover until the Chinook was two minutes out. I thought again about the brilliance of our doctor, and how we would certainly have lost Matanisinga without him. I took a moment then to pray for Paul Muirhead's health, the young lance corporal currently receiving treatment in a military hospital in Bahrain, who also owed his life to the doctor. I had been told that his mother had been flown out from the UK to be by his side, and I thought ahead to the day when I would meet her, and the parents of all the other young men who had been hurt under my command.

I shook my head to clear it. Now was not the time to think

on that, but to ensure that my casualties here were gotten away to surgical teams, and home, and so I got to my feet, and dropped my cigarette into dirt littered with broken link and empty cases. With a final prayer, I went to prepare my men.

23

Easy Company were on the walls. Once again they were a muzzled pit bull, ordered by me not to fire unless the Taliban kicked off a contact, and only then if they did so in a big way.

I called my commanders together. They'd fought a running battle for days on end, but none showed signs of slacking. They knew what was coming – what was at stake – and they were determined to see their boys onto the casevac.

After bringing them up to speed on the casualties, I broke down my plan in a set of quick battle orders; the working HMG was redirected so that it covered the northern side of the HLS, where I expected the enemy to be most thickly concentrated. Fast air was cued up, with likely firing points identified so that we could smash them the moment they engaged. The Outpost was bolstered with extra men and machine guns. The casualties and stretcher party would wait at the base of the Outpost, ready to sprint out and load the casualties onto the Chinook the moment it touched down.

'Remember to get off,' I felt obliged to tease the doctor.

Then I headed to the rooftop, where Ray nudged me. 'IRT should be wheels down here in figures five.'

I nodded, then ran through a checklist in my mind, desperate that there was no detail overlooked that could make even the slightest difference in this extraction. I ran through dozens of what ifs, but eventually, I had to admit to myself that there was nothing left to do but wait.

I heard the whump-whump-whump of the rotors a moment later.

'Here they come,' Abe whispered.

No sooner had the words left his lips, than the Taliban let rip.

Calls of 'Contact!' broke out as the zip of rounds passed over our heads.

Boom – 'RPG!' – Thud. A dud round crashed against the northern wall.

All about me, my men returned fire. They knew what was at stake – the survival of their friend – and they stood up into the storm of enemy fire without a thought for their own safety.

The whump of the Chinook fought to be heard over the deafening cacophony of rifle and machine-gun fire. Each stroke of the helicopter's heavy blades seemed to push both sides towards a new intensity.

'Fucking hell, this is going to be hot,' Ray groaned, listening into the Chinook's pilot on the air net. 'The Apaches are engaging. Chinook's taking fire.'

I could see it now, a lumbering beast lurching across the rooftops. Chinooks were known by their crews as bullet magnets for a reason, and I watched open-mouthed as green tracer slowly arced its way towards the machine. It would have been beautiful, if it hadn't meant death for my men.

With targets everywhere, the Apaches fought back. Hellfire missiles flew from their rails and ploughed into Taliban firing points; 20mm cannons chattered relentlessly.

The Chinook battled onwards.

'This is going to be hot,' Ray said again. 'Sixty seconds.'

I cleared my throat. Forcing my voice to be as calm as possible, I got on the company net. 'All Easy call signs, this is Zero Alpha. IRT is sixty seconds out. Rapid fire, rapid fire. Out.'

I heard NCOs shout my repeated order from all corners of the compound. Our rate of fire increased. It had to. We had to keep the enemy's heads down long enough for the Chinook to come in, and if we could buy them two minutes, it would be enough.

The IRT was close enough now for me to make out the

features of its cockpit. I saw the sparks fly as rounds struck its body.

'Fuck! They're taking fire, Ray!'

He made no reply, and said nothing into the radio – the pilot knew what was happening to his baby and did what he could to weave such a hulking frame away from the worst of the fire, his door gunners ripping long bursts from their Gatling guns.

I looked down towards the north wall, where Doc Stacey crouched alongside Matanisinga, whose throat was heavily bandaged. Our surgeon had been adamant that he couldn't guarantee his patient for any amount of time, and that he needed surgery immediately, and yet . . .

I turned. The Chinook was less than a hundred metres away now. The size of a bus, it looked like a target the Taliban could not miss. The flash of enemy strikes peppered its hull. If it went down, a crew and a surgical team would go with it. Already stretched, my men would have to fight out to recover the survivors – if there were any. It would mean fixing bayonets and fighting street to street. It would be carnage, and I couldn't expect to lose less than a section of men.

I took one last look at Matanisinga. It was the least I could do for the man I was likely to condemn. Then, I made the call.

'Hot LZ! Hot LZ! Call her off!'

Ray echoed the order into the radio. I had made my call, and now all I could do was watch, and pray.

The Chinook's nose pulled up, its movements so slow that it was as if a whale glided over the Outpost. I watched transfixed as rounds continued to crack against its skin.

Boom! Boom! – Two RPGs launched from no more than eighty yards away screamed through the air as they bracketed the Chinook front and back, mere feet from their struggling victim.

'Fuck!' Abe called out in as much relief as fear – we knew

that if only one rocket had found its mark, then the Chinook would be a burning hulk.

'Get her out! Get her out!' I urged the pilot, who must have been struggling valiantly at the helicopter's controls.

He did. I could not imagine what skill and guts it took to fly the beast through that storm, but the pilot dipped the nose, and pushed through the fire and out over the town. Trails of tracer chased after her, but the Chinook had cleared the danger zone.

'FUCK.' Ray exhaled, sitting down heavily.

Around us, the battle petered away. The Chinook had slipped through the Taliban's grip, mere feet from destruction, but they knew that the casualties were still inside the compound, and so their prey would have to return.

'Get the artillery on the net,' I told Abe. 'I want to smash these bastards.'

As one half of my JTAC went about this task, the other artilleryman turned to me. Ray was slumped against the sandbags, his eyes following mine as I looked at the casualties now being shuttled back to the ops room's hard cover.

'How the fuck are we going to get them out, boss?'

I said nothing. Instead, I looked at the fear painted on the young faces of my men. Not fear for themselves, but fear that their friend would die in front of them.

I could not let them down.

We would get Matanisinga out alive.

24

After the aborted casevac attempt I went to the ops room and called Battlegroup HQ with a clear message – Matanisinga gets extracted within the next few hours, or he dies.

No one at battlegroup wanted that to happen. Nobody wanted to lose a Chinook, either.

'We're working on a solution,' they told me, and then went on to give me the bad news that, although the IRT had got into Sangin after their aborted mission here, the Royal Irish soldier they had casevaced had died on the Chinook before he could reach a surgeon. The 'golden hour' had been stretched to four, and he had paid the price. I did not want the same fate for Matanisinga.

'I don't care what it takes,' I entreated. 'But we need to get him out.'

My commanders agreed. To make it happen, something unprecedented would have to take place.

'We're getting preliminary fires,' I told the officers and senior NCOs of my company. 'That means we don't need to be in any kind of contact to call in the air and guns. The lawyers have signed off on it, and Task Force Helmand is sending us as much air as we can use, including a Spectre gunship.'

There were wide eyes at that news. Prelim fires were the things of war, not counter-insurgency – though, of course, we scoffed at the difference – and the Lockheed AC-130 Spectre was a flying battleship that bristled with weapons. It was the most destructive force in the sky, and it was ours to use.

'Second casevac will be at 0130,' I told my men, refusing to say 'attempt'. 'Until then we smash every known firing point. Every known forming-up point. Anywhere that's even had a

sniff of Taliban, we smash it. Stand to will be at 0100,'
I finished, though I expected that the walls would be filled
with Easy Company's soldiers long before then – no one was
about to sleep through what was coming.

After some map work in the ops room, I made my way up to
the headquarters rooftop with the JTAC. The Afghan night
was still and silent. It was not to last.

'Who have we got first?' I asked Ray, knowing that high in
the skies above us, coalition aircraft were waiting like taxis in
a rank for their turn to come in and pound targets. The power
in our hands was formidable, and we were about to turn it
loose. To save Matanisinga, we would lay waste to a town.

'F-18s,' Ray spoke, and we looked to our list of targets.

'This one,' I pointed out.

And so it began.

It is hard to describe the few hours between the casevacs that
night. Never in my life did I expect to see such havoc, and
certainly I would never have believed that I would be at the
helm controlling it. Every strike had to be signed off by myself,
and for almost three hours I oversaw a rolling rain of bombs
from the sky. The explosions ripped through the air, the flashes
lighting up the entire horizon for a split second, followed then
by dust and debris tumbling and thudding to earth. We
brought the planes in again and again, a multinational wave of
firepower. Pilots waited patiently in line for their turn to join
in the chaos, and then they too delivered destruction onto the
Taliban's known positions and concentrations. In no time, fires
had broken out, one A-10 pilot drawling over the air net: 'It's
just nothing but a sea of fire down there.'

In no time, night had become day, the raging blazes casting
long shadows across rubble and ruin. I was so busy calling the
mission that the chaos was lost on me, recognition appearing only in the moments when we would switch from air to

artillery, and there was a pause between fire missions to allow a clearing of the airspace. It was the archetypal vision of hell, but it was a hell of our own creation, and for good reason – we wanted our comrades to get out alive.

And it was working.

From the very first bombs, the enemy's radios had been alive with chatter as they called in casualty reports, or simply exclaimed that a bomb had been a hundred yards short. We used these intercepts to steer our next fire missions, and many of the enemy that our terps had come to recognize over the radio were never heard of again. Others provided a source of amusement for us, men in the ops room laughing callously as we were told that one enemy mortarman was screaming that his beard was on fire. New voices would appear to say that the previous commander was dead or injured, only to be replaced themselves moments later. Through our interpreters we listened to our enemy bleeding and burning in the sea of fire that we had created. Did we feel guilt?

Not an ounce of it.

Our ears ringing and guts shaking from the constant concussion of explosion, we laughed instead. We knew that this would do it. We knew that our wounded would get out. With previous solitary air strikes, we had punched the enemy to the ground. Now, we were kicking him to death as he lay helpless on the floor.

'Get the company stood to,' I told my senior NCOs, though most of the men were already on the walls, watching the frenzied fire and explosions with open-mouthed awe.

The clock reached 0110 – twenty minutes to the arrival of the Chinook and her Apache escort, all of which were already wheels-up from Bastion. It was time to call off the fires.

The town was not silent when we waved off the bombers. Dogs barked frenziedly. Fires crackled and burned. We heard shouting in the distance, and all the time the mounting list of enemy casualty reports transmitted over the radio.

'We fucking smashed them,' Ray spoke, his smile lit up by the flames of the town.

'We're gonna get them out,' Abe agreed.

The whump of the rotors sounded a short while later. This time, there was no tracer arcing up to greet it.

'The Apache pilots just told me they've had to take off their night vision,' Ray shared. 'There's so much glare from the fires, they can't use them.'

The beat of rotors grew louder, and then we saw them, the beast and her guardians silhouetted in the sky by the blaze below them.

'Thirty seconds!'

I could feel the Chinook's presence now as much as hear her, dust whipping across my face. I looked down to the northern wall through my NVG, and saw that the stretcher party were already running out onto the HLS as the huge machine flared its nose and touched down at last. Within seconds the casualties were on. It would only take one RPG . . .

But then she was up! Nose dipping, weaving and lurching her way out and away.

The cheers began moments later.

'Fucking go on!' Ray celebrated beside me, and I felt my heart slip back into my chest – we had gotten them away. Ranger Panapassa Matanisinga would live.

25

A few minutes after the Chinook disappeared into darkness, the Taliban opened fire. It was a weak offensive that reeked of desperation and anger. The enemy had not only let their prey escape but had also been brutally mauled, taking appalling casualties. Buoyed by the success of the casevac, Easy Company beat back the attack within twenty minutes. Then, as Musa Qala burned, I made my way to the ops room to debrief and take stock.

The wounded had been evacuated, but I couldn't call the night a success. In order to get our men to safety, we had been forced to lay waste to the town we had been sent here to protect. It would take years just to rebuild what we had destroyed in air and artillery strikes. I did not regret a single bomb or shell that I had called in – with my men's lives at stake, nothing else mattered to me – but more than ever, I questioned our mission. What were we achieving by being here? We were 'securing' a ghost town civilians were afraid to enter. We were killing the Taliban by the dozen almost daily, and yet still they came.

On our own side, we were soaking up a steady stream of casualties. In less than a fortnight, our Afghan Police colleagues had seen their numbers reduced by 25 per cent. Easy Company had lost two men killed, and a dozen more injured. That number counted only the men who had been evacuated, as there were many young men in Easy who carried light shrapnel wounds, but who refused anything but the most basic care. So long as they were given the OK by the medical staff, I was happy for them to stay and soldier with their comrades – I knew how devastating it would be for me personally to be pulled out of combat for such a wound, and I would not inflict that on my men. It may be hard for a civilian to understand, but even a soldier who has lost both legs will feel guilty for leaving his friends whilst they still face danger. Far from being a relief, to quit the battlefield for a light wound is many a soldier's worst nightmare.

The thought of casualties troubled me most. I had come to Afghanistan – and Musa Qala especially – with the realistic expectation that some men would be injured and others would die. What I had not been prepared for was the scale of our casualties, nor the difficulty in extracting them to safety.

For the thousandth time I ran over our other options for a more suitable HLS. Again, I came back to the same conclusion – if we had to stay where we were, we needed more men so that we could send them out into the town to push back the enemy, and secure the HLS. At the same time I knew it would not be happening. We were lucky to have been able to get a section to replace the one we had lost, let alone increase our strength.

The lack of men puzzled me most. As I've said, there were battalions of troops in the UK. Even with our commitment in Iraq, there were soldiers to call upon. Two or three companies, used in a manoeuvre role, could provide great relief to fixed positions such as ours. I would find out later that such units did trickle into theatre, but invariably they were thrown into the same fixed positions as we were, and quickly pinned down. It was the 'ink spot strategy' that showed an impressive British presence when looked at upon a map of the province – NATO forces in every key town – but the reality was that each of these ink spots was an undermanned band of soldiers fighting for their lives, with those town centres turned into war zones.

But what was there to do? I was a company commander, and I had my orders. Easy Company would hold this position. With nothing else for it, I lay down and sought sleep. I had no doubt that tomorrow would bring more of the enemy. I could only pray that we would see it through without losing more men.

Their pride stung from the previous night, the Taliban attacked in force in the morning. They came from all directions, a blistering rate of fire. During the contact, the Taliban gave us a taste of what we had inflicted on them during the dark hours – six mortars and two 107mm rockets crashed into the compound, sending shrapnel flying as we pressed ourselves down into the ground, nothing but prayers to protect us from the metal that we could hear shrieking and whining through the air.

We survived the barrage with no casualties. It seemed miraculous. I thought that surely our luck would run out at some point that morning, and thought that I had seen it happen when the reserve section – racing across open ground – were bracketed by two RPGs that threw smoke and debris all around them.

The eight men of the reserve section ran on, untouched. After air and artillery strikes rained in, the contact was broken.

Paratroopers are not made to be static. As a concept we were developed – and as individuals we were trained – to be a rapidly deployable force. If the army were a boxer, then we are the sneaky jab, not the labouring right hook. That is not to say that we always assumed we would be on the move. Far from it. Our textbook mission was to swoop in, seize objectives, and then to hold on to them until the heavier infantry units could relieve us. At that point we'd be taken to the rear to be re-equipped before repeating the process. That was how the practice of deploying paratroopers was supposed to work, but of course, we'd all seen *A Bridge Too Far*.

'When are XXX Corps getting here, sir?' my men had taken to asking me, referring to the film's delayed reinforcements that were led by Michael Caine.

'Not long now, boys.'

For the Paras of Easy Company, the battle of Arnhem was deeply imbedded in regimental lore, and so it was easy to be self-critical when grumbling about our own position. Thankfully, we had not parachuted in on top of an SS Panzer division, and so the references to the much-loved movie were made in jest, rather than any serious belief that we were in the shit as deeply as they had been. *Zulu* was another target ripe for parody, and 'Do your tunic up, lad,' became the common quip to any soldier in the company who looked a little slow or lethargic.

I said it now to Signaller Jones. Usually a bright and upbeat soldier, the young man had become withdrawn over the past couple of days, and the reason was obvious enough: the steady rain of mortars was rubbing at the nerves of every one of us. Thankfully, the British army has a simple remedy for such issues.

'Let's get a brew on,' I suggested. 'Tea or coffee?'

Half of the company headquarters team were present in the ops room, and after considerable debate, we eventually came to a consensus of tea. As if waiting for the moment, the Taliban let us know that we were not forgotten.

'Incoming!' the sentries shouted from the fighting positions as they heard the dull thuds of enemy mortar firing.

'Here we go again,' someone griped as we pressed ourselves into the room's corners, anxious to be clear of the open doorway.

Eeerr – BANG!

Dust shook free of the walls. Someone groaned in frustration.

Eeerr – BANG! Eeerr – BANG!

A few seconds of silence passed. Hands moved away from ears. Bodies uncoiled from the floor.

I began a routine that was now well rehearsed, and moved to the doorway. 'Any casualties?' I shouted up to the fighting positions that were within earshot.

'Nah, sir,' an Irish voice came back. 'Rounds landed in the middle of the compound. They didn'ee hit nothing.'

I turned back to my HQ team. 'Sergeant Major, can you do the rounds please; make sure that a bit of shrapnel hasn't found its way into anyone. Jones, check the lines to all sangars please. Find and fix any breaks.'

'Yes, sir.'

'If you need me, I'm going over to our mortars. I'm going to take Corporal Harding and do a strike assessment.'

'Don't forget your pace stick, sir.' Captain Salusbury smiled. It was a line from *Blackadder Goes Forth*, and we were using it to death.

'Quite right. Wouldn't want to face a Jerry machine gun without that!'

Having done my finest impersonation of Hugh Laurie, and after taking a moment to check the fit of my helmet and body armour, I scuttled out towards our own mortar line. Conscious that more shells could come in at any time, I chose the route that offered me the most cover, always thinking ahead as to what depression or doorway I could throw myself into if I heard the thud of a launch, or the sentry's warning.

After collecting the pale-skinned mortar expert Corporal John Harding, we moved to the centre of the compound to examine three scrapes in the earth that showed where the enemy's rounds had impacted. Shrapnel and the flash of the explosion had left dirty, jagged black rings around each of them.

'Good grouping,' Corporal Harding noted, giving praise to his enemy's professionalism. 'That would have been a bad day if it had hit a fighting position.'

He was right, and my stomach twisted into a knot as I thought of such a situation occurring again, but short of abandoning the positions – a non-starter as it would leave us without defence against ground attack, and was precisely what the Taliban wanted – there was nothing further we could do to protect ourselves on the rooftops. I did not want to lose more men to the Taliban bombs, but I had no choice but to order them to hold in position, and to pray to God that we would not take another direct hit like the ones we had taken so far.

'What do you reckon, John?' I asked.

He took out his tape measure. Using this and his eye, he made his assessment of what kind of mortar the enemy had been using, and from which direction the rounds had been fired.

'Eighty-two mil, sir. From the north-west. Probably that same team as the six at dawn.'

He was likely right. I almost told him that there was not much point in the enemy changing positions when we were having no luck locating them, but I caught myself in time. Talking like that in front of the blokes would not do.

Harding and I split up there. As I moved back to the ops room, the elusive Taliban mortar teams were foremost in my mind. I almost found myself wishing that the enemy would switch tactics, and would come at us in their massed attacks as they had done when we first occupied the base. Deadly as those attacks could be, at least they offered the chance of fighting back. Having to sit patiently and wait for the next inevitable bombardment was mentally pushing all of my men towards snapping point. It was pushing *me* towards snapping point, which was something I dreaded happening in front of my men.

A day earlier I had sent a runner to repair a broken line and had seen the man standing in cover, head in hands, in that moment unable to make himself move out of safety.

'Come on,' I told him. 'I'll give you a hand.'

Every man amongst us will have fought and overcome his own battle with fear.

Merciless piss-taking and dark humour, as ever, were the soldier's antidote to these problems, but I knew that I'd be kidding myself if I thought that there would be no long-term repercussions from this kind of siege, which was as much a psychological attack as it was a physical one. I thought back to Bosnia and Kosovo and how it must have felt to have been a civilian under the relentless Serb bombardments. At least my helmet and body armour gave me the illusion of safety. My rifle the illusion that I could fight back.

Bloody hell, Adam, snap out of it.

I couldn't afford to be melancholy. Even thinking about *not* thinking about the mortars was a win for Terry, pulling me away from other tasks that I should be contemplating, the endless list of 'what ifs' and 'what do we do whens?'

I needed to be on the ball for my blokes, and so I stopped in the shelter of a doorway, and lit a cigarette. A couple of the Afghan Police walked by, and smiled hello. One of them wore thick make-up and stank of cheap perfume – the designated rent boy. Their culture was so very different from our own, particularly the British army's, where embodying masculinity and a sense of fearlessness was always keenly in our mind. With such thoughts of 'cracking on' and keeping a stiff upper lip I returned to the ops room.

Sergeant Major Scrivener arrived at the same moment as I did.

'The blokes are good, sir.'

'How about the lines, Jones?' I asked the signaller. 'All good?'

'All good, sir,' he told me. 'I've got a brew on.'

Jones moved to the fire outside the building, where there was a battered kettle perched atop the flames.

I had barely begun to debrief the sergeant major on the impact assessment when a roar of anger echoed across the compounds.

'You fucking cunts! You jack fucking cunts!'

I put my head out of the doorway.

Signaller Jones stood by the fire. The kettle was in his hand. From the way that he was waving it around his head, it was clearly empty.

'Jonesy, what's wrong?'

'Fuck this company, sir! Fuck this company, the bunch of fucking thieves!'

'Jonesy, calm down.'

'No, sir! No! They used the water and they never bothered filling it back up! No, sir! I'm fucking done with them, sir. Fuck them! I'll throw this over the wall and then no one can brew, thanks to that *jack bastard*!' Jones finished, screaming the last two words at the top of his lungs.

Helmeted heads had begun to pop out of doorways and over sandbags.

'Keep the noise down, yeah?' one of the Irish asked, smiling, enjoying the meltdown. 'I'm tryin' a enjoy my cup of tea in here.'

'Fuck you!'

'Hey, Jonesy,' a soldier on the rooftop asked. 'Did you say the kettle's out of water? I couldn't a hear you.'

'Even Terry's asking what's wrong,' a private called down from the fighting positions, and sure enough, Taliban voices were coming from the town. They must have been under the impression that this was another round of insult exchanging with the sangars.

It took another couple of minutes of good-natured piss-taking before Jones finally saw the ridiculousness of his explosion and stood down.

'Sorry, sir,' he apologized to me as he finally passed around the completed brew.

'It's all right, Jonesy.'

We were all on edge.

The enemy appeared again in the afternoon, but they made no effort to push forward. Instead, they seemed content just to sit back and to pour fire at us from mouseholes and windows. The attack was not much more than a nuisance, and we beat it back with strafing and rocket runs from RAF Harriers.

It had been a good day. Men were still elated that we had gotten Matanisinga away to safety – I had checked in on his progress via the satphone that morning and he was stable in post-surgery. Also, having seen the destructive firepower rained down onto the town the night before, Easy Company knew that they would not be abandoned should they become the injured party. Such knowledge is crucial for a soldier's morale and fighting spirit. On top of it all, we had come through mortar and RPG strikes that day without a single injury.

We should have been wary of such good fortune.

The news came at 1800 hours, when I turned on the radio and offered my report to Battalion HQ. 'Call Zero via secured satphone. Out.'

Thoughts of Matanisinga pushed into my mind as I called the battalion's ops room on our satellite phone.

'I'm sorry, Adam, but Lance Corporal Muirhead died in hospital today.'

'Muirhead? You mean Matanisinga?' I asked, perplexed. It had been days since Paul Muirhead was casevaced.

'Muirhead. He had injuries that were not survivable. I'm sorry, Adam.'

My shoulders slumped. I let out a breath. I knew there was more, and I asked for it.

'Yesterday was a bad day,' the ops officer told me candidly. 'As well as your incident, and the one in Sangin, we had a patrol walk into a minefield in Kajaki. One dead, several injured. Yesterday, the battlegroup lost three men, and had eighteen wounded. Three of those have lost limbs. It was a fucking awful day, Adam.'

I swore. Then, I asked for the names of the men. They would be comrades and friends of those under my command. With near disbelief, I wrote out the long list of casualties. Beside three of the names, I marked KIA.

'Everything all right, sir?' Sergeant Major Scrivener asked me, seeing the loss etched on my face.

I showed him the list. Then I told him that Lance Corporal Muirhead, beloved of Easy Company, would not be waiting for us when we got home.

News of the casualties was still spreading when two 107mm rockets came hurtling in from the north like freight trains, their explosions tearing huge gouts in the earth.

'Sir!' one of my men called me. 'The Alamo saw the firing point!'

I shouted for my JTAC: 'Ray! Abe!' Moments later, we were sprinting for the Alamo.

The keen-eyed sentry there showed us where the two rockets had shot into the sky. Within moments, my JTAC had 7 Para's guns in the desert booming. Dirt was kicked up into the air, and then –

BANG!

An enormous explosion that was followed instantly by further fireballs, some cartwheeling like fireworks.

'We hit their supply,' Ray said.

It was a big win for us, but no one was smiling. We had lost too much this day, and not even the destruction of the rockets that tormented us could offer solace.

The dusk was coming, and so it was time to stand to, and fully man the walls. I picked up my rifle and went up onto the rooftop, careful to keep my profile low to avoid giving Terry a silhouette against the sunset.

I looked out across the town. The ghost town.

There was no movement. No life. And yet I knew that they were all around us in their hundreds. They were waiting for their moment. The moment when we would succumb to their mortars, crawl inside our buildings, and allow them to sneak up to our positions, unseen and unopposed.

Across the compound I could see my men crouched behind

the sandbags and low mud-brick walls. The mortars had claimed their friends and shaken their nerves, but my men were steady.

Later that evening the Taliban prodded us again with RPGs. A mournful Easy Company unleashed fury on this provocation, and the contact died before it had begun.

I remained on the rooftop after ordering my men to stand down. Despite the absolute brutality of our air strikes the night before, the Taliban had still come again today, in force and determined. Radio intercepts also confirmed that they had received more ammunition and fighters. Despite all their losses, they were still coming.

When would it end?

26

The next morning was one of surprises. The first was the absence of any dawn attack – aside from intercepted radio messages regarding their wounded, there was no sign of our enemy.

The second surprise was delivered by our own side – we were to begin preparations to move.

The rumour mill is a powerful force in the army, and within moments it had gone into overdrive. Aside from the words 'be prepared to move', and a time frame of seven to ten days, we had no other information, and so into that void we poured our ideas, best guesses, and wild flights of fancy. We wondered if we would be rotated or simply relieved. Could the Marines be coming out to theatre early? Maybe it was the theatre reserve battlegroup, but weren't they already up in Now Zad? Could it be the Danes? Were they coming back? Surely they wouldn't return to a situation even hotter than the one that they'd left behind.

Speculation was rife, and answers free. In an attempt to be productive, my headquarters team began to make lists of supplies that we would recommend any unit brought with them during a handover, as surely the operation would require a large logistics move – the sneaky insertion that we had undertaken would not fly now that ammunition stores were dwindling.

Taking to maps and aerial photos, we marked out compounds that we thought would make better patrol bases. If the headshed were insistent on us holding on to the district centre, we came up with plans to occupy key compounds that could become platoon houses, enabling at least a degree of mutual support and providing the essential element of protection for the currently exposed and overlooked HLS.

The Taliban did not leave us alone during the day, and attacked three times with small arms and mortars, but their fire did little to distract our minds from the suggestion that soon – very soon – we could be leaving this place.

The next morning it was business as usual. The enemy attacked us at dawn and, with small arms and air strikes, we beat them back. Mid-morning, a Taliban mortar launch was identified and pounded by the guns of our own artillery – our own mortars were so low on ammunition that they were being held back for a moment when it looked as if we could be overrun. At lunchtime, a voice on the ICOM commanded his men to 'hurry up and start firing'. Soon after, RPGs and small-arms fire began to smack into our fighting position. A 107mm rocket hurtled in and chewed a huge hole on the Alamo's rooftop, but the angle of the blast was deflected from the men fighting there – had it been a metre higher, it would have been a butcher's yard. The enemy closed the day by hitting us with heavy machine-gun fire that punched tennis ball-sized holes into the walls. Following that, we heard over the ICOM that yet more of their commanders were dead. For the families of those 'martyrs', it would be a momentous day. For us, it was just one more amongst many.

Freddie called me over in the ops room. He had the mischievous look on his face that he always got when he had some juicy intelligence.

'Remember that professional they were bringing in a few days ago?' he asked me, and I nodded. 'Turns out he's an armourer. He's come to fix their weapons.'

'That's not as exciting as a hitman,' I complained.

It had been a good day for Freddie, and our LEWT team. Through radio intercepts, they had worked out the position of a particularly vocal Taliban commander. That man was absent from their airwaves now – his constant chatter had given away his position, and Ray and Abe had called artillery down into his big mouth. 'Loose lips sink ships.' Terry obviously hadn't seen those posters.

The ICOM had also gifted us the information that there were more fighters due into town the next day, and that they were seasoned professionals. Perhaps it was their reconnaissance that we saw driving wildly in the streets, circling our position. It was not the smartest of tactics, and a pair of hungry A-10s pounced to turn the pickups into scrap metal.

The enemy probably felt obliged to shoot at us that evening, but it was a tired effort at the end of a quiet day – at least, by the standards we'd become used to. To Easy Company, now even the strafing run of an A-10 was barely worth lifting your head to watch.

I wondered about the new fighters, and if they would be a cut above the enemy that we had been killing each day. I wondered too at how quiet it had been. Tomorrow would be the fifth anniversary of 9/11. If they were planning on making a show, then maybe tomorrow would be it.

The enemy did attack at dawn – RPGs zoomed overhead, and tracers sparked and ricocheted – but compared to the close-in frays of previous days, at no time did I feel that we were in danger of collapse. Easy Company had become as adept at beating back Taliban fighters as a goalkeeper is used to parrying away footballs. But if we had become blasé about combat, such an attitude died later that morning, when a circling jet announced a disturbing discovery. There was a gathering of men at the edge of town.

Three to five hundred of them.

Such news sent a shockwave through the ops room. We knew the enemy were expecting reinforcements, but five hundred? Ray was talking to the pilot, ready to call down artillery fire the moment we could confirm the gathering as hostile, but the pilot could see no weaponry or patterns that would suggest the mass of men were Taliban.

'Five hundred?' the sergeant major remarked to me dryly. 'Tomorrow could be a little tasty, sir.'

'Just a little,' I agreed. 'How are we on ammo?'

'I've dished the last of it out, sir. If we do have five hundred of them to kill, we'll be doing the last couple with bayonets.'

I didn't doubt that Scrivs could kill a dozen of them himself with a bayonet, but the fact that we had distributed the last of our ammunition was sobering. If these men were the enemy, and if they did press in a mass attack, then it truly would be down to the last bullet.

'Can the pilot see any weapons?' I pressed Ray, but the JTAC shook his head. Without positive ID, there was no way we could call down a strike on the gathering.

There was nothing we could do but wait. We received a radio intercept that a new commander had arrived with men, but it gave no clue as to their location. The only other information the enemy handed us was that their foreign fighters were allowed to go home for Ramadan, and that they'd transit via Gereshk. Again, we offered this intel up the chain of command, only to be told again that we were mistaken, and that we were fighting disgruntled opium farmers.

It was a tense day. Nerves on edge, I almost leapt from my skin as two mortar rounds crashed into the compound in the early evening. The gathering at the edge of the town finally broke, with no positive identification made. If they were the Taliban, I expected that we'd find out in the morning. I took a moment to myself to consider what that would mean.

The last of the ammunition had been distributed. Despite our requests for more, the battlegroup did not have the resources to bring it in by convoy, whilst the danger of flying in Chinooks made that method of resupply too risky. And so, we found ourselves down to a single fire mission for the mortars and enough bullets for one or two firefights. There were five hundred of the enemy, and eighty men under my own command. The statistics weren't great on paper, but they didn't take into account that my small number of British soldiers were amongst the best trained infantry in the world, and that they would fight like dogs. Indeed, more savagely than that, because we knew that surrender was not an option. We would not be taken prisoner, and that night, like every other man in the company, I took stock of my ammunition, and marked out my last magazine. It was so I would know when the time had come, when I was on my last few rounds, and I would make sure I died upright and fighting. Better that than the alternative, which was far worse than death. With such thoughts in mind, I recalled Rudyard Kipling's poem 'The Young British Soldier', and in particular, its final verse:

> *When you're wounded and left on Afghanistan's plains,*
> *And the women come out to cut up what remains,*
> *Jest roll to your rifle and blow out your brains*
> *An' go to your Gawd like a soldier.*

Not much had changed in Afghanistan in the last couple of hundred years. Not much had changed in war, either. Tomorrow, our enemy would come and try to kill us, and it was my job – my duty – to see that it was they who died instead.

Against all odds that night, I slept soundly. Surrounded by the enemy, with my back to the wall, and with no way out, I was exactly where a paratrooper wanted to be.

27

It was in the dead of night when the first movement was spotted, and a sentry let rip on a GPMG at Taliban fighters he had seen manoeuvring forward in a rat run. I was in the ops room, and scrambled to the rooftop in time to see red tracer from the Outpost zip and ricochet in the streets below it.

'Watch and shoot!' an NCO called. Low on ammunition as we were, we could not afford to fire at ghosts.

No fire was returned our way – the enemy had fled, or died.

'Stand down,' I ordered, feeling for the men who had been roused by shouts and by boots – there was no gentle way to wake a man when the enemy were closing in.

I returned to the ops room. I had snatched a half-hour of sleep, and I knew in my gut that it was all I would get that night. It wasn't something that fazed me, as I felt calmly in tune. Nothing sharpens the mind quite as much as the thought that there are five hundred men in the darkness who want to kill you, and that the ammunition you have to stop that happening is down to the final reserve.

'What are you smiling at, boss?' Sergeant Major Scrivener asked me.

'Nothing. Backgammon?'

We played through the early hours, breaking for the occasional brew or radio intercept from the Taliban – one made mention of a resupply of three hundred mortar rounds, and gifted us the exact grid reference. We passed it up the chain, and an aircraft was tasked with observing the space.

'Three hundred rounds?' the sergeant major mused dryly.

I laughed. 'That's a bad day for someone.'

We didn't need to point out that the bad day could well be

ours. Nor did we talk about how the long wait for battle was the worst. How those early hours dragged like days, and how we knew with dreadful certainty that the morning would see our men placed in harm's way once more. The reports on the gathering of five hundred Afghans was the elephant in the room – I would back my troops man to man against any Taliban fighter – even a handful of them – but against a force of five hundred there was the very real chance we would simply be overwhelmed by sheer weight of numbers. And then there was the ammunition . . .

Dawn crawled towards us, infiltrating our minds and robbing us of the little sleep that was on offer. Men stirred earlier than usual, gathering about protected flames to brew up and light cigarettes. A steady rumble of farts and tired insults announced the reveille of Easy Company's warriors.

Despite knowing what the day promised, the men were at ease, their early rising down to a desire to 'crack on and get the job done' rather than to any trepidation. Of course, they knew in their heads what could happen, but there had been no easy day in Musa Qala, and death was only ever a call of 'Contact!' away. These were as professional an infantry as could be found on the planet. Men who had trained rigorously for war, and who had then continued their education in a daily classroom of small arms, RPGs, mortars, and air strikes. There was not a man amongst us who could not be a salt or sweat, and I allowed a brief moment of pity for the fresh Taliban troops who would come against such competition. The typical British infantry soldier of today is young, short, and skinny, and was raised by a PlayStation as much as by any parent, but he is a fucking savage when it comes to war. I had no fear that morning. Worry for the safety of the men under my command, but no fear.

'Let's get into position,' I spoke aloud to the men in the ops room. 'Stand to.'

Every man was ready for the order. There was no hesitation

as they gulped down the remainder of their brews, stumped out cigarettes, and pulled their battered helmets onto their heads. Gaunt and bearded, they made their way to walls and rooftops, there to meet their enemy.

First there was a sliver of silver on the eastern horizon. Then, a hungry grey light began to eat away at the darkness, revealing the remains of compounds and shops. As the light grew, individual pieces of rubble could be seen in the streets, some walls caved inwards, homes and shops appearing as abandoned building sites. The sun began to rise, revealing loping hounds and pattering birds, but amongst the wreckage of what had been a bustling market town, something was missing.

'Where the fuck are they?' Ray whispered beside me.

There was no sign of the enemy. Not a shot fired. Not a dashing shape between buildings. The orange disc of the sun continued its shimmering rise into the sky, and such had been our position that I had almost come to associate that natural marvel with the crash of RPGs, and the clatter of PKs.

But there was nothing. Only dogs. Only birds. Only silence.

I raised myself to one knee, and held the pose for a brief moment – no one fired at me. Still, it would not do to be an idiot, and so I lowered myself back to the rooftop, and then crawled to a new position before peeking back out over the ghost town.

This was not expected.

Looking around, I could see the tension in my men as they fidgeted behind rifles and guns. They had pumped themselves up for the mother of all dawn contacts, and instead their sights were empty, and their adrenaline seeping.

It could all be a ruse. I kept the company stood to.

'What's happening on the ICOM?' I asked via radio to the LEWT team in the ops room.

'Nothing, boss. It's dead. Not a peep.'

The evidence of my eyes and ears told me that there weren't

a mass of enemy waiting to attack us – my gut told me that I would *feel* the presence of so many people within a hundred metres – but my head knew what had taken place the day before, and there must have been a reason for such a gathering, and the steady increase of resupplies. I couldn't believe that the enemy would begin its big offensive in the middle of the day, when we could see them moving into position, and rain down shells onto their heads. It just didn't feel right. Maybe today would not be the day, and the mass attack would fall tomorrow, or towards dusk.

Eventually, when the town was bathed in fierce sunlight, I realized that I could not keep my men as a coiled spring forever.

'Stand down,' I ordered, and as my soldiers crouched and crawled their way from the exposed rooftops, I looked out over the devastated town, wishing that I had the answer to just one question: Where the hell were they?

That day, it was as if my Omega watch had given up, the minute hand seeming to crawl around the face at an impossibly slow speed. There was a palpable tension in the air, but with the ammunition distributed, and sentries posted, there was little to do about it but smoke, brew up, complain about the flies, and play shithead.

'You're a fucking shithead!' Ray laughed in my face, throwing the cards down.

'Best of three, you fucker,' I challenged, and so the day went by, minute after minute, card by card. All the time we wondered what were five hundred enemy fighters doing in town if not to fight us?

Eventually, 1800 hours came around, and with it our scheduled radio report. Having turned on the radio and checked the net, the signaller passed me the handset, and I told Zero that we were ready to send the daily report. Instead of taking it, they again asked me to call into Zero via the satphone. After a minute of searching for a signal, it connected.

'Adam?'

'Hi, sir. What can I do for you?' I asked.

'Something quite out of the ordinary, actually. I'm not really sure how to tell you this, Adam, but tomorrow you need to leave the district centre, and meet with the Taliban to coordinate a ceasefire.'

I burst into laughter, wondering which of my friends in the headshed was impersonating Colonel Tootal.

'Nice try, you wanker.'

I hung up the phone, and returned to the card table.

'What's so funny?' Ray asked.

I was just about to tell him when the duty signaller called over.

'Boss, the CO is on the phone. He wants to know why you hung up on him.'

The men around me began to laugh, but any trace of humour had dropped from me now. If it really was him . . .

'Sir?' I asked, taking the phone.

'I can see why you would think it's a wind-up, Adam.' Tootal spoke stoically, and I had no doubt then that this was truly my CO's voice. 'But it's not. Tomorrow, I need you to leave the district centre. I need you to walk out, alone, and meet the Taliban.'

28

In all of the eventualities of our situation that I had played out in my mind, talking to the Taliban had never been one of them.

As Colonel Tootal's words soaked in, the first thought that crossed my mind was that I could be the next Westerner to feature in one of the Taliban's infamous YouTube videos, my head hacked from my shoulders and my death posted on social media. The Taliban were not a conventional force like we were. They did not respect any code such as the Geneva Convention, and had led the world in the use of media and torture as a weapon of war.

I tried to push such images from my mind, and concentrate on what the order actually meant – talking to the enemy was unheard of, not only here, but in any conflict that I could think of. Of course, the British army took prisoners, but a local ceasefire? How many years had it taken the British government and Sinn Féin to hammer out the Good Friday Agreement, I thought. But even that was an inaccurate comparison – for me to talk to the Taliban was akin to an officer in Armagh talking to the local IRA commander. It was simply unthinkable.

And yet it was the reality. Why?

Colonel Tootal had given me some clue after he had dropped the initial bombshell – the people of Musa Qala and its surrounding environs had simply had enough. Their vibrant town had been reduced to a two-way shooting range that was a death sentence for civilians to enter, and so a gathering of tribal leaders and elders had approached the British and Taliban with one simple message – stop destroying our town, and let us live our lives. Neither side could ignore the plea – the Taliban wanted control of a population, not a ghost town.

The same was true of our own mission – driving people from their homes was not the same as providing security for them.

The huge gathering of five hundred finally made sense. It could only have been a shura between tribes, villages, and the Taliban leadership – I could assume their involvement, for without their consent, there could be no talks, let alone a working ceasefire.

I called my company headshed to me, and explained to them that the mass concentration were not all enemy fighters.

'How do we know this, boss?' Freddie asked, his jaw dropping as I gave him my answer.

'A ceasefire?' Scrivs growled, the words unpalatable to the senior soldier.

'That's right,' I went on. 'Tomorrow at 1000 hours, they'll come to us, and I'm to go out and meet with them, and develop a cessation to the fighting.'

'What the fuck?' Freddie swore. 'I can't believe my ears. You can't go out, boss. That's fucking bollocks.'

'It's fine,' I told him, masking over every fear and doubt that I had. 'They want to talk. They wouldn't be here if they didn't.'

'Or maybe they just want to grab you as a hostage.'

'Maybe.' I smiled.

'This is fucking bollocks,' Freddie growled again.

'I'm going to need Naz,' I told my HQ group, referring to the interpreter. 'Scrivs, the meeting will be along the street from the main gate. Can you arrange gun teams and snipers up on the western wall?'

'Course, sir.'

I looked at the leadership of my company. The news had left them more shell-shocked than any mortar attack.

'All right, then,' I said, hoping that I appeared confident, and was hiding my true emotions. 'I know this is all a little out of the blue, but let's make it work. I don't want to talk to the Taliban any more than anyone else does, but let's look at the positive side here – a ceasefire means no more of our boys go out on casevacs. We came too close on that last one. This is the chance to avoid any more deaths in the company.'

Their grudging nods showed me that those words got through. Unpalatable as the idea of talking to the Taliban was, no one wanted to see more body bags loaded onto Chinooks – Chinooks that had been moments away from being shot out of the sky.

'We'll make this work,' I promised my men.

At 2120, Staff Wornham approached me with a radio intercept of an enemy transmission: 'Ceasefire now in place.'

The Taliban had put down their weapons.

Naz was one of our three interpreters, in his twenties, intelligent, and steady. He was also from the north of the country – with looks more Mongolian than the Pashtuns of Helmand – and was an Hazari. Raheem, our second interpreter, was as steady as Naz, but I worried that the Taliban would be more likely to be hostile to a fellow Pashtun who was fighting for the other side. For this reason, I took Naz aside and briefed him on what was to occur in the morning.

'And you want me to come with you?' he guessed, unflinching.

'I do.'

'OK. Can I have a gun?'

It was absolutely against the rules to arm a civilian, and absolutely the right thing to do. I gave him a 9mm pistol. He took it with the nonchalance of a man who has been raised amongst weapons since childhood.

'Here's what we're going to do . . .'

We talked for a long time. I had no doubt that the meeting would be tense, and if it did not descend immediately into chaos, then I wanted it to flow freely. To that end, I briefed Naz on exactly how I wanted our interactions to go.

'You'll stand on my shoulder. I'll look the person I'm speaking to in the eye, and make regular pauses for you to translate.

I trust you to know what I'm saying when it comes to tone and meaning, and to put that across. When you translate what they're saying to me, give me as much extra information as you can. How are they saying it? Is there something in their manner that we need to be aware of? Any bit of information you see, pass it on to me during the translation.'

Naz nodded slowly at my words. I had no doubt that, after living in each other's pockets for three weeks, he knew me well enough to carry over the tone of my words into Pashtun, even if there was no direct translation.

'The tribal elders are going to be there,' I told him. 'They're facilitating the meeting, and they're the people I want to greet first.'

From shuras in Sangin, and experience meeting tribal chiefs in Africa, I had some idea of how the decorum of these gatherings should be handled, but now Naz briefed me in detail on the customs, ensuring that I would pay the proper respect to the proper people. With tensions high, we could not risk an unintended slight.

'Treat them like you would an uncle or a favourite cousin,' Naz insisted. 'Be respectful, but be friendly and open. They'll like that. They probably have never talked to a man from England before.'

'And how should I greet them? Handshake?'

'Yes. A good handshake.'

I practised with Naz. Nothing could be left to chance.

'No kissing, then?' I asked.

We laughed a little too hard at the bad joke. It was impossible to forget what we were preparing for.

'If it all goes bad,' I told the young Afghan, 'it's down to you and me. Pull your pistol, put down any Taliban that are close enough to grab us, and then sprint to the main gate.'

'OK.' He smiled, knowing as well as I did that if anything went wrong, we would never make it back to camp.

My rehearsals with Naz over, I placed my hand on the man's shoulder.

'Get some sleep. It'll be fine,' I assured him.

'Inshallah.' He smiled.

If Allah wills it.

I joined my team in the ops room.

'Let's work up as much as we can on the Taliban commanders,' I told them. 'See if we can start putting names to faces and so on, once we get a look at them tomorrow.'

A half-dozen patient smiles were raised at my optimism – *Crazy boss. He really thinks he's going to live through this.*

We set to work, but the usual banter and piss-taking of the ops room was missing. Instead, the men of Easy Company seemed stunned. Sucker-punched.

I could see that Freddie was desperate to speak.

'What's on your mind?' I asked him.

'Well, for one, obviously, I don't like the idea of you going out alone, boss,' he explained. 'And the other thing is . . . well . . . a ceasefire? Feels a bit like getting on the jack wagon, doesn't it?'

The jack wagon was the truck that followed any route marches, and picked up any soldiers who fell behind or were forced to drop out. In the army, it was synonymous with failure and dishonour. A good soldier would rather tab until he died on his feet than be put onto the jack wagon.

'I know where you're coming from, Freddie, but this isn't jacking. We've fought them to a standstill, and now we can help set the terms for the people here to get back to their lives.'

I delivered the words with outward sincerity. Did I believe them? It didn't matter. We were soldiers, and our mission had been switched from killing the enemy, to talking to them. It was my duty to see that this was carried out as professionally and to the utmost of our ability as any other task. I may not have liked the taste of it, but I reminded myself that we were first and foremost in this town for the people of Musa Qala, and not for ourselves.

'I think it's going to go well,' I said.

But I didn't think it was going to go well. I didn't think it was going to go well at all. I thought that I was going to walk out of the gate, be grabbed by the Taliban, and then be killed inch by agonizing inch. But I couldn't let my men know that. Instead, I found myself a quiet space in the headquarters building. Alone, I allowed myself to fully accept the danger of the situation I was about to put myself in. The danger, and the madness. What kind of idiocy was it to walk into a gathering of men who for weeks had been trying to kill my soldiers – and on some days, succeeding? For my part, I had overseen the death of hundreds of the enemy. Some had died from my own fire. I remembered hearing what the mujahideen had done to Russian prisoners, and in that moment I was terrified that my lifespan now certainly could be measured in single hours. What would my family say? What would the papers say – *Idiot Para walks out to meet the Taliban for tea and gets his head hacked off*? It was absolute madness, I told myself, and I felt my legs shaking with nerves. For a moment, I almost felt as if they'd give underneath me.

My God, I have a wife and two kids, and I'm never going to see them again. I'm never going to see them because I'm being sent on a fool's errand. A suicide mission. I always knew that I could die in Afghanistan, but I always thought that it would be in combat, and with my rifle in hand, like a Viking with his sword, not offering myself up to the enemy to be butchered in cold blood. Adam, what the fuck have you gotten yourself into? You wanted a challenge from the army? Well, here's one for you. Find your way out of this one.

I'm not sure how long my fatalistic funk lasted. Maybe five minutes, maybe ten, but then it was gone, replaced by a calm acceptance – in the morning I would be dead, but if I was going to go, I'd go out like a Para.

With no way to change my fate, I lay down on the floor and tried to sleep.

29

I slept fitfully, and was almost relieved by the time stand to arrived, and I had something to occupy my mind. Dawn came and went with no sign of the enemy, and so there was nothing to do but wait for 1000 hours. Certain that I would be dead a few minutes after that time, I made an effort to pack my kit as neatly as possible, placing on top the items that could be distributed amongst the men. Then I cleaned my rifle again so that it was immaculate, and laid my shemagh over the top of it. That rifle had been an extension of my body for weeks, and to move about the compound without it felt as though I'd lost a limb. I knew that, walking into the town, I would feel not only naked, but as though I had bullseyes tattooed onto every inch of my skin.

'Morning, boss,' Ray greeted me. 'How you feeling?'

'Like you should get the brews on,' I answered him. 'Game of shithead?'

What better way to spend the final hours of your life?

Ray won the first game. 'You're a shithead,' he mumbled. Certain that I was a condemned man, he was holding back on his usual glee at being able to insult his boss.

I looked at my watch – 0930. Time to get ready.

I found Naz with a gaggle of ANP men. I didn't need his help in translating their body language. These men had spent a lifetime fighting the Taliban. The only time they wished to talk to them was as they were tying a rope around their necks. The night before I had tried to impress upon the ANP's officers that a ceasefire was a good thing, but my words had fallen on deaf ears – they had travelled from their homes in the north to kill Taliban, and nothing less. When I told them that the talks would go well, they looked at me as one would do a child that believes in Father Christmas – *Of course they will, Adam Khan. Of course you'll be fine.*

'How are you feeling, Naz?' I asked the man who would be key in what was to come.

'Good, boss. I'm honoured to do this.'

'You're a good man. Happy with the pistol?'

'Sergeant Major has shown me. No problem.'

'OK, then. Let's go and wait by the gate.'

We walked to the main gate, which was an eerie feeling in itself when previously all movement in the open parts of the compound had been at a sprint. I considered that the enemy could still snipe at us now, but decided that if they were planning treachery, then better I discover it at distance rather than within a few metres of them.

Coming to the western side of the camp, I saw the wall there thick with my men, under the command of Sergeant Major Scrivener. Sentries were still posted in every corner of the compound, giving us all-round defence, but Scrivs had repositioned a few of the gimpys so that they could now shoot straight down the road to where the meeting would be. My 3 Para snipers were also there, already looking through their sights for danger.

'Crowd's beginning to build up, sir,' Scrivs called down to me. 'About a hundred of them. Looks like a mix of civvies and Taliban. Don't see any weapons. None of them are wearing webbing, or anything like that.'

'Thanks, Sergeant Major.'

I looked at my watch. Ten minutes to go – bollocks. I'd come out too early, and now I'd have to stand here in public as the nerves crawled inside my stomach and my brain, telling me to turn round. Telling me that this was idiocy, and that I shouldn't throw my life away so carelessly. I've got two kids and a beautiful wife to live for, for fuck's sake. What am I doing?

I turned to Naz. Doubtless the same thoughts were going

on in his own mind. Like him, I was certain that I would meet my maker when I did pass, and there was at least a comfort in that, but the thought of never seeing my family again – not seeing my children grow up – was terrifying.

'*Starray mashay.*' I spoke the Pashtun phrase aloud, as much to myself as to Naz – Be encouraged. Be a man.

A four-man fire team from the reserve moved in and began to pull away at the motley collection of bedframes and scrap that formed our front gate. I joined them, clearing a path to my own fate.

'Sir, no offence, sir,' one of the young Rangers said, 'but this is fucking bollocks, sir. You can't trust them, sir. You shouldn't go.'

'He's fucking right, boss,' his NCO chimed in. 'Chin this off. We don't want you going out. We don't want to talk to them.'

The young men were the voice of almost every single member of Easy Company. There was not a man on the walls who wanted to reach an accord with the Taliban – despite our predicament, Easy felt as though it was winning the battle. It was my task to explain to my soldiers that, though that was true, we risked losing the war, and the people of Musa Qala.

'We have to do it for the people of this town,' I told the men on the gate. 'We came here for them. If this helps them get back to a normal life, then this is what we have to do.'

'I think Captain Salusbury would make a better OC anyway,' one of my men joked darkly.

I laughed. Such humour was exactly what I needed to get me out of the gate. 'I'm sure he will, you fuckers.'

I glanced at my watch: 0958.

A last look about my person. I wanted to step forth like a professional soldier, and now I checked myself over, ensuring that not a single pocket was undone, that the pistol on my thigh was devoid of dust, that my sleeves were rolled to the elbow neatly, and that my helmet sat snug and level.

'How do I look?' I asked the four young soldiers at the gate.

'Good, sir,' they mumbled, and I could see in their eyes that they were taking their final mental picture of me. The final chapter to their OC's story that they would pass on over pints to the other men of their battalion.

'Ready, Naz?'

'Ready.'

I took a steadying breath, and allowed myself a final moment to think about my family.

'Good luck, boss,' my soldiers told me.

I walked by them with a smile, and squeezed out of the gate, seeing for the first time the mass of men ahead of me.

I had been a guardsman before I had been a paratrooper, and I put that to use now, striding towards the gathering with perfect posture, confidence in my every step. I wanted the elders and the enemy to see a professional soldier who was full of swagger, as if I viewed the entire affair as something wholly normal, not a skulking conscript who had been beaten out of his hiding place and who was seeking clemency.

Despite my outward appearance, I had never felt more scared. No number of bullets, RPGs, mortars, or rockets, could have generated the terror I felt as I left the womb of the district centre alone but for Naz. From the number of people at the gathering, one thing was immediately clear – if I were grabbed, there would be no way to escape. In such a situation, the men on the western wall had their orders – let rip. Do not let us be taken alive.

Memories flashed into my mind of my time with the Canadian soldiers. They had told me how one of their officers had sat down to talk at a peaceful shura, only to have an axe buried in his head. It was an unsettling reminder to me that, even if the Taliban did want to talk, it would only take one man to kill me.

This really is going to be my legacy, I suddenly thought to myself. *My legacy, and Naz's. We're going to be remembered as those two clowns who thought they could saunter out of the gates, and talk to the Taliban.* Fuck. Is this what it felt like to be shot at dawn?

'Taliban are on the left,' Naz whispered as we walked.

There was no mistaking the enemy. Their garments were universally dark, their faces young and arrogant. The civilians were distinguishable by the lighter colour of their cloth, and their more open demeanour. Afghan society is very structured and hierarchical, and by the way that some men showed deference to others, it was easy for me to pick out their tribal leaders. I was ten metres from them now. Close enough to engage in eye contact. There was no backing down. As I walked, I removed my helmet, a deliberately staged act to show that I was unafraid.

I made a beeline straight for the eldest.

'That's him,' Naz confirmed. 'Greet him first.'

'As-salaam alaikum,' I greeted the elder tribesman, shaking his hand firmly as I smiled.

The elder responded with his own greeting and warm smile, Naz translating that his name was Haji Ramatoulah. In essence, he was the mayor of Musa Qala, and more. He in turn introduced me to the elders on his shoulders, detailing at length which villages they were heads of, pointing into the distance and using our own forces as waypoints. 'This is such and such, and his village is by the crossroads where you have your big guns. This is such and such, and his village is over here, where you have your men in the tanks.'

So it went on, and with each introduction, I felt my trepidation slip away. I had survived the first twenty seconds, which I had always foreseen would be the most dangerous, and I could not smell or see an ounce of agitation in the men around me – they had come to do business. They were not about to explode into violence.

'They're very happy this is happening,' Naz confirmed,

tagging it onto his translations. 'He's treating you very well. He asks about your beard, and if you are Muslim?'

I explained that I was not.

'Well, all the same, it is a very fine beard,' Naz translated in my ear. 'Now, he wants to introduce you to the Taliban.'

The Taliban. There were some thirty or more of them in a group, but ahead of this gathering stood a knot of four men, their leaders. They were hard-looking bastards to a man, gaunt-faced and sunbaked, with thick black beards beneath faces of stone. To see them so close and unarmed was more bizarre than frightening. A reminder that I was in totally uncharted waters.

Haji Ramatoulah made the introductions, finishing with the man who, as was clear from his bearing, was the enemy's commander. His name was Mullah Ghulam Sadiq, and as Naz translated the introduction, he also gave me the careful reminder of a radio message we had intercepted the week before – Sadiq's son had been killed in the fighting.

Sadiq's handshake was firm, his eyes penetrating, but he displayed no outward hostility towards me. I expect he was as curious as I was to see who he had been trying to kill, and who had been killing his men.

For my part, I did not greet the Taliban with the same warmth as I had displayed to the village elders. I wanted to be dispassionate, almost mechanical. I wanted them to know from my manner that they could do business with me, but as a solider, I would rather be fighting. I imagined Sadiq felt exactly the same.

Our handshake over with, I felt as though I should be the first to speak.

'We are here because of the fighting,' I said, directing my words to Ramatoulah, who nodded, and to Sadiq, who simply stared into me.

'I understand that we can stop fighting in this town.' At this, I gestured to the elders. I wanted this notion to be coming from them, and they nodded vigorously. 'We can stop the fighting here, and allow the people of this town to come back.' I finished with a deferential nod to Ramatoulah, who took up the clear invitation to continue, beginning a long speech that berated both sides for the fighting, and the destruction that it had caused. Ruin by ruin, the elder pointed out the devastation, putting stories and names to piles of rubble.

'This was the most famous baker in Helmand! This butcher had been here for sixty years! This shop belonged to my cousin, who was forced to flee, and lose his livelihood!'

So it went on, building after building. I had never been in denial about the effect that our fighting had on the local populace, but to hear it from a local's mouth was a chastening experience. Sadiq seemed unmoved, his death stare intact.

It was at this point that I realized the crowd had closed in around us. To better hear the elder speak, they had formed a tight circle with us at its centre. I would be lost to the eyes of my men on the wall, but my gut feeling was that I did not have to worry – this was going well, and I had faith that it was going to work.

Ramatoulah finished his impassioned speech. After a moment for Naz to finish his translation, I looked to Sadiq, inviting him to speak. He said nothing. That was fine by me, as it would allow Easy Company to be seen as the side driving for stability for the townspeople.

'This is what needs to happen,' I said, directing my words towards Sadiq in a calm but firm manner. 'We won't come for you. Not because I don't want to, but because I've been ordered not to. You won't come for us either. If you don't come for us, then there's no need for us to fight.'

Sadiq thought over the words, then growled out a few of his own.

'He doesn't want to stop either,' Naz translated, 'but he has been ordered, too.'

'We don't need to be happy about this,' I told Sadiq. 'But we need to make it work for them.' I gestured to the elders, then turned my attention to their leader.

'I promise that we can stop shooting. There will be no artillery. No bombing. I can do this,' I said, turning back to Sadiq and pointing towards him with an open hand, 'because you will not come for us. Agreed?'

After a few moments to pull at his beard and think, Sadiq gave a begrudging nod.

It was at that point that the shouting began. It came from the crowd and several voices. Too many for Naz to count, but he gave me the gist.

'They're asking about their businesses. Casualties. They want to know who will pay for repairs, and so on.'

The calls ceased immediately as Haji Ramatoulah barked angrily for silence, a demonstration of the elder's sway over the people of the town.

'We will talk more about these things, I promise,' I told the elder, who seemed satisfied with my words. 'Can we meet here again tomorrow, at the same time?'

Haji Ramatoulah agreed. After a moment, so did Sadiq.

I felt as though a final impression needed to be made on the Taliban commander, and so I put out my arm to encompass the nearby buildings that had been the favoured firing points of his fighters. 'We won't come for you, because you will no longer be here. You don't come for us. We don't come for you. There will be no shooting, no mortars. No bombs.'

The big man said nothing, but nodded. I put out my hand, and he shook it.

The ceasefire had begun.

30

Many more handshakes and farewells were needed before we could leave the meeting without causing offence. Once that was done, I walked with Naz towards our gate, seeing for the first time how our compound looked from the outside – the walls were pockmarked from the fighting, and bristled with the guns of my men. It was an impressive show of force – the defiant garrison that could and would fight on if needed.

The walk back seemed a lot shorter than the one out. Coming through the gate, I wanted to just lie down, and thank God that I was alive, but there was no time for relief as we made our way in through the tangle of scrap.

'Naz, come with me. I want to write down as much as we can.'

Taking notes during that first meeting would have been at odds with the warrior-like image I was trying to project for Sadiq's benefit, and so now, in a quiet part of the headquarters building, we set to work on recording every detail we could – who was who? Who was most friendly? Who was most quiet? How many fighters? Which of Sadiq's subordinates could we identify? There was a lot of ground to cover, and I filled reams of pages with scribbled notes.

'Great job today, Naz,' I told the Afghan as we finished. 'You were brilliant. Really brilliant.' It was easy to forget that he was not a soldier.

'Thanks, boss.' He smiled proudly.

'Ready to do it again tomorrow?'

'Of course!'

And the truth was, so was I. Walking out of the gate, I had felt as though I was heading for the chopping block, and yet as the meeting had gone on, I had been overtaken by a tremendous sense of calm. With the first moments survived, I realized that there was a very real chance of this process working, and though the idea of a ceasefire with my enemy stuck in my throat, I could swallow it because I did not want to see any more of my boys going home broken or in bags. Casualties were often a price that needed to be paid, but we were taking them and simply not achieving our mission. We had been sent here to provide security for the town in order to carry out CIMIC projects, and whether I liked it or not, it seemed clear now that the only way that was going to happen – barring the appearance of a non-existent battlegroup dedicated to Musa Qala – was through talking to the Taliban.

I shook my head. It all seemed so surreal. I could see that Naz, too, was floating on a cloud of disbelief.

'Let's go get a brew,' I suggested.

Never have I felt like more of a celebrity than when I came out of the headquarters room with Naz, and found half of the company waiting for answers. I had already sent the word that we were weapons tight – no firing unless fired upon – but now came a barrage of questions concerning anything from the elder's manner to Sadiq's beard. I answered a few quickly, but there were other men in Helmand who were desperate to know how the meeting had gone – Colonel Stuart Tootal and Brigadier Ed Butler, the brigade commander.

I called in on the satphone. After being told 'well done on not buggering it up or dying,' we got down to business. With the phone now insecure (it had long since 'dropped its fill'), I had to be cautious with what I said, keeping to broad outlines and atmospherics, and being careful not to say anything that could tip our hand. Though there was next to no chance that the Taliban had the technology to hack our calls, the same was not true of the Pakistani intelligence services, and we had to work under the assumption that they would be feeding intercepts to the Taliban in what was an undisclosed but well-known dirty secret.

'What's your gut feeling, Adam?' Brigadier Butler asked me. 'Will they hold by it?'

'I really think they will, sir,' I answered optimistically.

And I *was* optimistic. Haji Ramatoulah had struck me as an honourable man of his word, and though Sadiq seemed unhappy with the ceasefire – a feeling that, as a soldier, I shared – there had been no indication from him that he would not stick to it.

'If I'm going to start meeting with them to discuss rebuilding the town,' I pressed the officers, 'I'm going to need to know how much rope I have. Money, resources, and so on.'

'I'm afraid we'll have to hold off on giving you that just now, Adam,' the brigadier replied. 'Now that you've set the groundwork, I have a meeting with your local ACM's two-up in the desert.'

The local ACM's two-up was Sadiq's equivalent in Taliban rank to Brigadier Butler. It seemed as though, now the men on the ground had agreed to stop killing each other, their commanders could meet to discuss the bigger picture.

'We'll call in after your scheduled report at 1800, Adam. Great job today. Out.'

I hung up the phone, and saw the patiently waiting faces of two dozen Rangers and Paras.

'All right.' I grinned. 'One question at a time.'

Not a shot was fired that day, and the hours passed in mistrusted silence. Out of habit, men darted from cover to cover, but a few struck out to sit in the shade – a pastime that had been prohibited since the mortars had begun, and had required us to be either on a fighting position or in hard cover.

There was a sense of confusion and frustration in Easy Company that day. I made an effort to speak with every man, and their questions were universal – 'Why the fuck are we talking with them, boss? They killed our mates. Have we done all of this for nothing?'

I did my best to convince them otherwise, but soldiers are full of pride – we have been raised that way by the army for good reason – and 'ceasefire' smacked of 'surrender'.

'That's not what it is,' I insisted. 'We've fought them to a standstill. We've done our job. Now, we can see this town gets back to normal.'

That task began the next day, with a second meeting between myself, the elders, and the Taliban. The procedure was the same as the first, with formal greetings, but with the addition that Haji Ramatoulah suggest that we sit beneath the half-ruined veranda of what had been the bakery. We agreed, and I was pleased to see that when the elder ordered a group of Taliban fighters to clear the area of rubble, they did so immediately and without question. It was an encouraging sign. For his part, Sadiq showed no sign of irritation that the civilian would think to give orders to his men.

The talk on that second day was of bakers, butchers, and shopkeepers. The bakery was highest on the list of priorities, as the flatbreads it produced were a staple of the Afghan diet, and the Taliban were as keen as we were to see it back in action.

'Three hundred loaves a day,' was Sadiq's request, which made it a reasonable assumption that he had at least that many mouths to feed in the town.

I added our own order, and with the promise of a minimum four hundred loaves a day, there was great business to be had for the baker who would come in and set up shop. However, with the town encircled by both ISAF forces and the Taliban, there was a risk for anyone who would make the journey, not only to their life, but also to their wallet – regardless of which side Afghans were on, there was a high chance they would levy 'taxes' on anyone coming in and out of the town, and so I worked with the elders and Sadiq to come to an understanding that such bribery would not be enforced on the merchants.

'I want this marketplace to be busy again,' I said to the elders, who nodded earnestly. 'We will buy bread, meat, and other supplies, and we will do so regularly.'

Sadiq chimed in to add that his men too would also like to make use of a market, once it was established.

'If my men and your men meet in the market,' I told him, 'there must be no fighting. The ceasefire applies to the entire town, not just what we can see from our walls.'

'Agreed,' he said, after a pull at his beard.

We were both curious about each other, and questions of soldiering began to work their way into the conversation. Sadiq pointed to the sky, where a refuelling tanker circled in a lazy pattern. So positioned, we always had aircraft mere moments away.

'We hate your planes,' he admitted. 'In particular, "the horn".' At this, he mimicked a sound that I guessed immediately – an A-10 strafing run.

'How do they know where we are?'

I gestured to my personal role radio, which was only good for talking to my men who were within a short distance of me. 'We each have one of these. Any one of my men can call in my planes.'

Sadiq raised an eyebrow in appreciation. 'We hate them,' he said again.

Good, I thought to myself.

One of Sadiq's lieutenants pointed at the Para wings on my sleeve.

'What is this?' he inquired through Naz.

'It means I'm a paratrooper.'

There was much nodding at the word. They were familiar with and fascinated by the concept, and for the next ten minutes I fielded questions on what it was to be a paratrooper.

'But you did not come like this here?' Sadiq asked.

I shook my head, and told him a harmless story about the insertion exercises that took place from Scotland to Salisbury Plain. The chance to talk to Sadiq and his subordinates was fascinating and enjoyable, and I almost forgot for a moment that these were the enemy who had not only killed and injured my men, but also were prone to committing such acts as drowning men in buckets should they have been found talking to, or supporting, ISAF forces.

I was in the company of killers, and I needed to remember it.

Later that day, with the ceasefire twenty-four hours old, I decided that there was trust enough in the agreement that we could begin to carry out the work on the compound that we simply could not have done when the Taliban were in the surrounding buildings. Repairing the Alamo was the first task, and soon my men were crawling over it like ants rebuilding a nest. We did not have the supplies to make a great job, but it had been agreed with Sadiq and the elders that we could order building materials through local merchants, and repair the damage that had been done to our home.

With such industry, the days passed quickly. Freddie in particular was in his element, the assault pioneer/Para taking to the work with infectious enthusiasm. Manual labour in the Afghan sun was tiring, and the anger at the ceasefire soon dwindled – men were simply too busy, or too asleep, to vent their spleen. The promise of bread – and a break from rations – seemed to do enough to douse any further vitriol.

Then, on the third morning, negotiations hit an impasse. It had been agreed that no other NATO forces would enter the town, but I wanted more medical supplies. Some of this was needed to replace what we had used, and others were basic items, such as antibiotics, that we simply did not have. One soldier had been pissing blood from a urinary tract infection for a fortnight.

'If we can't bring it in on a helicopter,' I offered Sadiq, 'I'm quite happy for it to come through the elders.'

'No supplies.' Sadiq shook his head.

I held his look, and thought over the position. If the cease-fire went south, then the provisions Doc Stacey had requested could mean the difference between life or death for my men. It was a point that I could not back down on, but neither was there anything to be gained by a stand-off of egos.

'I'm going to go back to my men,' I spoke gently, but firmly. 'This resupply has to happen if this ceasefire is to continue. I'll be back in an hour to hear your decision.'

When I returned, there was tea, and half-smiles – the resupply could go ahead. Medical items only, and to be delivered by the elders.

Over the next few days, the market of Musa Qala began to show signs of life. Rubble was cleared from the streets, shopfronts repaired, and traders began vying for the business of both Easy Company and the Taliban. Entrepreneurs can make a great profit by following in the footsteps of war and disaster, and it was these men who began haggling with me over crates of Mountain Dew and Coke. At one point, we received a radio intercept between Taliban commanders complaining that their men were being turned away at the shops. I waited for them to bring it up at the next meeting – not wanting to raise suspicion as to our source – then made it clear to the elders that the Taliban's men must be welcome in the market. This was no good deed on my part, but a simple understanding that for the ceasefire to work, both sides must feel the benefits. It would only take one pissed-off fighter to murder a shopkeeper, and then the whole town would suffer.

It took five days from the first meeting for the market to truly flourish, with civilians coming in to buy, as well as the combatants. Certain items like canned drinks were readily available – and likely looted from ISAF stores. Others, like mobile-phone SIM cards and top-ups, were much harder to find. The Taliban had made being caught with a mobile punishable by death – with the exception of a few professions, such as long-distance drivers – but I was keen to get these into the hands of my Afghan Police so that they could call home, and so I reached an accommodation with Sadiq. I also suggested that he, I, and Haji Ramatoulah all took a phone that we could use as a hotline in case of emergency. Sadiq was sceptical at first, but I explained that it was important we could talk at once in the instance of a gas canister exploding, or some other unforeseen incident that could be misinterpreted as hostile action. He agreed, and the hotline was put to use a few days later, when some out-of-town civilians engaged in celebratory fire.

It was a strange period for Easy Company and myself. I was free to wander the marketplace – taking with me Naz or Raheem – to order the stores and food that would make the company's life more palatable. On one occasion I took four of my men to help carry the canisters of oil back to the compound, but such was the unease of the locals at the sight of five soldiers that I did not repeat the venture. Instead I walked alone with my interpreter, and often we would bump into Taliban fighters who were in the market to purchase their own provisions. At such times there would be a moment to accept the bizarre situation before we would exchange 'salaams' and then both go on our way. Of all the situations I had foreseen happening on this tour, being alongside the Taliban as we bartered for goats was not amongst them.

31

The next three weeks passed without a single shot being fired. The ceasefire held, and the morning ritual of meeting with the Taliban became as ingrained and as casual as fighting them each morning had been. At times I would catch myself at the bizarre situation I found myself in, but more often I would simply get on with the day.

Life was very different in the district centre. My men were still bitter about the ceasefire, but they were beginning to see its benefits. It took some time for the town's butcher to be found – we discovered later that it was because he had lost so many of his family to the Taliban that he refused to do business with them, until Haji Ramatoulah insisted – but eventually there was a steady supply of goats and sheep being herded inside the compound to be slaughtered. This work was carried out masterfully by the butcher, Sergeant Major Scrivener then dividing the cuts between platoons. On one occasion we also bought chickens, but these all died within a day, and the rumour mill was strong with the suggestion that they had been poisoned. Firewood was a priority on the shopping lists, men cooking their meat over open flame, everyone fancying themselves the new Bear Grylls. Potatoes were bought, skinned, and fried in oil so thick it could have gone into the quad bike's engine. Somme Platoon requested courgettes, and were bitterly disappointed when the market traders had no idea what they were.

As well as the butcher, a mechanic was also provided through the elders, giving some much-needed TLC to the ANP's pickup trucks, and our own Pinzgauer and quad. Diesel was hard to come by, and so although the generator was given some attention, we still had to remain on scheduled broadcasts for the sake of our limited supply of charged radio batteries.

Rebuilding the damage done during the fighting, and improving the sangars, took up most of our days. We bought concrete mix from the locals, and began to fill the gaping holes in our walls that had been torn out by rockets and RPGs. Seeing that this work would be completed before we were pulled out, I decided that something else was needed to occupy idle minds, and so I gave my platoon headsheds the task of running a Junior NCO cadre – not only would this keep the Toms busy, but it would give my leaders something to plan and execute.

One morning, Haji Ramatoulah brought the town's religious leader, an old imam, to inspect the damage to what had been his mosque. Having been forewarned of the visit, I had taken a section of men into the rubble, and there we had marked any unexploded ordnance, and cleared away bags full of bloodied dressings, RPG tail fins, empty cases, and grenade pins. It was a cosmetic effort on what was still clearly a battleground, and as the imam was led around and saw the destruction, tears streamed over his cheeks. I tried to think of something I could say to console him, but in the end I could think of nothing. This had been his pride and joy – his connection with heaven – and now it was a bloodstained ruin.

Once it was clear that the ceasefire was solid, I began to ask Haji Ramatoulah about civic projects he would like carried out in the town. I was careful to avoid timelines and promises, but I collected his wishes, and passed them up the chain. Afghans do not have the same training in interpreting maps and aerial photos as we do, and so I would be required to visit these sites on foot, which invariably led to me being some distance from the compound. Though I was alone with my interpreter, I never once feared for my safety. Naz and the ANP officers had impressed upon me that in Afghan culture, honour demands that you must not only treat your guest with courtesy but also safeguard his life. This was *nanawatai*, and it meant something to our hosts. Whilst I was Haji Ramatoulah's guest, his militia were the guarantee of my safety, he said. Should anything happen to me, he would go to war with the Taliban, and nothing less. It wouldn't be the first time they had clashed, as it was Ramatoulah's militia that had propped up the ANP in the district centre in June as the Taliban had come close to over-running it. Clearly, here was a man who wanted his town governed without their zealous overlordship.

Haji Ramatoulah was a thoughtful man, but like all Afghans, he was tough in the way that he did not hold the same individual values as Westerners – I once saw him whip a boy mercilessly with a birch branch for some transgression. He was not afraid to stand up to the Taliban, and he had seen the Russians come and go, and doubtless thought that we would be yet another army that would insert its fingers into Afghanistan before getting them burned and running for home.

One day, whilst walking with Naz, Ramatoulah, and some of the elders, we came across a mass grave. I could smell it before I saw it, the pungent aroma of bodies cooked beneath a blazing sun. The trench appeared to have been excavated by a JCB, and I asked about its whereabouts now – we could use it for clearing rubble from the streets. Ramatoulah shook his head, then told me that the grave was for the Taliban dead. Making a quick calculation of its length, I figured that there were scores of the enemy buried within it. Had the men I had killed myself finished their jihad here? I was curious about the enemy's mechanics, and nothing more.

'How many in here?' I asked the elders.

They didn't know. The Taliban had dug the graves, and they were continuing to do so now – as civilians returned to the town and their homes, bodies were being found on a daily basis. Soon, the repatriation of those Taliban dead became a staple of our morning meetings. A townsman would return to his compound and begin sifting through the rubble of his home. He would find bodies and, not wanting to approach the Taliban directly, he would tell his elder. His elder would bring it up in the meeting, and then Sadiq and I would try and make sense of where the place was, so that a time could be arranged for his men to recover their dead. I would like to say that the Taliban were as callous about the fate of their own dead as they were towards the people that they sought to control, but the truth is that they were fastidious in the recovery of their fallen comrades. I probably passed the mass grave another half a dozen times in those weeks, and each time, it had grown longer, what had been a parallel grave to the track being forced to dog-leg into the field. I do not know exactly how many bodies went into the ground there, only that it was well above a hundred.

The bodies were a reminder of why we were in the town, and what we had been doing in those first few weeks. Now that there was a lull, I made certain that I found time to talk to each of my soldiers man to man. It was informal, over a smoke or a brew, but I wanted each one to hear from me why we were now in the position that we were in. There was still anger that we were talking to the enemy, and I wanted them to know that this had nothing at all to do with the company. That it was coming from way, way higher up the chain, and that this was simply another constraint in the list of rules of engagement.

'I feel like we're jacking,' men would tell me.

It is said that to complain is a soldier's prerogative, and questions like 'Why are we here?' or statements along the lines of 'This is shit' were often thrown my way during the days of the ceasefire, but the soldier you should worry about is the one who isn't moaning.

Such feelings were not softened by the fact that the rest of the battlegroup was still heavily engaged with fighting the enemy. It seemed as though we were the only company ordered into a ceasefire, and that gnawed at my men's spirit. I know for certain that it did, because it also gnawed at mine. I could see the logic behind the decision, but like all the men of Easy Company, I was keen for us to be redeployed elsewhere if our fight had finished here. There was not one man in Easy who wanted to 'wait out the war' here, and then go home. We were straining at the leash, desperate to join our brothers in Sangin, Now Zad, or Kajaki.

Twice, it seemed as though our wish would be granted. 'Prepare to move' was given to us over the net, though never with any detail about how it would happen. We knew that 3 Commando Brigade had already begun assuming duties from 16 Air Assault, and we wondered who would replace us here. The Taliban were vehemently opposed to any military units entering the town, and so it seemed most likely that defence of the district centre would fall to Haji Ramatoulah's militia. I hoped that would not be the case, as it had been the skill of my men, air power, and artillery that had kept the enemy from overwhelming us with sheer numbers. Without wanting to be disparaging of the militia, they were not trained British infantrymen. Neither would they be able to call on A-10s and 105mm guns. If the Taliban decided that a ceasefire no longer suited them, then I did not like the militia's chances.

Then, almost a month after the initial meeting with the Taliban, it seemed as if we'd finally be getting back into the fray.

'Prepare to move in three days,' Zero told me over the sat-phone.

'Roger. How are we extracting?'

There was a pause at the end of the line. For a moment, I thought the line had gone dead. When Zero gave me my answer, I wished it had.

'Cattle trucks.'

32

Cattle trucks. If not for the already bizarre situation we were in, I probably would have thought someone was trying to get one over on me.

'What are they saying, boss?' I was asked by a dozen young Irish voices.

'Prepare to move in three days,' I told them, holding back the bombshell until the evening orders group.

'Bollocks!' my men scoffed. 'That's what they said the last few times.' Then, their curiosity satisfied, they melted away to their shaded spots, and I was left to think.

Cattle trucks.

'For fuck's sake,' I muttered to myself.

I knew that we would not be collected from Musa Qala by helicopter or ISAF vehicles – the ceasefire terms prohibited it – but I had been pushing hard that we should be able to patrol out of the town, and to link up on the western side of the wadi. Our force was light enough that we could carry our gear, and we would be leaving nothing behind but the sangars' field telephones – a decision I had received permission for from Zero. The idea of being in trucks slightly sickened me, thinking of the many vulnerabilities that we would have, but in the next few days, the headshed would insist on it, telling me that a convoy of vehicles would be far easier for them to manage than a company of men on foot. The decision to leave Musa Qala went as high as the president of Afghanistan, and NATO in Brussels and London, and so there was no room for me to insist on another way – we would be leaving in cattle trucks, and so as company commander, it was down to me to make sure that it worked.

I gave the warning order to Easy that night. There were the expected mumbles of 'This is shit' and 'They wouldn't do it themselves, would they?' I found it hard to argue either point, and so I concentrated on the positives: we're getting out of here; we're going back to Bastion, and then we can be sent back out to fight. The promise of action, at least, did something to dampen the anger.

Of course, action during the extraction was the last thing I wanted. This entire enterprise had all the ingredients of a total disaster, and we had not gone through weeks of ceasefire to lose men on the last leg.

'We're all going to have to work together to make this happen,' I told Haji Ramatoulah and Sadiq at our meeting the next morning.

'How many trucks do you need?' the elder asked me.

'Eight,' I told him, and he nodded in agreement. My next words, however, left him and Sadiq in stunned silence.

'And I'm going to need eight drivers, and an elder or a Taliban commander to sit in each vehicle. We're not going in the trucks alone.'

'This is not possible,' Ramatoulah said eventually, shaking his head.

'Not possible,' Sadiq agreed.

'Look,' I told them, 'we have had peace here for a month now, but all of that means nothing if we are attacked leaving the town. If even a single bullet is fired at my men, we will be going straight back into that compound, and there will be no more ceasefire. There will only be fighting, and there will be air strikes, and there will be artillery.'

I let those words sink in. For Sadiq, it meant losing more men trying to crack a nut that had not shown the slightest sign of yielding. For the elders, it meant their home reverting to a bombed-out ghost town.

'I want this to work,' I impressed upon the men. 'But you have to work with me.'

'You have my word you will not be attacked,' Sadiq said.

'You have shown that you're a man of your word,' I answered delicately, 'but mines in the road do not know about the promises of Mullah Sadiq. We need people in those trucks who know the area, and we need a route that has been proven to be clear. No mines. No bombs.'

One of Sadiq's lieutenants whispered into his ear. Sadiq pulled at his beard, then spoke himself.

'He says that this is a plan for you to know where we have prepared for your tanks,' Naz translated.

I shook my head. 'It's not. I'm not asking where you have your mines, I just want the track that we will be using to have been cleared. The route can be a long way to the desert. It doesn't have to be the shortest one through the wadi.'

Sadiq pulled at his beard some more, and then nodded. Ramatoulah took that as his moment to speak.

'Mullah Sadiq, will you provide men to show us the tracks? Some of my elders will drive them with you, so that we can show that the route is clear.'

Sadiq nodded.

'Are you both agreed that there will be an elder or Taliban in each truck?' I pressed.

After much deliberation, the men nodded.

'Which trucks?' Sadiq asked.

'I'll decide who goes in which truck on the day,' I told them. I could see that neither man was happy with this, so went on to explain. 'I trust each of you, but there are some who will not be happy with this ceasefire. It will only take one man firing, and we are back to fighting. Just one gunshot, and no matter how far we have gone, we will fight our way back into town.'

'Surely there is a point where you have gone so far it is not worth you coming back?' Sadiq asked.

'No, Mullah Sadiq. At any time, we will fight our way back. You have seen my soldiers fight. You have seen what our aircraft and guns can do. You know that you can hurt us in an ambush, but you won't win the fight, and then you'll have us back in this town.'

Sadiq conceded the point.

'My men will be silent,' he promised.

And with a shake of hands, it was decided.

Easy Company would be leaving Musa Qala.

Once the meeting had broken up, all three sides set to their tasks to facilitate the move – the elders and Taliban to find the trucks and clear the route, and myself to preparing the set of orders for what had to be one of the most unorthodox missions I had ever heard of within the British army.

'I think this is really going to go ahead,' I told Scrivs. 'We need to make sure this place is ready to hand over to Haji Ramatoulah's militia. All the shit burned. All the brass picked up.'

'I'll see to it, sir,' my sergeant major promised. 'Feels like the end of a really intense range package.'

'It does, doesn't it?' I agreed. 'Fucking bizarre.'

As I set to work on my orders, Scrivs got down to what sergeant majors do best – getting soldiers to bring shitholes up to acceptable living conditions. Acceptable for Afghanistan, that was.

To this end, several large bonfires were lit. These would rage until we departed, stacks of accumulated rubbish having built up during our occupation of the compound. It wasn't that we were dirty, but it simply was not worth the risk of a man getting shot out in the open to burn old ration boxes. The Taliban noticed the flames and the soot, and declared over the radios: 'The foreigners are really going. They're burning all of their stuff.'

Sandbags full of empty brass cases were collected from the fighting positions, and would make a tidy profit for the first Afghan to come across them. Unexploded ordnance was marked as well as we could, but without an EOD team, there was no way for us to clear it. I had requested one during our meetings, but Sadiq had been unmoveable – no ISAF forces to enter the town for any purpose.

One of the most heart-rending tasks of breaking camp was painting over the murals and engravings that the men of Easy had worked onto every flat surface within the compound. Anything from Para cap badges to 'Ozzy's bedspace' had to go, and it was with a real sense of loss that the men obliterated the symbols that had given them pride, or just a taste of home and identity. The whitewash was a symbol that our time was drawing to an end, and it pained the soldiers to know that there would be no physical trace of them left behind in a place where they had given so much. Last to come down were the flags, the Union Jack, Red Hand of Ulster as well as the Welsh Dragon and our Para/Pegasus flags. Only the Afghan flag remained. We really were leaving. It was almost over.

On the morning before the extraction I met again with Sadiq and Ramatoulah, the two men confirming that they had worked together to reconnoitre a route, and that it was safe. It took me some time to translate their directions into a path that could be marked on a map.

'Any attack on my men, either deliberate or from a mine, and we stay,' I stressed again. 'You've seen the men in the desert?' I asked Sadiq, referring to the company of 42 Commando, and the Estonian mechanized squadron that had moved into place to support our move.

Sadiq nodded. The Taliban's network of spotters were experts.

'If anything happens to us, they come in, too,' I told the Taliban commander.

'I understand,' he assured me, and I was certain that he did.

The day before departure passed in a blur of burning the last of the rubbish, drawn-out orders, and the constant challenge of 'what ifs' and 'what do we do whens'. As evening drew in, Haji Ramatoulah and Sadiq asked for a meeting, informing me that the route would need to be changed. This was fine by me, as a proven route was my only concern, and I impressed upon Sadiq that, if he needed more time, we could wait.

'No,' he promised. 'This route is good. There will be no fighting.'

'If that changes, tell me. We have come too far with this for it to fail now.'

The men agreed, and Sadiq took his leave. He would return in the morning with seven of his commanders – one man for each of the cattle trucks.

The first of these transports arrived in the dusk. Seeing it bounce its way down the highway towards the district centre brought home to me that we really were about to leave here on the back of Afghan cattle trucks. How the hell had it come to this? Had we done something wrong?

I tried to tell myself that these doubts were unfounded, and that we had done all that had been asked of us, and more, but the thoughts still nagged at me. Soldiers are proud men, and the thought of leaving the town on these decrepit vehicles was embarrassing at best, and dishonourable at worst. I knew that what was happening here was an anomaly within the army. I had never heard of anything like it before, and I realized in that moment that there would be fallout – I didn't know what, exactly, but my gut told me that Easy Company would be in for hard times even after we had cleared the town, and had reached the relative safety of the desert.

Haji Ramatoulah arrived with the first truck. Although I had reservations about what was to happen, he was elated. It was clear that he wanted the British out of his town, and in that delight there was a further blow to my own ego. We had come here to help the people of Musa Qala, and every single one of them I had talked to could not wait to see the back of us. It was a kick in the teeth, to say the least.

One by one, the trucks rolled in. As they came, Scrivs and Freddie fell on them like the military version of *Pimp My Ride*, stripping back some areas of the truck, and building up others. By pulling sandbags from the compound's defences they were able to layer the beds of the trucks to help protect against mine strikes, though there was little that could be done to shield the sides against small arms – the best that we could do there was to give the men clear fields of fire, and hope that a strong defensive posture would deter attack.

The Afghan militia began arriving late in the evening, ready to take over from us when we left in the dawn. Our NCOs tried to brief them as best as they could on the fighting positions, but the militia were disinterested and distant. Like all the locals, they just wanted to see the back of us.

'How are you doing, boys?' I would ask the men as I moved around the compound, eager to talk to my troops.

'Pretty shit, to be honest, sir,' was the common theme of the replies. 'We didn't ask for this,' they'd add, and I would try and explain once again that they had fought the enemy to a stand-still, and now we had provided security for the locals.

'And how long will that last, boss?' men would snort. 'Can't trust these fuckers. They'll probably ambush us as soon as we clear out.'

'They've had loads of chances to shoot at us, lads,' I pointed out. 'How many times have you been standing on top of the Alamo? Easy shot for them. I've been right into town, and they could have killed me, but they didn't.'

'I suppose, boss,' my soldiers would shrug.

'They want us gone from here, lads. They know they're not getting into this place so long as we're here, and they know that if they try anything on the extraction we're coming right back. They don't want that, and so they'll leave us alone.'

Did I believe that? In all but my most pessimistic moments, yes. The truth was that we had been easy targets on the compound's rooftops. I *had* been totally alone in the marketplace. The Taliban had shown remarkable restraint, as had my own men, and I did not believe that they would throw that patience away by attacking us on our way out.

Mines were another story, and I pressed Ramatoulah on the subject again that evening.

'You have worked incredibly hard for this peace,' I told him. 'Are you certain of the route?'

'I am.' He nodded. 'And of course, I will be driving you. I will drive the first vehicle.'

I couldn't ask for a better assurance than that.

'Not long.' The elder smiled. 'Not long, and you will be home.'

I didn't sleep much that night. There was simply too much to be done, and when there wasn't, my head was alive with too many thoughts for there to be any possibility of sleep. If walking out to meet the Taliban had been the most reckless moment of my life, then tomorrow was the most important – I had to get my men out, and I had to do it in the back of cattle trucks, on routes cleared by locals, and with the Taliban sitting beside our drivers.

Well, I had joined the army for a challenge, hadn't I?

The flat light of dawn began to seep into the darkness, and into the grey came the figures of my men. A lot had changed since our arrival. Once, the dawn's touch had been the herald of RPGs, contact, and air strikes. Now, rather than crawling into their fighting positions, my men were stoking fires and loading their kit onto cattle trucks. The smell of cigarettes joined the acidic tang of the burning rubbish to rasp throats. Perhaps it was for that reason that Easy Company's men kept their mouths closed, the usual banter between comrades absent.

Perhaps.

Looking around the compound, with the procession of trucks lined up towards the gate, I felt a deep sense of sadness. In this place we had stood against an enemy as a collective of men, and not individuals. Here, we had fought in some of the most intense combat the army had seen for half a century. The experience of Easy Company – the good and the bad – was one that I would never have again. I knew that for certain, and the sense of loss at that fact far outweighed my sense of relief that we were leaving alive.

Of course, leaving the compound alive wasn't necessarily the same as staying that way until we reached the desert. As well as assuming as defensive a posture as possible, we had to rely on both the elders and the Taliban for a proven route, and silenced weapons. To that end I greeted both sets of men as they entered the compound, and assigned each to a truck, Sadiq making no comment when I sent him to the third truck back, where he would sit alongside Dean Whiten. I did not inform the young Para captain of the identity of his travelling companion – everything about Sadiq said that he was Taliban, and Dean was professional and cool enough to take his enemy's presence in stride. I left the pair fully confident that there would be no incident amongst them. For my own part, I would be in the vehicle driven by Ramatoulah, with one of Sadiq's lieutenants as well as Naz and my JTAC – Ray and Abe. There would be stacks of air covering us from above, and Apaches from afar – no helicopters over the town, as per the agreement – and Ray and Abe would be busy controlling it all. They would also be crucial in us fighting our way out of any ambush. I had promised the Taliban continuous air strikes if we were attacked, and I would follow through on that threat.

'Don't go getting that fucking radio shot,' some of the lads joked to the JTAC, knowing its importance, and deliberately excluding the air controller's own life. 'We need that thing.'

With the Taliban commanders divided – all faces that had taken part in the shuras – I took a moment to watch my sergeant major and platoon sergeants at work as they hustled men onto the trucks, or dispatched them to some final errand, like dousing fires, or cleaning up the ablutions area.

'What the fuck are you doing with that?' Scrivs asked a teenage soldier who was carrying a green plastic garden chair.

'Want to be comfy in the truck, sir,' the lad replied, straight-faced.

After a moment, the older soldier shrugged. 'Go on then.' And why not? It would be a long ride.

I popped my head into the back of one of the cattle trucks. The sides were low enough that my men could look over them. With about a section to each truck, and the GPMGs split amongst the company, there was a good weight of firepower in each one.

A knot of young soldiers called for my attention. 'Sir, look what we found.'

'Bloody hell!' It was a pair of heavy machine guns, Soviet-made Dushkas. 'Where did you find those?'

'Underneath that scrap, boss.'

'Ask the sergeant major to make them safe,' I told the lance corporal amongst them. 'Then put them on the trucks.' A pair of working heavy machine guns were not a gift to be left behind.

Dawn was almost fully upon us now, and so I took the satphone from my webbing and called Zero, now a Royal Marine colonel by the name of Matt Holmes. He had replaced Colonel Tootal now that 16 Air Assault Brigade had handed over to 3 Commando, and the command net was full of new and unfamiliar voices. This wasn't my first call to the commando officer and, as usual, he made me feel totally confident in the plan, and my part of it.

'The go or no-go is yours, Adam. If you don't like the feel of it, you don't have to go. We can hold off until it feels right.'

'The elders and the Taliban commanders have come in as I asked,' I replied. 'Atmospherics are good. They've also kept the town quiet. There's nobody out, so we should get a clear run.'

'OK then. I'll see you in a few hours. I'll be on the command net.'

'Roger, Colonel. See you then. Out.'

I sought out Sadiq, who sat calmly in the truck's passenger seat.

'Mullah Sadiq,' I spoke through Naz, 'are you happy with this route? There will be no mines? No fighting?'

'I am.'

'I will be in the first vehicle,' I informed him. 'If I hit a mine, then there will be no holding my men back. The soldiers in the desert will join them, and they will fight back here. There will be three infantry companies in Musa Qala, and not one.'

'I understand.'

There was total confidence in his manner. Of course, there was always the chance that he was prepared to martyr himself and his commanders, but for what – an ambush on the convoy? They could have ambushed our compound at any time over the past month. It didn't make military sense to do it as we were leaving, and a force such as the Taliban does not conquer a nation of warriors like Afghanistan without having a deep understanding of tactics and strategy. Like it or not, I would have to go on his word, and my gut. There are no guarantees in war.

'Sergeant Major. Are we good to go?'

'We're good, boss.'

'Ready for this?'

'Oh yes.'

I thought about shaking the man's hand, but decided against the gesture – it was a little too much like admitting there was a chance a mine was going to tear my truck apart.

'Mount them up, please, Scrivs.'

'Mount up! Prepare to move!'

Those who had not done so already scrambled onto the trucks and took up their positions, the vehicles soon bristling with weaponry. Final drags were taken on cigarettes, Sergeant Major Scrivener falling on anyone who blatantly threw the butts on the ground in front of the elders – we would leave this place in better order than we found it, as ridiculous as that notion might seem when the walls were still pockmarked by fighting.

The elders and drivers got the message as to what the scurry in activity meant, and began to fire the belching engines of their trucks. The local mechanic had worked all night to ensure each was ready for action – or at least, as ready as fifty-year-old machines in the desert could be.

'All right, guys?' I asked my JTAC as I arrived at my own transport.

They smiled. 'Looks like fucking *Mad Max*, boss.'

I couldn't argue the point. Three pickups and eight cattle trucks, all filled with stern-faced Afghan Police and teenage boys from Britain and Ireland. It was some sight, and I allowed myself a moment to capture it as I weighed up the final decision.

To go, or not to go?

With the route guaranteed by the elders and the Taliban, stacks of aircraft in support, and two companies of troops ready to punch in to our aid, I knew that there was no point in delaying things. Being a soldier meant taking risks, and this was just one more of them.

I climbed into the Hilux, and took my seat beside Haji Ramatoulah. He did not need an interpreter for what I asked.

'Let's go.'

Smiling from ear to ear, the tribal elder put the truck into gear, and we lurched forward towards the gate. After weeks of toe-to-toe combat, the death and maiming of our comrades, and an uneasy peace, Easy Company were leaving Musa Qala.

33

The market was deserted as we rolled out of the gate. I had requested that the elders make it known that today was a day for civilians to stay indoors, and off the tracks and streets. This was to make the job of our I-STAR easier, giving them less activity to keep tabs on, but there was also a more personal reason — I was worried how a farewell from the locals would look. Leaving in cattle trucks was hard enough on the pride of my men. I did not want them to suffer hate-filled looks and thrown stones.

It was an eerie feeling to be driving through Musa Qala. The road was a killing zone, overlooked on all sides, and such a disadvantage will always raise the hairs on a soldier's neck. We'd had a degree of *Soldatenglück* in the fighting, but this was different, like totally uncharted territory. And the damage wrought on the town through coalition bombs and shells was painfully clear. It was little wonder that they wanted us gone.

I used the company net to keep in touch with my commanders in the other vehicles, whilst Ray and Abe talked to the air net. Thousands of feet above us, jets with high-powered cameras gave a top-down view of the space around us. Kabul and London were watching. Apaches, skirting the edge of the no-go area, scanned the road ahead of us. A few minutes after leaving the gates, a group of men was spotted approaching a junction. I halted the convoy until Ramatoulah could confirm that they were his men, moving into position to ensure that no civilians blocked the key points with their trucks.

Moving at not much more than jogging pace, it took the convoy twenty minutes to snake its way out of the town. They were the longest twenty minutes of my life, when any window could have hidden a gunman; any rooftop could have been the launch point for an RPG, or grenade toss. As we drove, I scanned the buildings ahead and aside of me. *If we come under contact right now, what do I do? If there's an RPG on the rear vehicle, what do I do?* I constantly played over these changing scenarios, knowing that every second would be vital if the Taliban broke their word.

It must have been torture for my men in the trucks. I had been meeting the enemy face to face, and had walked amongst them in the marketplace. Such actions had built my confidence in the enemy's honour, and I had tried to impart this view to my men, but nothing speaks so loudly as personal experience, and my men's experience of the Taliban was of being attacked by and then killing them. If the twenty minutes felt like hours for me, then it was days for my brave men. But, as ever, they showed courageous restraint in their actions, keeping weapons tight, as disciplined as ever.

Leading in the front truck, I did not want to think about what a mine strike would mean to me. I could only hope that, if it did happen, it would be a quick end, and that my men behind would all make it to safety. There was no mine-detection capability in the company – not a single metal detector or any IED-jamming equipment – and so we were totally dependent on the word of the elders and Taliban, and the driving skills of Ramatoulah and his men. At several points, the elder took a route that was far from being the most direct, and it was obvious we were avoiding some mines or booby traps. At these times Ray and Abe would tell the I-STAR to mark the area so that other units could be warned off. There was no way for the Taliban lieutenant who rode with us to know this, but the enemy were savvy fighters, and I expect that they relocated their mines as a matter of course.

As the buildings began to thin, and we entered the more rural area, the threat of small-arms and grenade ambushes diminished, but we were far from free and clear. The route that had been proven for us would first take us south before heading west, then north, then west again into the desert, and, quite aside from the threat of mines, the roads were a danger merely from being in such poor repair. Many times it was impossible to travel at more than walking pace, and several vehicles became stuck in the sands, and had to be pushed free by their occupants, Taliban commanders sweating alongside eighteen-year-old soldiers from Banbridge or Newry. It was just one more oddity in a mission that had become like no other.

As we travelled north through the wide gravel wadi, we were afforded the best view yet of the territory we had been fighting over. To our right lay the sprawling mass of compounds that made up the town of Musa Qala, to the left was the climbing green zone that terminated in desert, and our sanctuary. The exit points from the wadi screamed 'mines!', and it was several cuts into the rising terrain before Ramatoulah turned onto the track that would see us climb out of the wadi and begin our leg through the dense tangle of vegetation that was as ideally suited to ambush as the built-up streets of the town. At least, with every metre, we were coming closer to the men of Kilo Company and the Estonian mech squadron. If it did go noisy, each lurching step of the convoy meant less time fighting alone.

'How's everything on the I-STAR?' I asked Ray.

'We've picked up about five vehicles.'

'What?'

'They've joined on to the convoy. Pickup trucks. No weapons seen.'

I asked Ramatoulah about them. He explained that they were more elders and their children. They wanted to see the foreigners in the desert.

For fuck's sake, I thought to myself. *We're going to turn up to meet the Marines looking like a travelling circus.*

I looked at my watch. It had been four hours since we had left the gates of the district centre.

'Not far now,' Ramatoulah said excitedly.

It was the final hill, Naz translated for me. Once we were over that, it was a flat drive in the desert.

The last climb took its toll on the engines, and as we cleared the lip of the wadi, I decided we had best pause to allow the straining power plants to cool. Ramatoulah was glad of this, and took the chance to pray with the elders. The ANP did likewise in their group, and the Taliban in theirs. Though ostensibly united by a common faith, the three clusters were quite distinct. There was little talk or warmth between them during prayers or at any other time. The Afghan Police looked on at the Taliban with loathing. No amount of talk could persuade them that the ceasefire had been a good thing.

The short break over, we rumbled onwards. It wasn't long before fear of ambush began to subside, and hope was ignited.

'Boss. Look.' Abe prodded me. 'Look ahead. There!'

He pointed into the distance. After a moment for my eyes to adjust, I realized that I was looking at the dark shapes of the Estonians' vehicles. Confirmation of our deliverance came a moment later, two Apaches dropping from the sky. At ten feet above the ground they buzzed the convoy, pilot and gunner waving. Even over the sound of the rotors and engines, I could hear my men cheering in the wagons behind me. It was the moment when we dared to say to ourselves, 'We're really getting away with this! We're going home!'

The feeling of elation and relief grew as the shapes of the Estonian squadron loomed larger. Soon we could see the gun line of the 105mm artillery pieces, now under the command of 29 Commando. This was 'Commando RV', our meeting point. The place where we would climb down from the cattle trucks and onto two Chinooks.

I could see them now, and I realized instantly that their engines were shut down – a rare sight and further proof that, far from being a disorganized rabble piling into lorries, our extraction from Musa Qala had been a deliberate op, and well planned. We were the battlegroup's main effort, and 3 Commando Brigade's first deliberate operation in Helmand Province.

'Look at those fucking beauties.' Ray grinned, staring at the Chinooks.

'Look a lot better without bullets bouncing off them, don't they?' Abe joked. 'Fuck me, I can't wait to have a shower.'

'And shit in a flushing toilet.' Ray smiled. 'You looking forward to a shave, boss?'

'Actually, no,' I laughed. 'I've grown quite attached to this beard.'

The good mood in the truck's cab was infectious. Only the Taliban lieutenant – stone-faced as ever – was without a smile.

'This is very good,' Haji Ramatoulah repeated through Naz. 'Very good.'

He was delighted to see the helicopters that would mark the end of the journey from their town, and I now shared in his enthusiasm. Other emotions would come later, some of them soon after, but in this moment there was only relief at knowing that no more of my men would be killed or injured. Our pride may have taken a hit in those cattle trucks, but pride can be restored far more easily than gunshot and shrapnel wounds can be healed.

Haji Ramatoulah pulled to a stop at a gesture from a commando. We had reached our destination. Under the watchful eyes of the Royal Marines, we climbed from our vehicles. Some men from Easy were smiling whilst others were simply blank-faced in disbelief. Others finally found the humour in the situation and began to bleat and moo like the truck's usual occupants.

'Eh! Keep the fucking noise down!' the sergeant major ordered. 'Royal are watching.' He gestured to the men of Kilo Company.

The words struck a chord with the men, and they began to unpack their meagre kit from the trucks with suppressed smiles, laughter, and the odd sly punch into their friends' ribs. Clear of danger, they were beginning to slide into the true skin of who they were out of war – teenage boys. But how could they be looked on as that, after what they had endured?

'Some drive that, sir,' Sergeant Major Scrivener greeted me.

'Wasn't it?' I replied, shaking his hand. 'Let's get Somme and the ANP out on the first shuttle, Scrivs. I'll go and tell the ANP myself.'

Leaving Ramatoulah at the truck, I quickly went to find the Afghan policemen who had stood and bled alongside us. It had been a rough time for them, losing a quarter of their number to either death or injury, and then forced into a ceasefire that burned them with shame.

'You take these first Chinooks,' I told their commander. 'We'll follow on the second shuttle, and meet you in Bastion.'

I shook the man's calloused hand. There was no delight for him to be leaving Musa Qala, and I pitied the next of the enemy that he would meet, as they would surely pay the price of his disgust.

As Austen and Raheem gathered the Taliban together, I collected Ramatoulah from the truck – it was time to find Colonel Holmes. It was not a difficult task, the CO of 42 Commando made clear by his bearing. As we approached, I rehearsed in my mind the Pashtun greeting that I had been practising for days. I was adamant that I would present the tribal elder in his own tongue, a final thank you for his work in bringing a peaceful resolution to his war-torn town.

'Good to see you, Colonel,' I greeted the commando, my follow-on in Pashtun earning me a deep nod from the already smiling elder. Interpreter on his shoulder, Colonel Holmes launched into praise for the Afghan, the punchline of which being that, without Ramatoulah, there would still be nothing more to Musa Qala than shooting and air strikes. To prove his point that battle there had truly come to an end, Colonel Holmes then held up his hand, and on that gesture, the guns of 29 Commando went 'out of action', an impressive display of military skill and precision. There were shouted orders, and the loud snaps of the guns' mechanics as they were limbered ready to move, and then joined on to Pinzgauers. In mere moments, the 105mm guns had been turned from threatening gun line to departing afterthought.

The action moved Ramatoulah deeply, an exclamation point on the process that he had begun. I knew too that such a display of soldiering would have been intended for another audience, and the message to the Taliban was clear – we are the professionals here, and as quickly as we packed these guns up, we can set them back down. Do not break this truce.

'The Chinooks are on their way back,' the mild-mannered colonel informed me. 'I'll see you in Bastion, Adam.'

I turned to Ramatoulah and said my goodbyes. I had talked to this man daily for a month, and though I was certain that we respected one another, I was under no illusion that we were friends. Easy Company had been party to the destruction of large parts of his town, and I knew that the elder would be happiest if he never saw me, or any other British soldier, again.

I did not seek out Sadiq and his subordinates. Ceasefire or not, the man was my enemy. I had tolerated our meetings because I had been ordered to. Though there had been moments of insight that were intriguing between soldier and fighter, I would sooner exchange bullets with the Taliban mullah than farewells.

We had been at the RV for an hour and a half before the whump of rotors announced the return of the Chinook pair. They came skimming across the desert like huge dune-beetles, sand churning beneath them. We stood clear as they landed, and as they flared, I could not help but think back to the moment I had seen strikes ricocheting off the length of the casevac, and how the RPGs had bracketed her nose and tail. That moment, I knew, would define our time in Musa Qala. It was the moment when there was no denying the severity of our situation. The moment when, had one of those RPGs been a yard more on target, we would have suffered one of the greatest British army tragedies of recent decades.

We had gotten away with one, I knew. Small consolation to Jon Hetherington, Paul Muirhead, Anare Draiva, and their families, but under the conditions, Easy Company had escaped lightly. It seemed almost incredible that, with all that lead in the air, only one bullet had hit my men. Their individual battle skills had been a great factor in that, but a soldier also needs luck. I knew that, despite our casualties, Easy Company had been graced by the fortune of war. Now, as the Chinook's tailgate yawned open, it was time to leave Musa Qala behind.

I stood back and watched as my men began their crouched approach up and onto the tailgate's ramp, where one of the Chinook's loadmasters handed each of them a can of Mountain Dew. If the RAF crews had not won the men's respect by flying into a storm of shrapnel and lead, then they had just done it with a crate of cold sodas. RAF, Royal Marines, Estonians, Afghan Police, American aircraft, and several sub units of the British army were involved in our extraction. It was a coalition, just as it had been when we were fighting the enemy who were ten yards away. At no time had we been alone, but to see the evidence of that face to face made me glow with pride, not only at being Easy Company's commander but also at being a soldier. A *British* soldier.

'After you, sir!' Scrivs shouted above the sound of the rotors. We were the final two to board. The last sets of Easy Company boots on the ground.

I laughed at my sergeant major, and gave him a playful shove towards the ramp. 'No you don't, you fucker.'

I had been the first person off on our insertion, and I would be the last man to leave on our extraction. For a commander, there was no other way that it could be.

I stepped onto the metal and took my place on the ramp. I gave a thumbs-up to the loadmaster, and as his words were relayed to the cockpit, the whump of the engines grew louder. Within moments we were in the air, and through the frame of the Chinook's open tailgate I saw the force of men who had been witness to Easy Company's final action – the limbered guns of 29 Commando; the infantry of Kilo Company; the Strykers of the Estonians; the pickups and cattle trucks that had ferried us from a besieged battleground to the desert.

As the Chinook cruised through the pale blue sky, the desert behind us now nothing but an unremarkable blanket, it struck me at last that this was the end of our adventure. I was not alone in the thought – several of my men had smiles stretching from ear to ear. Others were stone-faced. A few were crying tears of joy, and relief.

Because we were alive.

We were going home.

The logisticians of Bastion had been warned of our arrival for weeks, and it showed. As we came off the ramp of the Chinooks and onto the hot tarmac of the camp's helicopter pan, I saw that half of the company had already handed over their remaining ammunition. My own count was four magazines of rifle ammunition, a grenade, and a mag and a half for my pistol, a truly miserable amount, and proof that we would indeed have been fighting to the last round had the Taliban chosen to continue in pressing their assaults.

A few green berets moved amongst the herd, Royal Marine officers who were anxious to glean what they could from soldiers who had faced the Taliban enemy. They were good leaders, not above asking the most junior Tom for advice. Advice that could save the lives of their own men, who would soon be pressing into fierce engagements of their own.

It took almost no time to hand over our meagre ammunition, and 42 were not about to hold us back for bullshit's sake. We were shown quickly to tents where our follow-on baggage was waiting. There would be showers, and laundered uniforms, but first there would be food, the Marines providing a guard to watch our weapons so that we could go to the scoff-house unencumbered. It was yet another welcome gesture on their part, and caused us to marvel at how strange it felt to be without our weapons within arm's reach.

Bearded and gaunt, we were the oddity in the air-conditioned tent that served as the cookhouse, but no remark was made about our appearance. Everyone knew who we were, and where we had come from. We were simply the last remnants of 3 Para's battlegroup, and I could imagine the questions that were going through the minds of Marines newly into the country – what had they been through? Would I look like that in six months?

We fell on the food like a pack of vultures, many of the soldiers simply unable to eat the piles that they had built on their plates, stomachs and waistlines much smaller than their eyes.

'The RSM left me a note,' Scrivs told me as we destroyed our second bowls of custard and sponge pudding. 'Everyone to be clean-shaven before we leave Bastion.'

That would be in the morning. We would not be re-deployed, and in lieu of that, what we all wanted was to come home. No man wanted to linger in Bastion's soldiering purgatory.

'We'll do a service in the morning,' I told the men at the table. 'The HCR have built a memorial, apparently. It's out by the JOC and it's got the boys' names on. We'll meet up there, and have a short service before we go to Kabul.'

That evening was a hurried blur of admin, showers, phone calls home, and debriefings to 42's staff. The next day, for the first time in months, Easy Company slept through the dawn. There was no stand to. No enemy to face, or expect. Many a man woke on instinct, but could smile to himself within his sleeping bag, and allow sleep to retake him.

To sleep in was bliss. Then, following a big breakfast, and

in clean combats, Easy Company formed up in front of the monument that marked the sacrifice of our comrades. Brass plaques had been etched with the names of our three killed in action. There were other names, of course, many known to us, and testament to the fighting that had taken place that summer. What was more telling was the number of plaques that lay empty and awaiting. Each engraving would mean tragedy for a family, and painful memories for comrades.

I gave a short talk to my company. I told them that I was proud of them, and that they had done all that was asked of them, and more. I told them that it had been the greatest honour of my life to command them, and I would miss every single one of them. Then, from the Para's prayer card that had lined my helmet throughout, I gave a reading from the Bible, Ecclesiastes 3: 1–8:

> *There is a time for everything, and a season for every*
>   *activity under the heavens:*
> *a time to be born and a time to die,*
> *a time to plant and a time to uproot,*
> *a time to kill and a time to heal,*
> *a time to tear down and a time to build,*
> *a time to weep and a time to laugh,*
> *a time to mourn and a time to dance,*
> *a time to scatter stones and a time to gather them,*
> *a time to embrace and a time to refrain from embracing,*
> *a time to search and a time to give up,*
> *a time to keep and a time to throw away,*
> *a time to tear and a time to mend,*
> *a time to be silent and a time to speak,*
> *a time to love and a time to hate,*
> *a time for war and a time for peace.*

It was a short service, concluded with the Lord's Prayer. We fell out where we were, and men broke into groups to talk, and to point out the names in brass. The remembrance would be our final action in Helmand. A few hours later, we boarded a C-130, and flew to Kabul.

The airbase at Kabul had not changed since I had arrived in country, and yet, to me now, it could not have been more different. It had been the first stepping stone on my way to the challenge that I was seeking, and now its signposts of orders, unsullied uniforms, and strict adherence to 'discipline' were the clear indicators that the adventure was over. With every step from Musa Qala, rules had become more rigid as the danger had waned. I had been invigorated by this place five months ago, but now it was an irritant to be put up with on my transition from frontline to family.

Easy Company went to the Toucan bar that night. We had been given an allocation of two cans per man, but the quartermaster had worked from our original headcount, and so there were extra cans for the men we were missing. These buckshee cans we drank with toasts to the soldiers they had been intended for. Prior to the drinks, I had been politely asked into the office of the base's commandant, a signals major who was both welcoming and clearly on edge – he saw an incoming company of infantry from the frontline, and expected trouble, but the men of Easy wanted to do nothing more than relax. They'd seen enough fighting. Enough destruction. What was smashing a bar stool when you'd killed more enemy and seen more A-10 gun runs than you could remember?

At one point in the evening I took a break from the bar and made my way up onto the same rooftop from where I had watched the sunset over the mountains during my first day in theatre. Those mountains had remained unchanged for centuries as wars were fought and armies marched through the country. I was just one more soldier who passed beneath their gaze. One more soldier who was leaving a different man. Alone on the rooftop, with no responsibility except to ensure that my men got on their plane in the morning, I finally had the chance to think freely, the momentous achievement and experience of what we had endured laid out openly in front of me. I did not know what to make of it then – nor, in all honesty, do I now. I can only say that any relief in my body that I had survived was matched – or possibly even outweighed – by a longing to return to combat, and that, I was certain, was an inevitability. I would like to have said that it was different, and that 3 Para had opened and closed the books on the Taliban in a single summer, but there was no denying on that rooftop what I knew deep down – we were sliding deeper into this war. There would be more contacts, more air strikes, more casevacs, and more deaths.

But what there would never be, was another Easy Company.

34

We did not fly home directly from Afghanistan to the UK. With a staggering display of common sense, the army insisted that all soldiers returning from theatre must attend 'decompression', an ominous-sounding term that was actually looked forward to with great enthusiasm by the men. It took place at the remote Blood Hound camp on the island of Cyprus, and began innocuously enough. At first there were the mandatory briefings about not beating civilians or family members, and then we were unleashed on the nearest beach. There were nervous giggles as the psychiatrist told us we may have seen and done things that would take time to understand. Some soldiers chose to sit in small groups and watch the waves. Others ran banana boats. It was a few hours of freedom, and then we were shepherded back to camp, where sheepish-looking chefs fired up BBQs, and waited nervously for what was to come.

I had to credit the officer that came up with the idea. They knew their soldiers well, and understood that a man returning from combat wants to drink, and the first time that happens he is liable to be rowdy, rebellious, and possibly even dangerous. Better to admit as much, and let that happen with his comrades in a remote base. And so Easy Company were gifted with lager much as a tiger is fed slabs of meat at the zoo, the handler retreating a safe distance and allowing the animal to feast. I'm proud to say that there was little infighting in the company. As for what else happened, it is best left from this book, and in the memories of those who were there.

The next morning, with red eyes and sore heads, Easy boarded a chartered aircraft for our flight home. Despite the hangovers, men were jubilant, and Abe the RAF regiment gunner suffered a lot of abuse as the infantrymen harassed him for being 'a trolley dolly,' demanding that he bring them nuts and beers.

I spent the flight going from man to man, sharing memories and wishing them all the best. I wanted them to know how proud I was of every individual, and how they could contact me once we were home. I knew that, for some of us, the war had not ended when we left Afghanistan.

Engaged as I was in conversations with soldiers that I had come to respect and love, the flight passed quickly, and it seemed that in no time we had touched down at Stansted. It was here that the Paras and signallers would depart, the Rangers flying onwards to their base in Scotland. Those final farewells were a blur of waves and good-natured insults. One moment I had been with the full company of my men. The next, I was with a handful. I felt like I had on the final day of school, but I was cheered to know that, as saddening as it was to say goodbye to my men, I was one step closer to my family.

It was a short, quiet drive to Colchester. So close to their families, men become introspective. Almost nervous. It all seemed like a dream, now. The gunfire, the bombs, the fear. It was hard to reconcile it with the English countryside that rolled by. The cars that filled the road, their occupants likely oblivious to a war that was being fought in their name on the other side of the world. I knew what to expect, and none of this was a surprise to me.

And yet still . . .

Our bus came to a stop. Outside it were two dozen families, balloons, smiles, and tears. There were laughing children and crying children. There were the overjoyed wives, and the stoic-faced ones who were the bastion of the home front. The matriarchs who held the line when their men were at war, veterans in surviving deployments as well as their husbands.

My family were not amongst them, but we had planned it

that way. I was Easy Company's commander, and until my men were all squared away, I wanted my attention to be on my duty. I would not see my own family until each of my soldiers was with theirs. When that was so, I began the walk home.

I hadn't got far out of camp when I was spotted by Pete Balcombe, a friend from the Army Air Corps. He was on his way to my homecoming party, and laughed as he offered me a lift. We had a couple of minutes to catch up before he pulled up outside my home.

'Go on,' he told me. 'I'll follow in a few minutes.'

He had been in this position himself. He knew that there should be one person on the step when the door opened.

With a smile on my face, I pressed the doorbell.

The door swung open immediately.

I was looking at my ex-wife.

'Oops! Wrong wife!' Chrissy laughed, stepping back. Wrong wife or not, I greeted her with a hug, then searched out my family. They came for me, Jacqueline and Livvy – my eldest – with enthusiasm, Conrad with some reluctance, wondering who this emaciated, tanned man in the doorway was. I held them both in my arms, kissing them and loving them. It was worth every hellish moment to experience the joy of holding my wife and two children against my chest. To do my job as a commander, I had compartmentalized my family away with so many things. Now, that box sprung open.

'I've missed you so much!'

I saw my parents and sister next. Then dozens of friends. They fussed about me, and I slipped away from the unwanted attention by asking them about all the things I had missed. It was bliss to hear about a broken fridge, a new job, or a bad school report. There was a sense of relief knowing that, during my absence, prayers had been offered and candles lit in St Malachy's Church in Armagh, but otherwise the world had gone on without me, and my deployment had caused no huge upset. Pleased that this was the case, and with a beer in hand, I smiled as I began to settle back into the routine of British life. Then, suddenly aware that I was still in uniform, I slipped away and changed, feeling awkward and strange to be in civilian clothes.

My army friends screwed the nut and left after a couple of drinks, knowing that I would want my peace. Family took a little longer to disperse, and I was not about to push them out of the door. They questioned me about my time, having no idea what we'd been through. When my wife had heard gunfire down the phone, I'd simply told her that I was running the ranges at Bastion. Now, I gave her the roughest of ideas, but no detail. That was a problem shared amongst friends. Others who had been through it.

That night, feeling exhausted and a little numb, I collapsed onto my bed and thought about what lay ahead. Easy Company was no more, and I was Support Company OC again. Men under my command were injured and in hospital. I would need to meet the grieving parents of those who had died.

The war had not stopped when we left Musa Qala.

As I lay watching my beautiful wife sleeping, I did not know if it ever would.

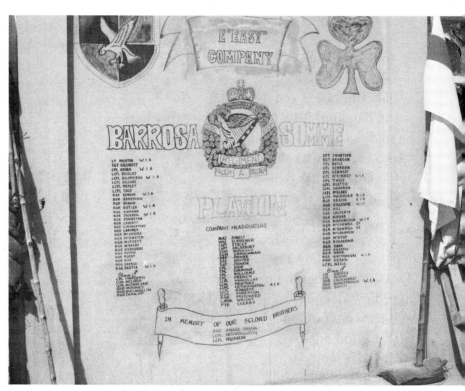

British Airborne: The company's mural on the side of the clinic.

Epilogue

September 2016

We gathered in the cemetery where Paul Muirhead had been buried. It was late summer, and beautiful. Nervous smiles and handshakes between old comrades steadily gave way to man hugs and laughter. It was the first time in a decade that many of the soldiers of Easy Company had stood face to face with the men who had been as close to them as brothers in Musa Qala. Why was that? Why so long?

Coming home from war is never easy. That is no secret. Our fight with the Taliban had forged bonds that could never die, but in that same instance they had created memories that were painful and unwanted. To see and talk with an old comrade was something that was desired and cherished, but every soldier knew deep down that it would come at a price. Pandora's box would be opened. The bad memories would creep out as the good ones were enjoyed. Then, the soldier would be ambushed. He would wake covered in sweat. Perhaps he would wake screaming. He would be edgy. Angry. Withdrawn. Maybe this would last for hours, maybe weeks, but there was no denying that it would come. For this reason it was often easier to remember those fierce days of combat alone, and from a distance. But then, in the case of Easy Company, there was something that kept us apart that we could not have foreseen when we were fighting for our lives from rooftops and alleyways.

Musa Qala was forgotten by all but us.

The first signs of it appeared quickly. The men of the Royal Irish platoons were split up and returned to their original companies, counter to all medical advice on how best to treat soldiers who are returning from war. They were two of the three platoons from that battalion who had seen action in Helmand, and the men of Somme and Barossa platoons were treated as curiosities rather than heroes. I saw it as a case of envy and insecurity from those who had remained on the home front, classic 'green-eyed' stuff, nothing more, but the riflemen of Easy Company soon found that they could not talk about their time in Musa Qala without being lambasted for it. 'You're not with the Paras now,' they were told whenever they tried to speak up. One of the Rangers, injured by mortar shrapnel, was chastised for making a scene, and playing up his wounds as he struggled to step down from a bus.

Easy Company's mission, the contentious ceasefire, and our unorthodox extraction was regarded as something of an embarrassment, or even joke, although the punchline was not one that anyone found amusing.

We were only a few months returned from Afghanistan when the Taliban broke their word and retook Musa Qala, overrunning the militia garrison at the district centre with ease. I do not know exactly what happened to Haji Ramatoulah and the other elders whom I dealt with but, given the Taliban's track record, I imagine that they suffered horrible deaths. This was a deep blow to myself and every man of Easy Company who had fought and bled for the place. And from the hushed jokes to the pointed fingers, there was no doubt that *we* were being blamed for the accord, our unusual extraction from the town, and the subsequent recapturing of it.

At first I thought that perhaps I was being oversensitive, and that the snide remarks about us being driven away in cattle trucks were nothing more than the army's usual level of harsh banter. But then, the honours list was disclosed for the tour, and I saw in those lists of medals and commendations a truth that I could not ignore. Whereas the battlegroup received a good handful of hard-earned Military Crosses and Mentions in Dispatches, not a single one of the men I had written up for awards received official recognition for their heroism.

Not one.

It seemed as though the official message was that it had been tough across all of Helmand that summer, especially in the platoon houses of Sangin and Now Zad, just not in our town.

Then, at the end of 2007, an operation was launched to once again wrest Musa Qala from the hands of the Taliban. It was a success, and seen by many as correcting the situation that 'the Paras' had left in their wake when they 'tactically retreated'. It said a lot to me about the accuracy of the information that the people pointing fingers had no idea that brave men from the Royal Irish had made up the lion's share of our force. Nor did it seem to matter to them that these same soldiers had baulked at the idea of talking with the Taliban, but, like all good soldiers, they had bitten their tongues and obeyed their orders.

The wider army was blissfully unaware of our trials in Musa Qala. During a pre-deployment brief in 2008, an Engineer major briefed us on the 'Ground Truth' in Helmand that we were soon to return to. All eyes turned to me as the Engineer officer, ignorant as to who I was, went on to explain that we had beat a hasty retreat from Musa Qala in 2006 after being unable to hold off the Taliban attacks. I waited until questions to correct him.

'I was the OC of Easy Company,' I said calmly, burying my anger, 'and we weren't kicked out. There was no withdrawal. We fought them to a standstill.'

Whether the words used were 'kicked out' or 'retreat', both cut deeply to the professional soldier, particularly when I knew that neither was true – on the part of the soldiers fighting on the ground, at least. In time, a number of books would refer to the 'withdrawal' or 'hasty retreat' from the town, and through repetition these statements became accepted as truth – something that became increasingly hard to swallow. Easy Company, against all odds, had fought the enemy to the point where they chose a ceasefire above more casualties. The local peace had been ordered from the highest levels, and we had obeyed despite our personal desire to fight on. To see my men – who had fought so bravely – be tainted by others' decisions made my stomach turn. A few years later, a pair of senior British diplomats were expelled from Afghanistan after it emerged they had been talking to the Taliban – it was still something that we just did not do, apparently.

Some of Easy Company's soldiers left the army as quickly as they could. Others felt like they had nothing left to prove, and followed suit. For my part, I intended to remain in uniform for my entire career, and looked forward to a further twenty years' service. In mid-2012, I was a defence attaché in eastern Europe when the axe fell on me, courtesy of the Strategic Defence and Security Review. Along with many of my comrades, I was now seen as surplus, and was forced into early retirement. I was so white with rage that it was only thanks to my wife hiding my medals that I didn't mail them back to the faceless staffers in the Army Personnel Centre in Glasgow. I could not believe that, despite my service, the swipe of a bureaucrat's pen had seen the entire plans for my life turned upside down. In my mind, I was being treated the same way as a soldier who failed a drug test, or was simply being got rid of like a knackered Land Rover. Even the pointed fingers and sensational remarks about Musa Qala had never once made me think about leaving the army. Back in 2008 I had returned to Afghanistan with 3 Para, this time operating out of Kandahar, and I would have continued to return for the rest of my career had I been asked, because there is no higher honour in life than serving alongside British soldiers. That was my purpose, and they tore it away from me.

*

It was the reunion of Easy Company in 2016 that helped me realize how much worse it could have been. Many of the men who fought under me in Musa Qala were now struggling. One was homeless. One of my JTAC pair had been discharged from the army due to his extreme PTSD. Others from Easy, I was very proud to see, had found great success both in and out of the army and continue to thrive: Jon 'Scrivs' Scrivener commissioned, as did 'PJ' Brangan; Freddie is a television personality specializing in fixing vintage military vehicles, and spends his spare time restoring Second World War-era motorbikes; Paul Martin made a full recovery, and commands his own company; Ranger Matanisinga overcame his wounds and returned to his family in Fiji; the unflappable Mike Stacey is still an army doctor.

Then there were the families of the fallen, whom I had first met at their sons' inquests in late 2006 – traumatic days in court during which we had had to relive each moment, explaining to grieving families how their sons had died on the field of battle. The loss of my beloved career could clearly never compare to the loss of a beloved son. My family was intact, and I could not ask for more than that.

Following a short service at Paul Muirhead's graveside, we relocated to a sports and social club where the drinks flowed, and with them came loosened tongues and war stories. The reunion was a happy affair, punctuated by moments of melancholy and loss. The sadness was felt not only for the loss of our comrades, but also for ourselves, for a man is a soldier for only a short period of his life, and his time as a soldier at war is even shorter. In the grand scheme of our lives, those long weeks in Musa Qala were but a slither of time, and yet they came to dominate all other years and moments. When again will we experience such simplicity in our lives, the daily tedium burned away until you are left with the ultimate dichotomy of live or die? When will we experience such comradeship, knowing that a man we met only days ago will risk – and give – his life for us? When will we experience such adrenaline, trading rounds in close combat, A-10s screaming down from the sky to churn the enemy and buildings around us into bloody rubble? When will we feel that our actions are at the centre of the world, and that what we are doing really *means* something?

Soldiers have been asking the same questions following war for millennia, and I don't like my chances of being the first to find the answers.

Many of my friends have asked me if I'd go back to Musa Qala, and to those days in the summer of 2006. Invariably, these questions come from civilians. My military friends already know what my answer would be.

Yes. Absolutely yes.

I hope that, having read this, you will understand the reasons why I would put myself back in that position, that danger. There is only one higher honour than standing shoulder to shoulder with brave men, and fighting a common enemy, and that is leading them. I will forever be blessed and humbled that I was given that opportunity. There is not a day goes by when I do not think of those young Rangers and Paras, and how they defied the greatest odds to beat back an unrelentingly barbaric enemy. There is not a day when I do not think about their courage, their grit, and their sheer unbreakable spirit. There is not a day when I do not think about their comradeship, their humour, and their love for one another.

And, of course, there is not a day when I do not think about my men who did not come home alive – Jon Hetherington, Paul Muirhead, and Anare Draiva. Their sacrifice needs to be known. It needs to be acknowledged, it needs to be praised, and it needs to be remembered. These men gave all, and there was not a single soldier in that battle who did not give something of himself to defend his brothers. I will remember them always with fierce pride, love, and loyalty.

They were my men.

They were, and always will be, Easy Company.

ACKNOWLEDGEMENTS

I would like to thank Geraint 'Gez' Jones for his superb writing talent, and my agent, Rory Scarfe of Furniss Lawton, who got us working together. From the start I had the pleasure of working with Ingrid Connell and her stellar team at Pan Macmillan, who expertly guided me through the process. I am indebted to Charles Heath-Saunders and Colonel Paddy Jackson of Army Media Communications for their guidance and help throughout.

Finally, to 'every man Jack' of the company, especially the NCOs, Rangers, and Paras. Without their grit and selflessness, it would have been a very different book.

'Utrinque Paratus'

Picture Acknowledgements

Page 1, *top*: Musa Qual'eh FIBUA map © Crown Copyright

Page 1, *bottom*: CONPLAN WOUTAON © Crown Copyright

Page 3, *middle*: © Mrs S Cherry

Page 3, *top and bottom*: page 4, *top*: page 8, *bottom*: © Freddie Kruyer

Page 5, *middle*: page 7, *bottom*: © David Pepper

Page 7, *middle*: page 13, *top*: page 14, *middle*: page 16, *middle*: © Lee Simmons

Page 8, *top*: © Adam Jowett

Page 8, *middle*: page 9, top: © Ian Wornham

Page 15, *top*: © Gaz Faulkner

Page 16, *bottom*: © Conrad Jowett

Page 16, *top right*: © Karl Newton

Every effort has been made to identify the owners of copyright material reproduced in this book. The author would like to apologize for any ommissions and will be pleased to incorporate missing acknowledgements in future editions.